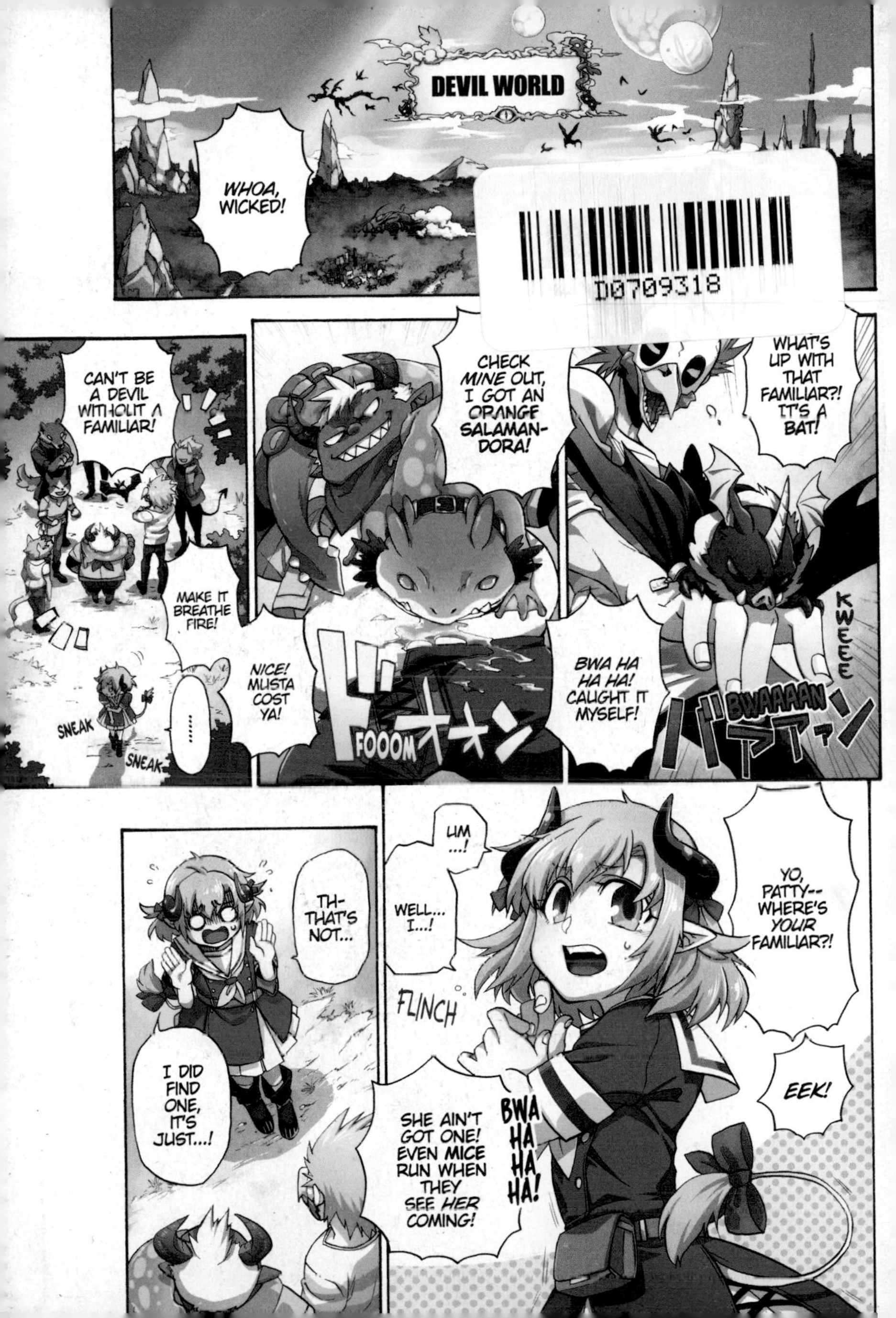
DEVIL WORLD
WHOA, WICKED!
WHAT'S UP WITH THAT FAMILIAR?! IT'S A BAT!
KWEEE
BWA HA HA HA! CAUGHT IT MYSELF!
BWAAAAN
CHECK MINE OUT, I GOT AN ORANGE SALAMANDORA!
NICE! MUSTA COST YA!
FOOOM
CAN'T BE A DEVIL WITHOUT A FAMILIAR!
MAKE IT BREATHE FIRE!
......
SNEAK
SNEAK
YO, PATTY-- WHERE'S YOUR FAMILIAR?!
UM ...!
WELL... I...!
EEK!
FLINCH
BWA HA HA HA HA!
SHE AIN'T GOT ONE! EVEN MICE RUN WHEN THEY SEE HER COMING!
TH-THAT'S NOT...
I DID FIND ONE, IT'S JUST...!

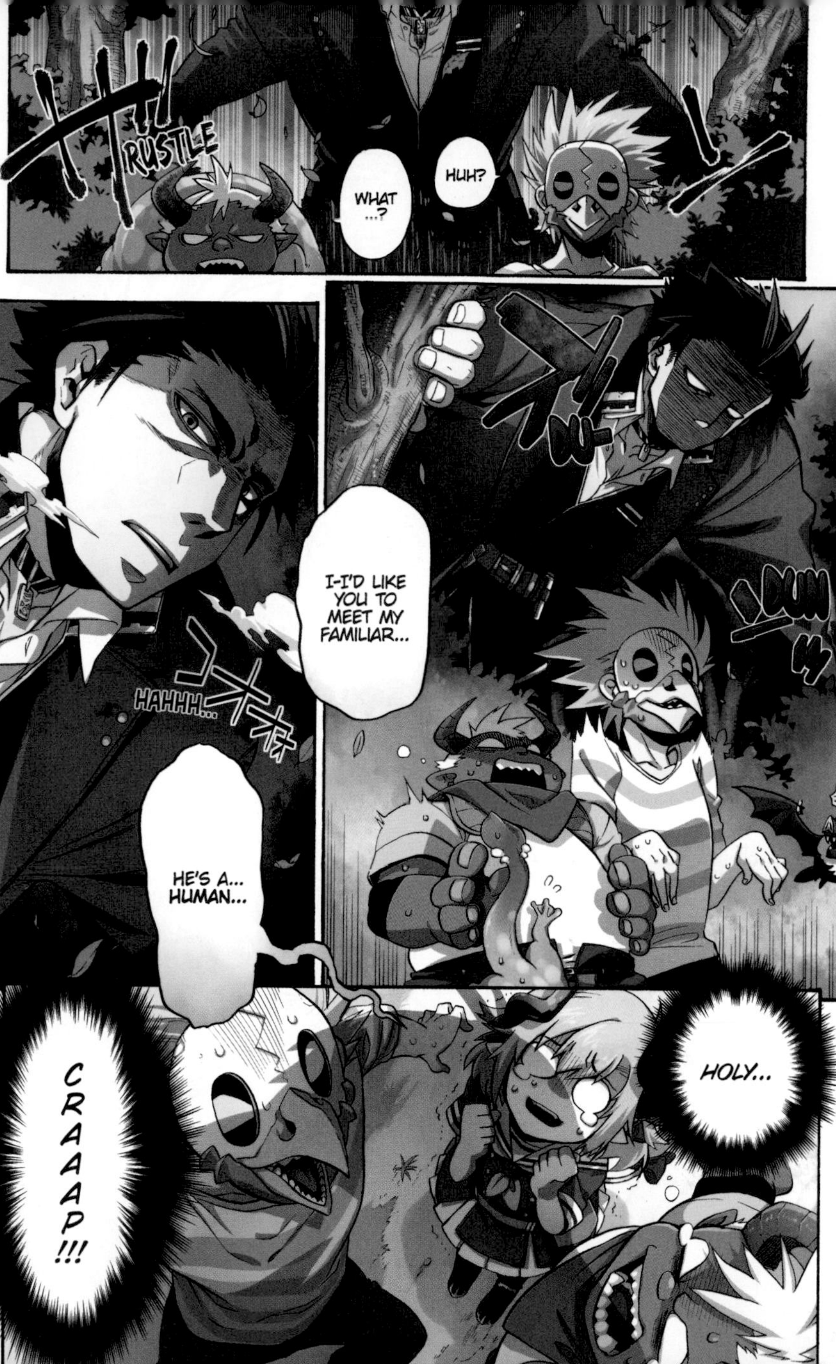
HUH?
WHAT ...?
RUSTLE
DU-
DUN
I-I'D LIKE YOU TO MEET MY FAMILIAR...
HAHHH...
HE'S A... HUMAN...
HOLY...
CRAAAAP!!!

FILE 1: Starting Village

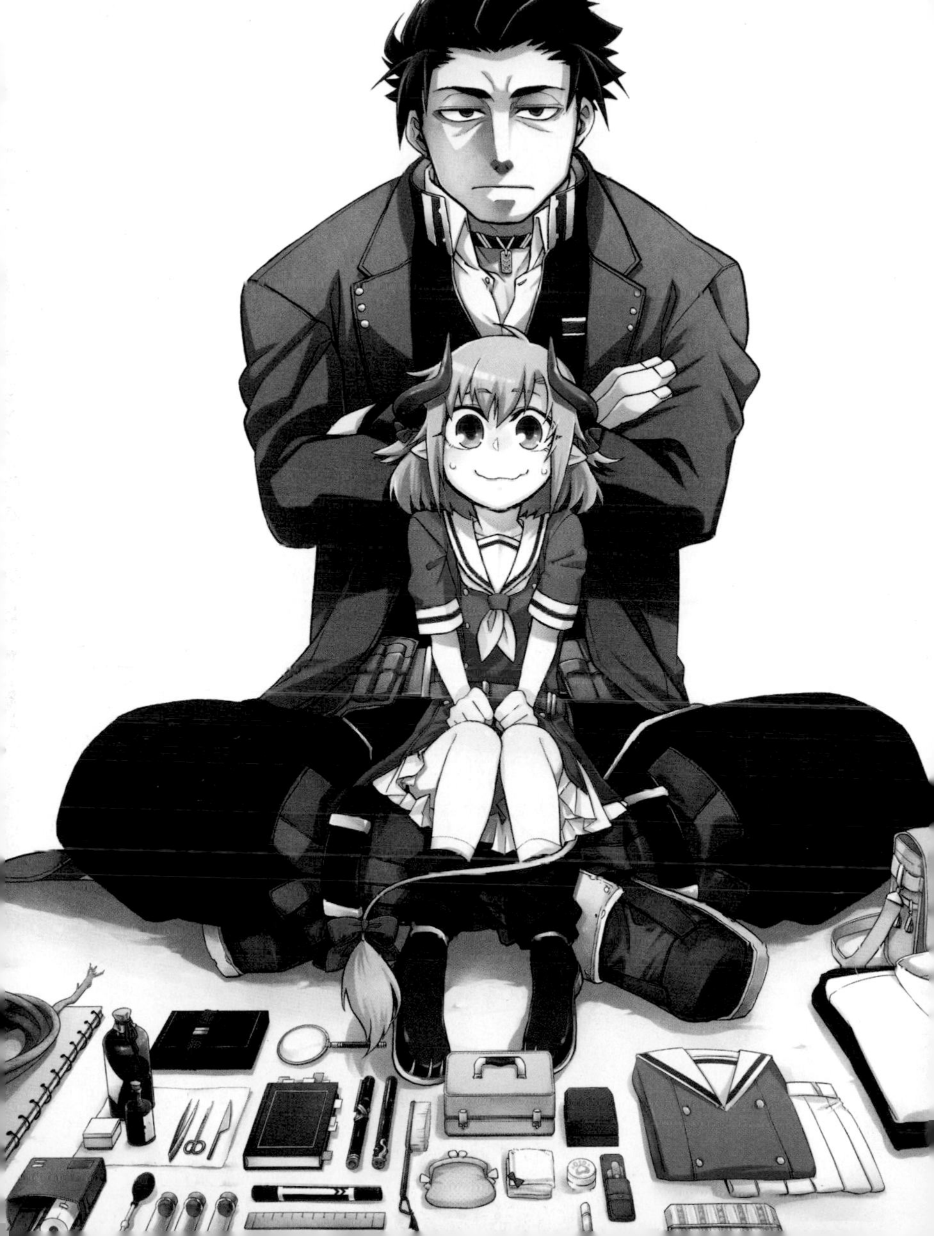

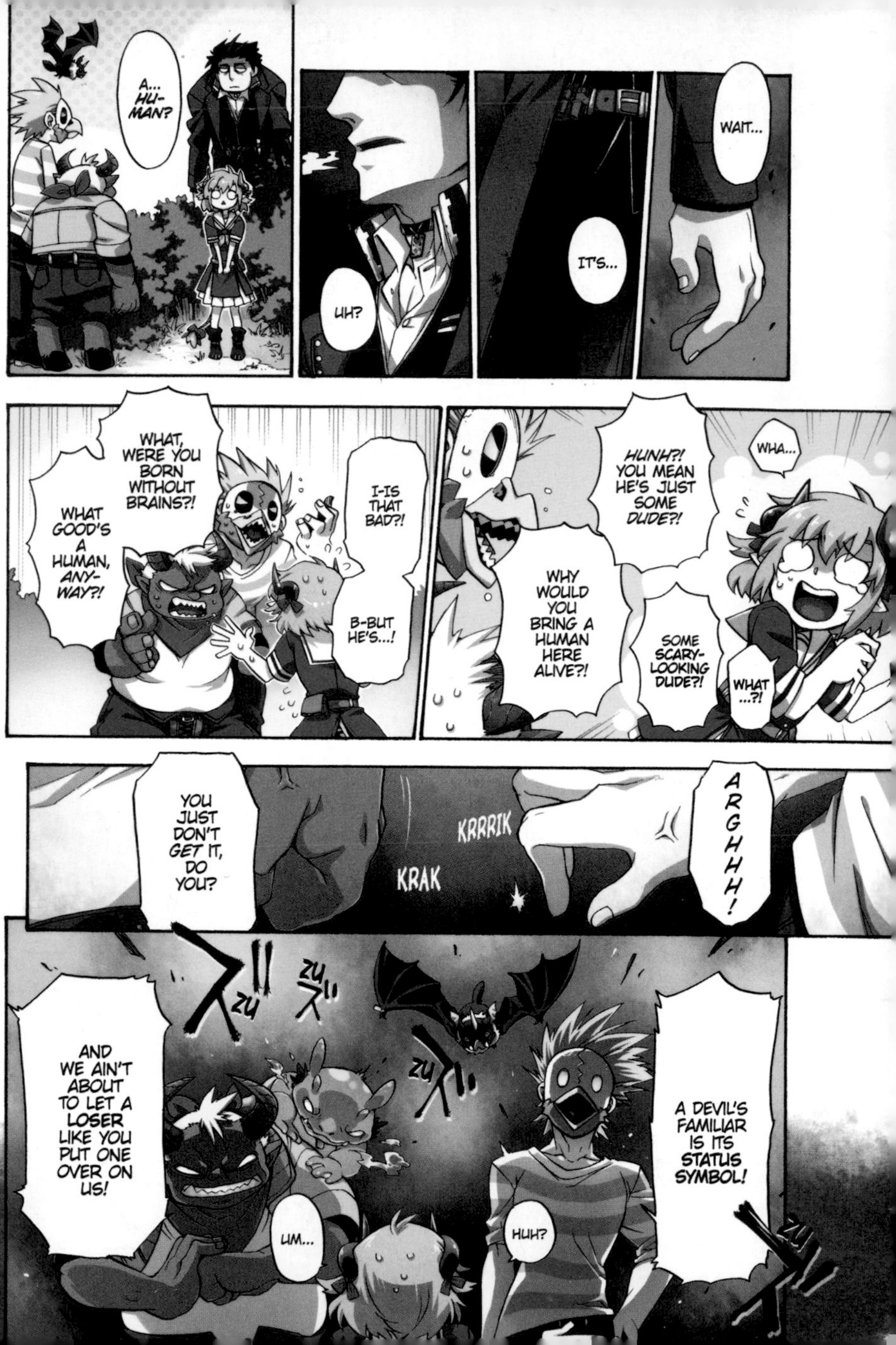
WAIT...
IT'S...
UH?
A... HU-MAN?
WHA...
HUNH?! YOU MEAN HE'S JUST SOME DUDE?!
WHAT ...?!
SOME SCARY-LOOKING DUDE?!
WHY WOULD YOU BRING A HUMAN HERE ALIVE?!
I-IS THAT BAD?!
B-BUT HE'S...!
WHAT, WERE YOU BORN WITHOUT BRAINS?!
WHAT GOOD'S A HUMAN, ANYWAY?!
ARGHHH!
KRRRIK
KRAK
YOU JUST DON'T GET IT, DO YOU?
ZU
A DEVIL'S FAMILIAR IS ITS STATUS SYMBOL!
HUH?
UM...
AND WE AIN'T ABOUT TO LET A LOSER LIKE YOU PUT ONE OVER ON US!
ZU
ZU
ZU

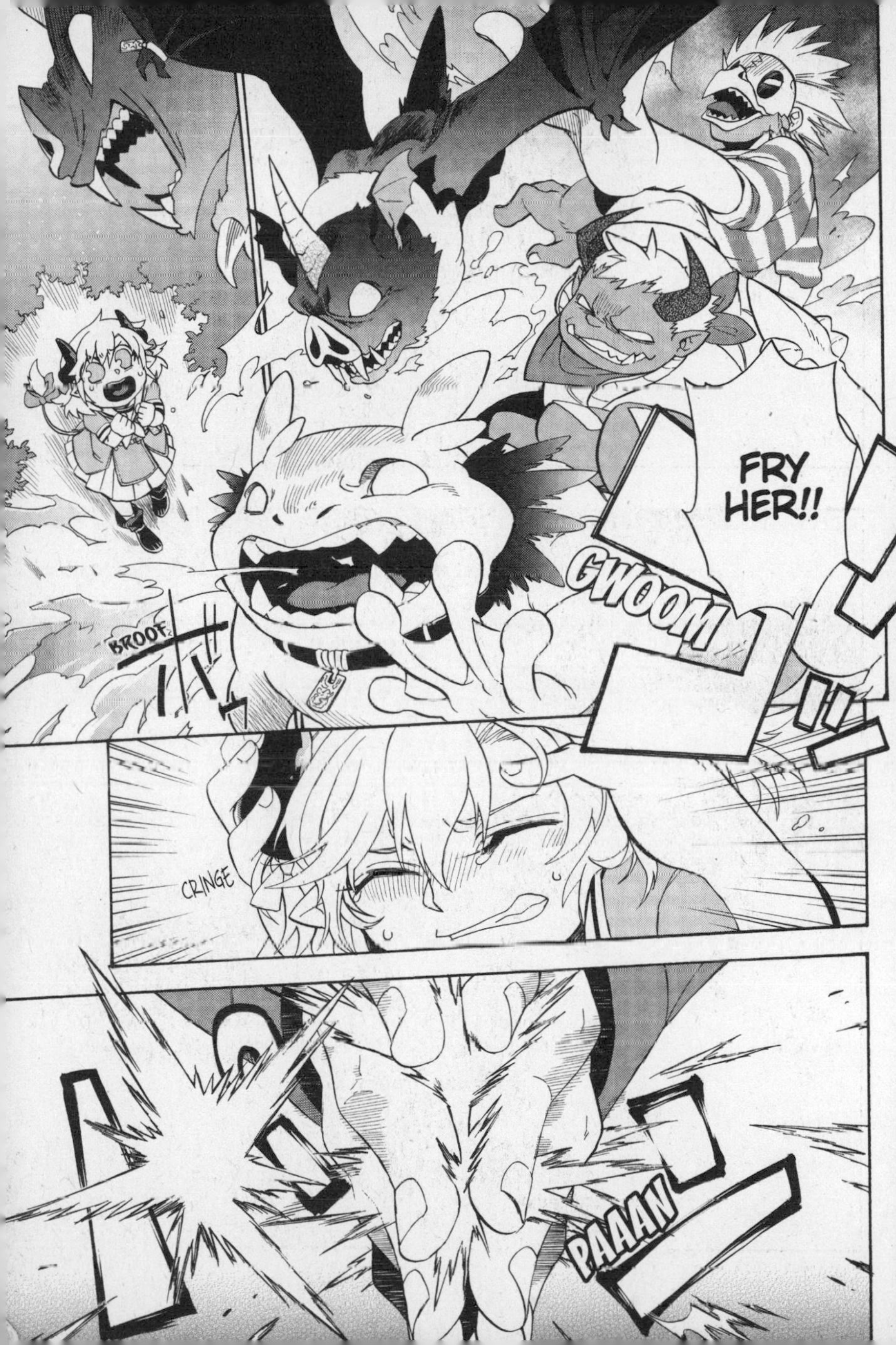
FRY HER!!
GWOOM
BROOF
CRINGE
PAAAN

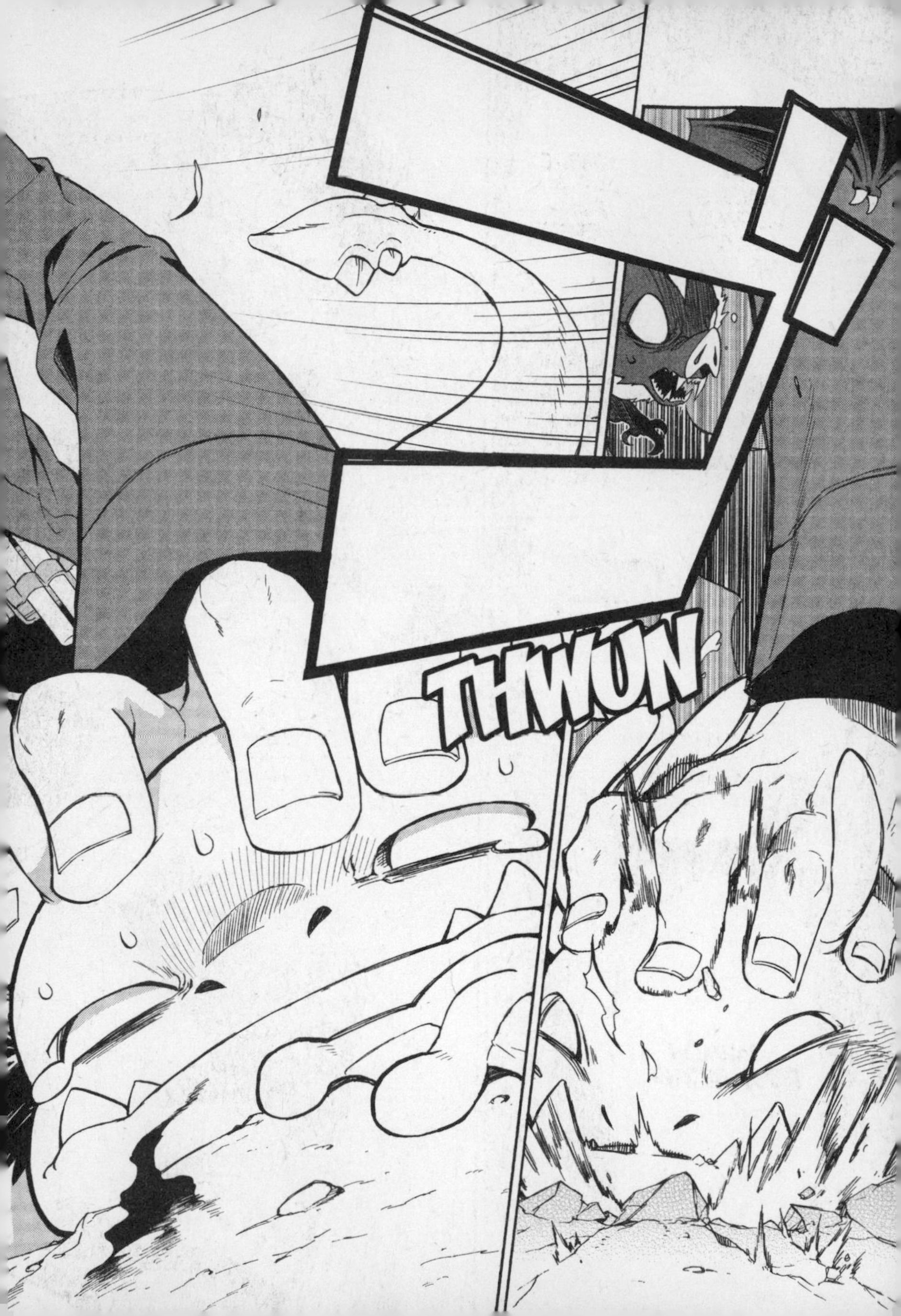
THWUN

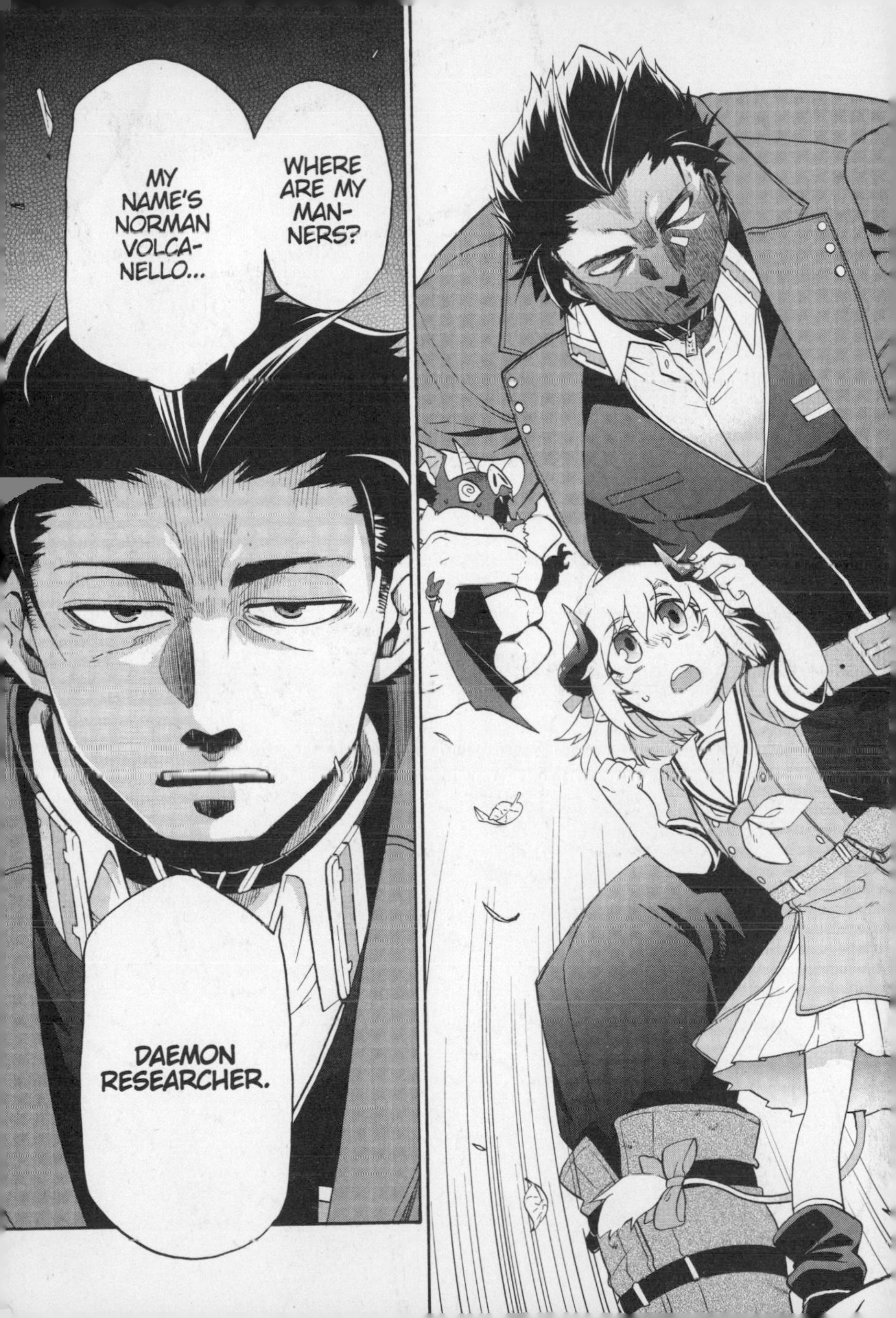
WHERE ARE MY MAN-NERS?
MY NAME'S NORMAN VOLCA-NELLO...
DAEMON RESEARCHER.

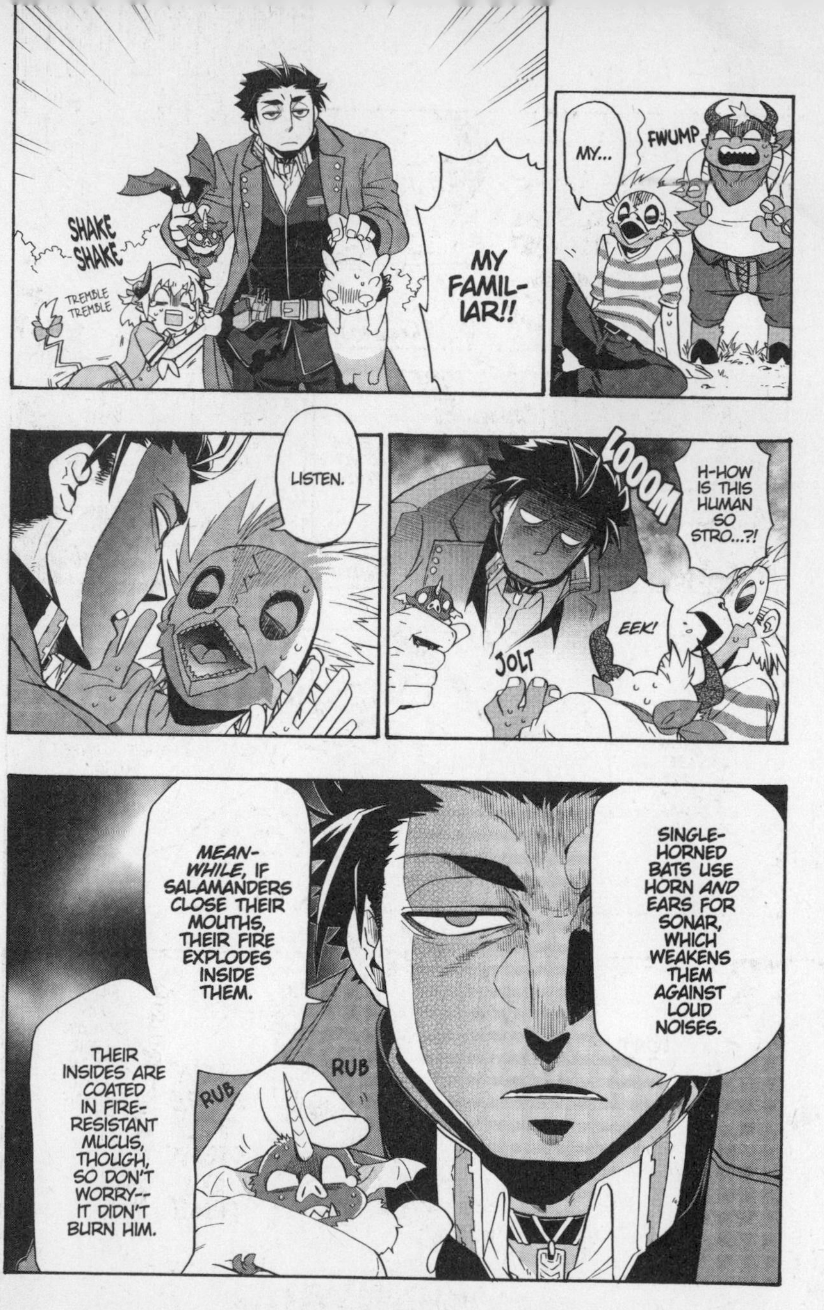
MY...
FWUMP
MY FAMIL-IAR!!
SHAKE SHAKE
TREMBLE TREMBLE
LOOOM
H-HOW IS THIS HUMAN SO STRO...?!
EEK!
JOLT
LISTEN.
SINGLE-HORNED BATS USE HORN *AND* EARS FOR SONAR, WHICH WEAKENS THEM AGAINST LOUD NOISES.
MEAN-WHILE, IF SALAMANDERS CLOSE THEIR MOUTHS, THEIR FIRE EXPLODES INSIDE THEM.
RUB
RUB
THEIR INSIDES ARE COATED IN FIRE-RESISTANT MUCUS, THOUGH, SO DON'T WORRY-- IT DIDN'T BURN HIM.

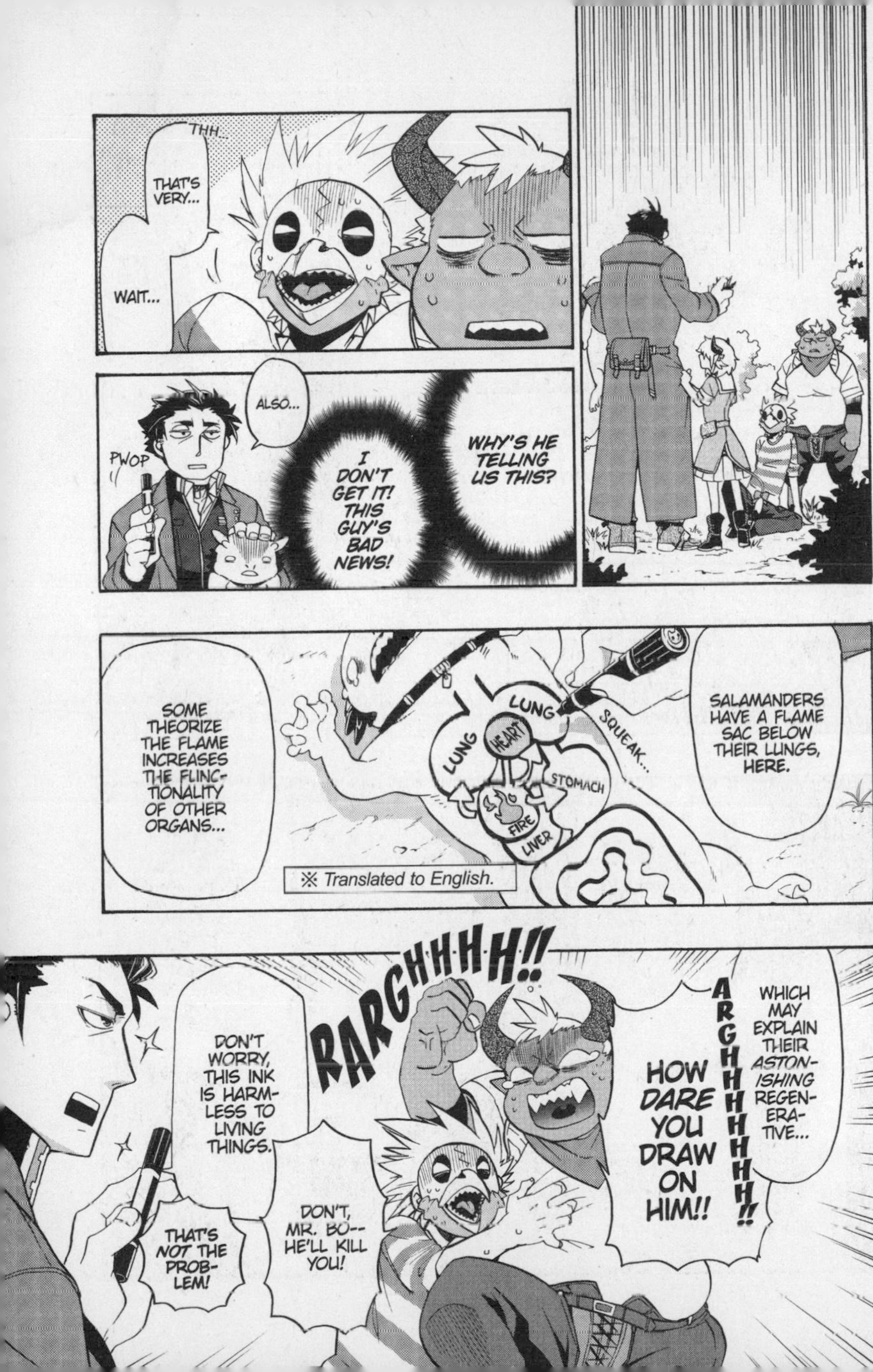
THH...
THAT'S VERY...
WAIT...
ALSO...
PWOP
WHY'S HE TELLING US THIS?
I DON'T GET IT! THIS GUY'S BAD NEWS!
SALAMANDERS HAVE A FLAME SAC BELOW THEIR LUNGS, HERE.
SQUEAK...
LUNG
HEART
LUNG
STOMACH
FIRE
LIVER
SOME THEORIZE THE FLAME INCREASES THE FLINCTIONALITY OF OTHER ORGANS...
※ Translated to English.
WHICH MAY EXPLAIN THEIR ASTONISHING REGENERATIVE...
ARGHHHHHHH!!
HOW DARE YOU DRAW ON HIM!!
RARGHHHHH!!
DON'T WORRY, THIS INK IS HARMLESS TO LIVING THINGS.
DON'T, MR. BO-- HE'LL KILL YOU!
THAT'S NOT THE PROBLEM!

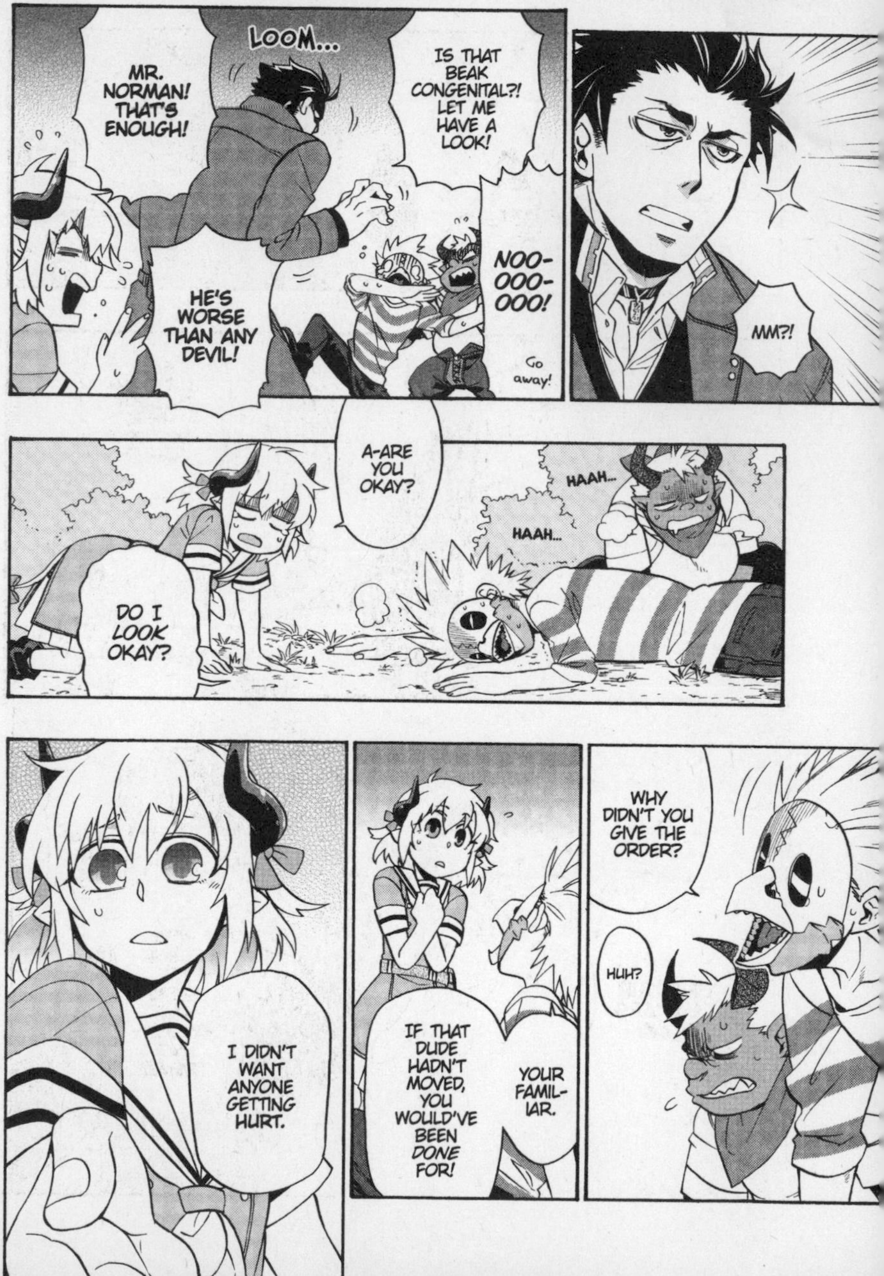
MM?!
IS THAT BEAK CONGENITAL?! LET ME HAVE A LOOK!
LOOM...
MR. NORMAN! THAT'S ENOUGH!
NOO-OOO-OOO!
Go away!
HE'S WORSE THAN ANY DEVIL!
A-ARE YOU OKAY?
HAAH...
HAAH...
DO I LOOK OKAY?
WHY DIDN'T YOU GIVE THE ORDER?
HUH?
YOUR FAMIL-IAR.
IF THAT DUDE HADN'T MOVED, YOU WOULD'VE BEEN *DONE* FOR!
I DIDN'T WANT ANYONE GETTING HURT.

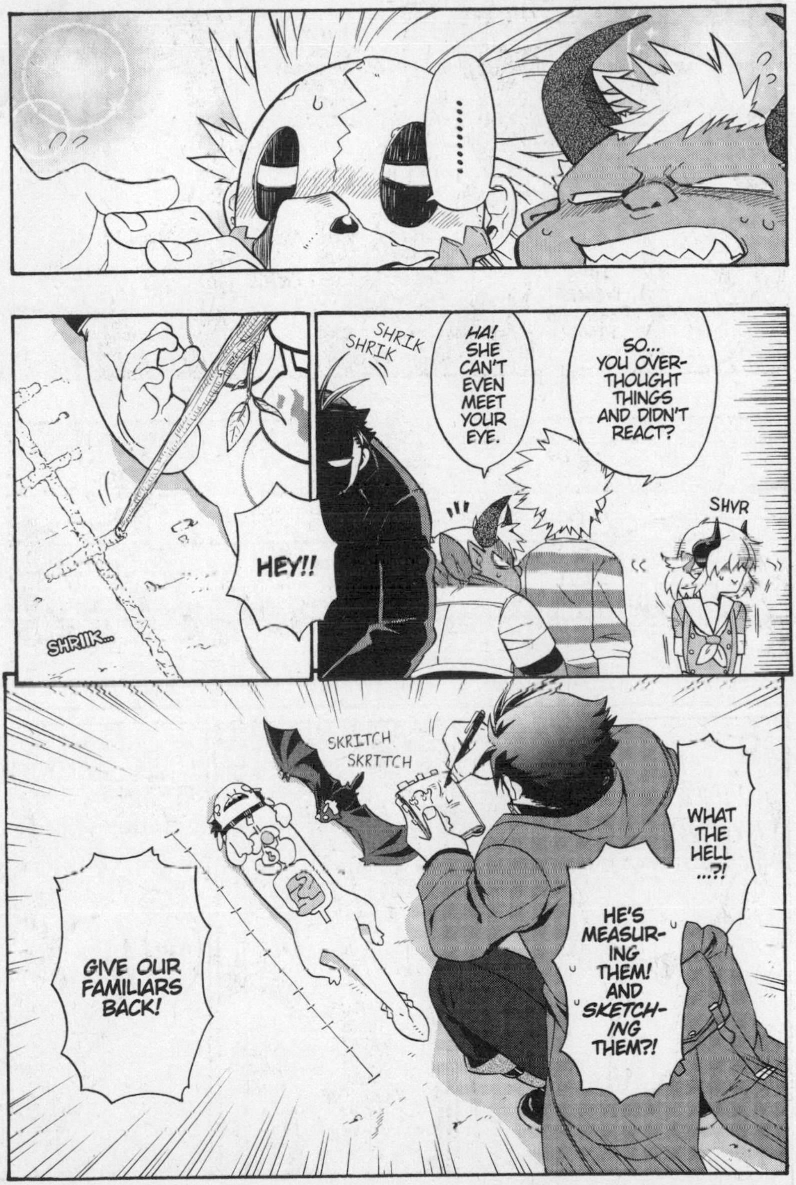
......
SO... YOU OVER-THOUGHT THINGS AND DIDN'T REACT?
HA! SHE CAN'T EVEN MEET YOUR EYE.
SHRIK SHRIK
SHVR
HEY!!
SHRIIK...
WHAT THE HELL ...?!
HE'S MEASUR-ING THEM! AND SKETCH-ING THEM?!
SKRITCH SKRTTCH
GIVE OUR FAMILIARS BACK!

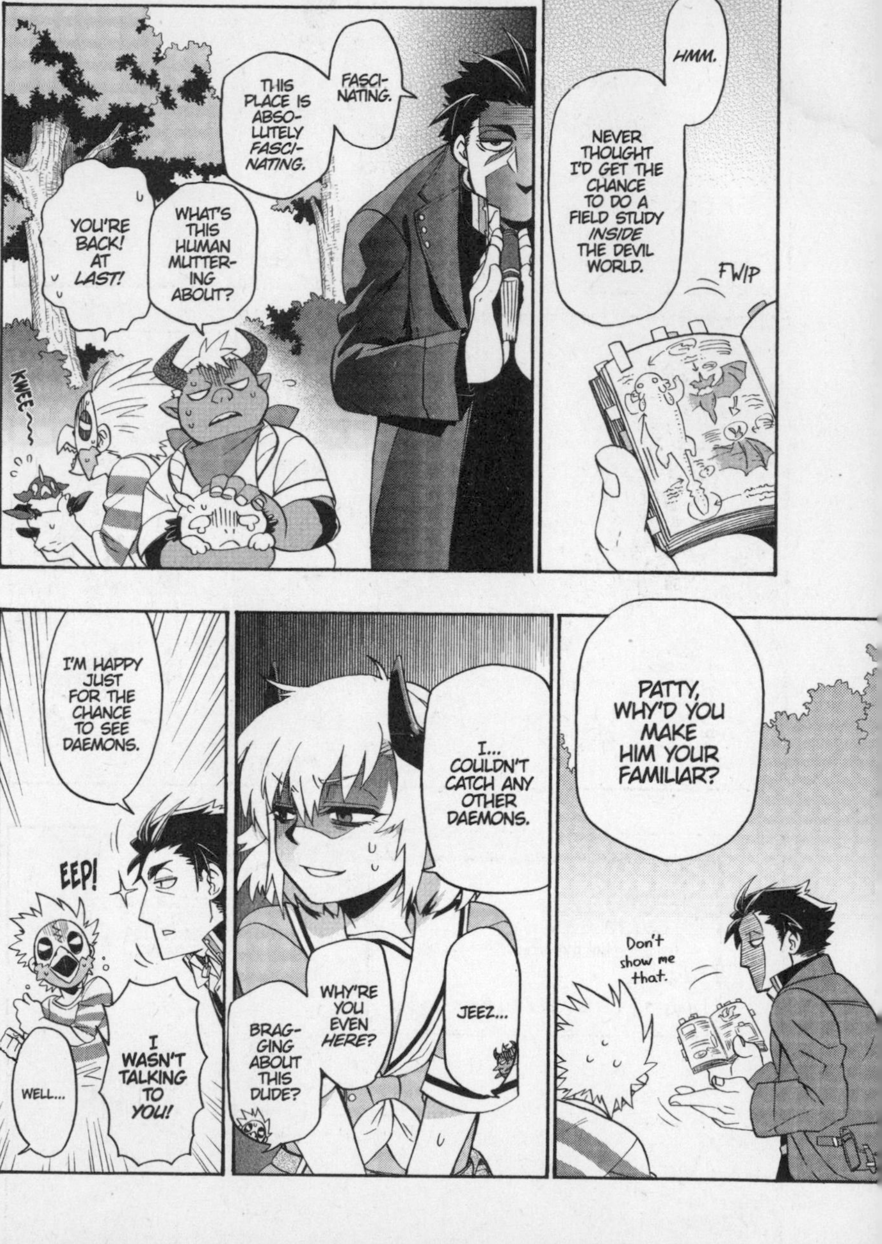
HMM.
NEVER THOUGHT I'D GET THE CHANCE TO DO A FIELD STUDY INSIDE THE DEVIL WORLD.
FWIP
FASCI-NATING.
THIS PLACE IS ABSO-LUTELY FASCI-NATING.
WHAT'S THIS HUMAN MUTTER-ING ABOUT?
YOU'RE BACK! AT LAST!
KWEE~
PATTY, WHY'D YOU MAKE HIM YOUR FAMILIAR?
Don't show me that.
I... COULDN'T CATCH ANY OTHER DAEMONS.
JEEZ...
WHY'RE YOU EVEN HERE?
BRAG-GING ABOUT THIS DUDE?
I'M HAPPY JUST FOR THE CHANCE TO SEE DAEMONS.
EEP!
I WASN'T TALKING TO YOU!
WELL...

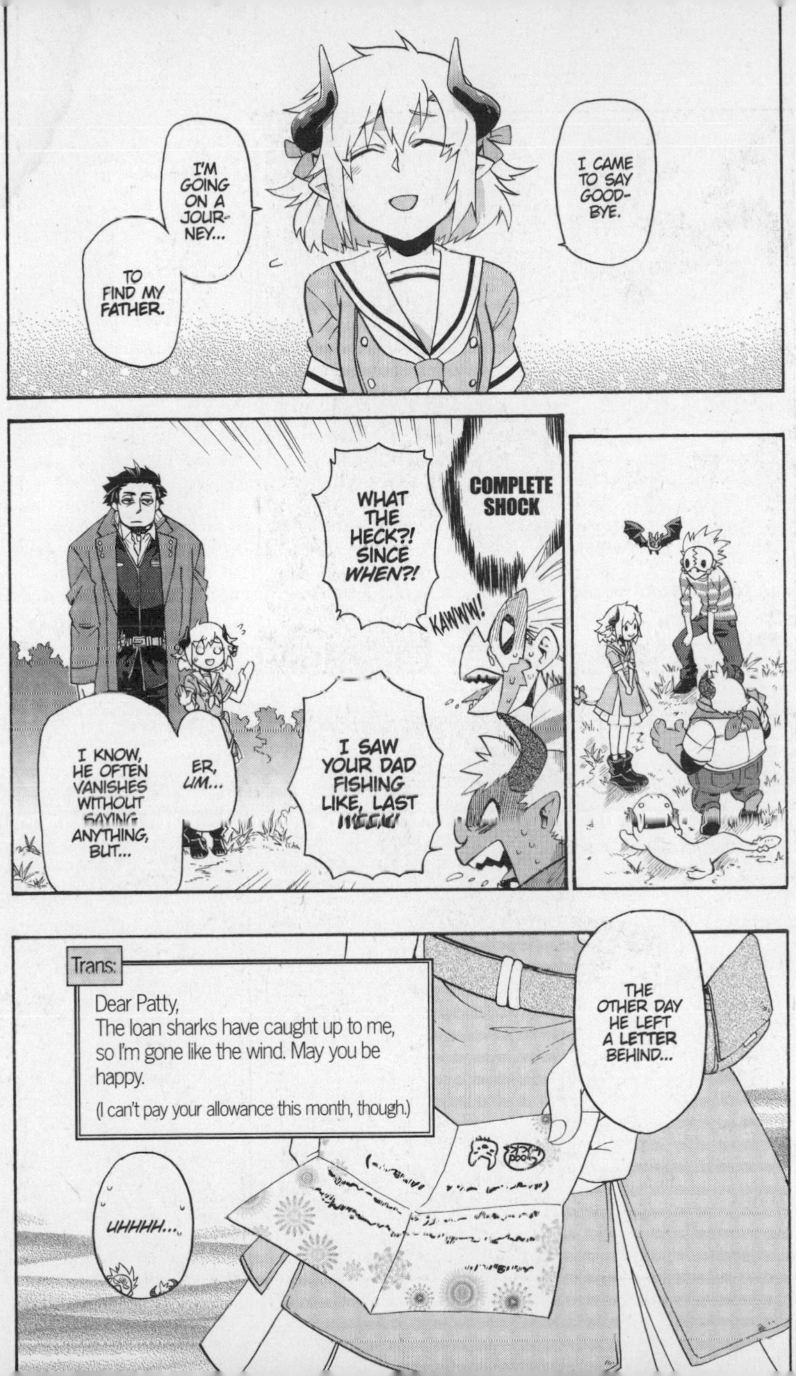
I CAME TO SAY GOOD-BYE.
I'M GOING ON A JOURNEY...
TO FIND MY FATHER.
COMPLETE SHOCK
WHAT THE HECK?! SINCE WHEN?!
KAWWW!
I SAW YOUR DAD FISHING LIKE, LAST
ER, UM...
I KNOW, HE OFTEN VANISHES WITHOUT SAYING ANYTHING, BUT...
THE OTHER DAY HE LEFT A LETTER BEHIND...
Trans:
Dear Patty,
The loan sharks have caught up to me, so I'm gone like the wind. May you be happy.
(I can't pay your allowance this month, though.)
UHHHH...

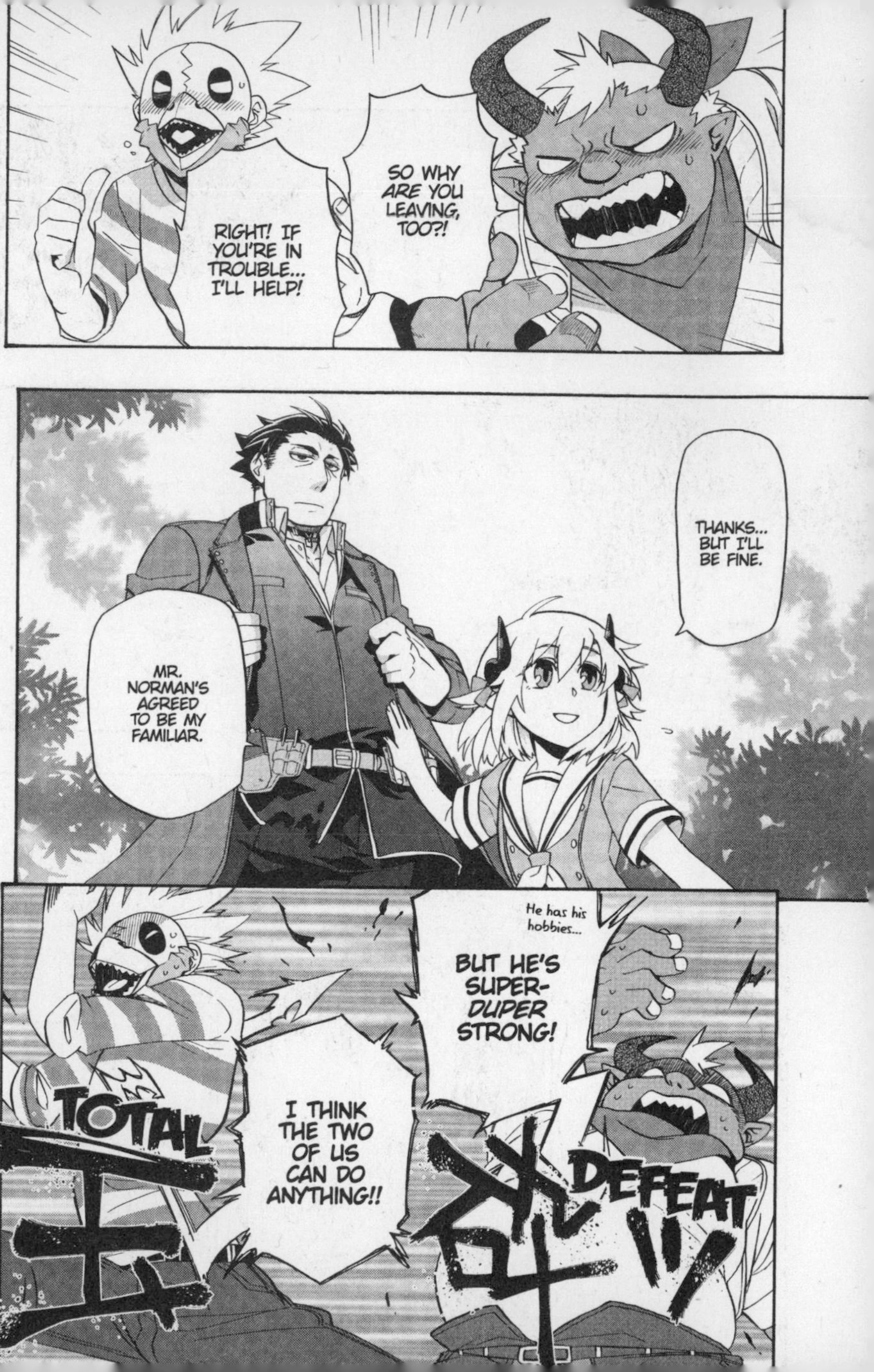
SO WHY ARE YOU LEAVING, TOO?!
RIGHT! IF YOU'RE IN TROUBLE... I'LL HELP!
THANKS... BUT I'LL BE FINE.
MR. NORMAN'S AGREED TO BE MY FAMILIAR.
He has his hobbies...
BUT HE'S SUPER-DUPER STRONG!
DEFEAT
I THINK THE TWO OF US CAN DO ANYTHING!!
TOTAL

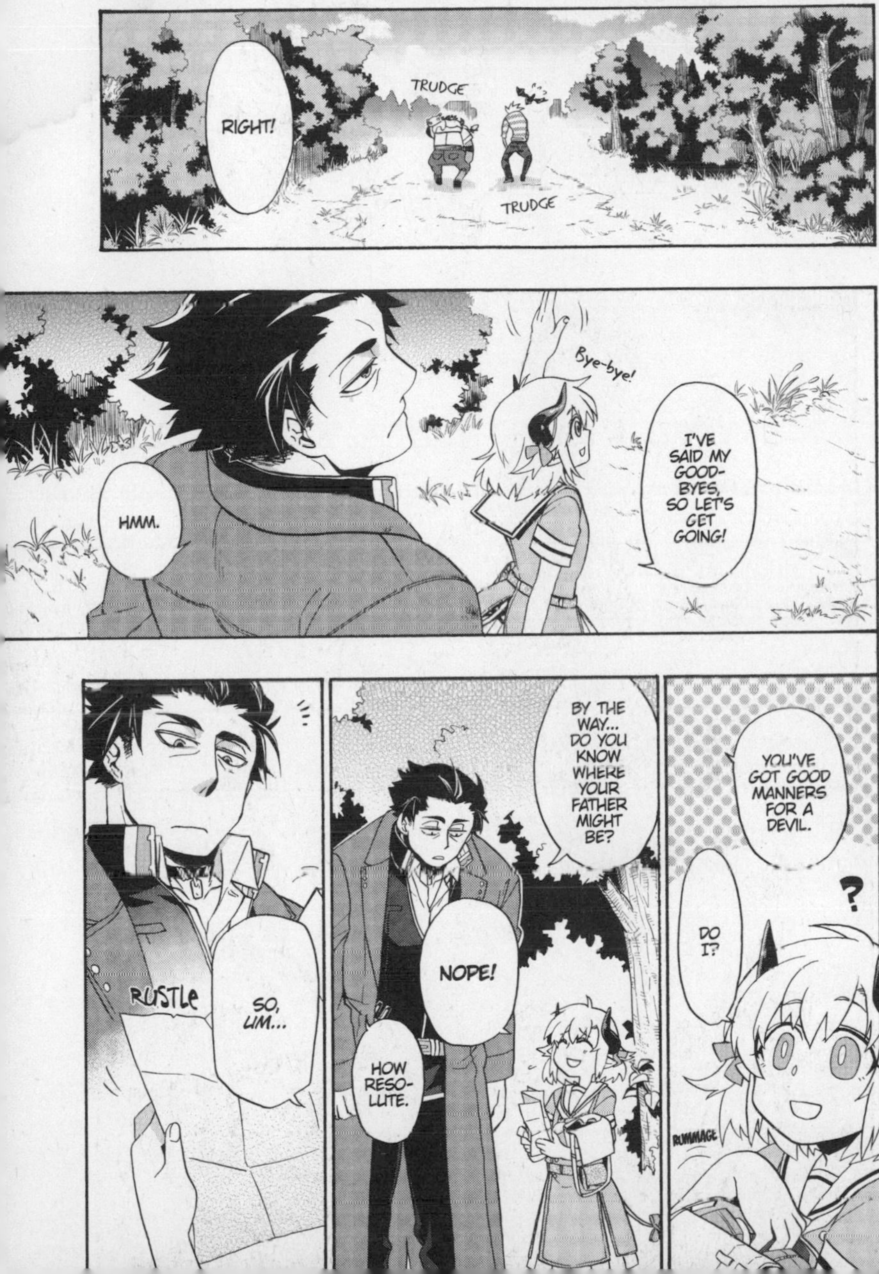
RIGHT!
TRUDGE
TRUDGE
Bye-bye!
I'VE SAID MY GOOD-BYES, SO LET'S GET GOING!
HMM.
YOU'VE GOT GOOD MANNERS FOR A DEVIL.
DO I?
?
RUMMAGE
BY THE WAY... DO YOU KNOW WHERE YOUR FATHER MIGHT BE?
NOPE!
HOW RESO-LUTE.
RUSTLE
SO, UM...

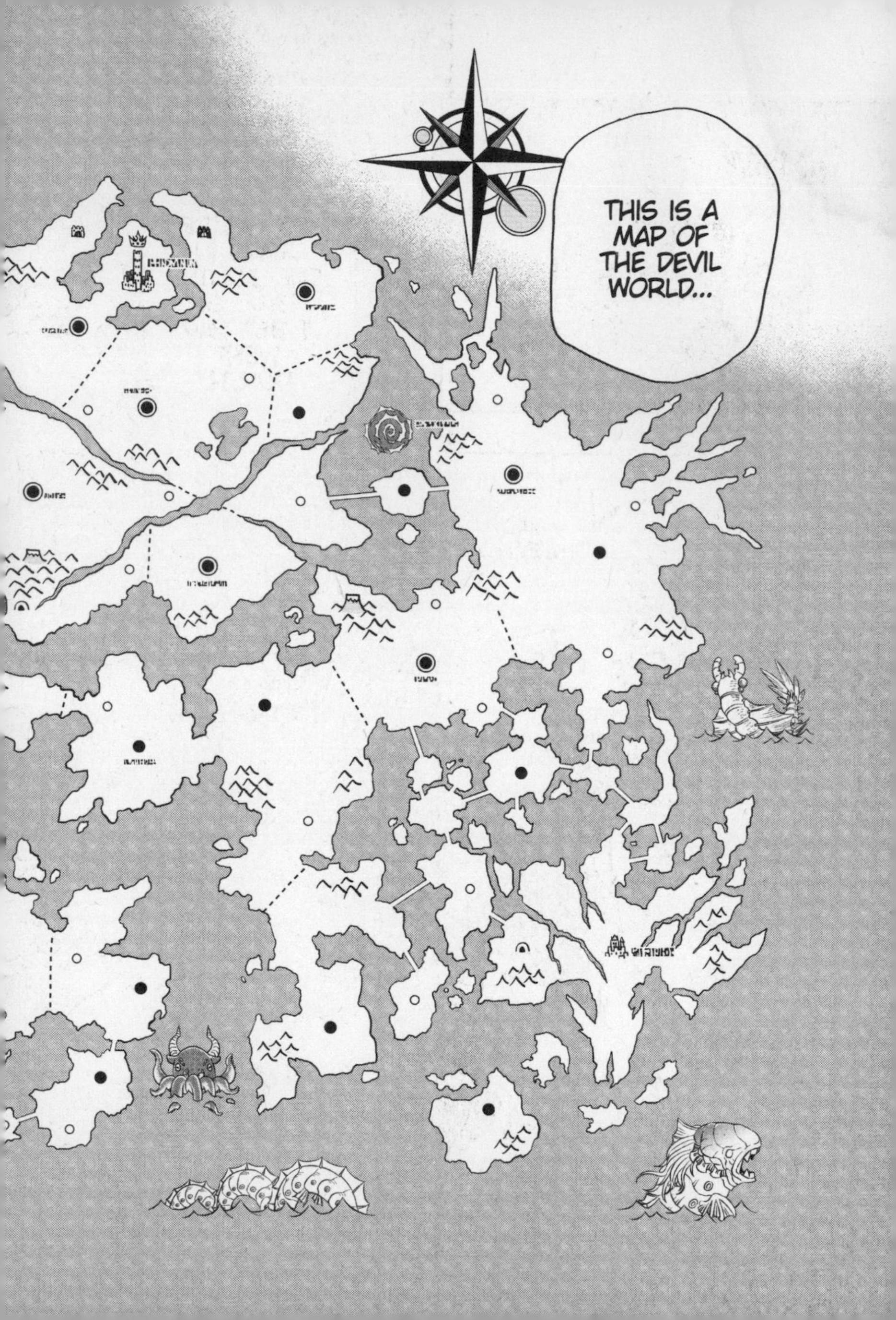
THIS IS A MAP OF THE DEVIL WORLD...

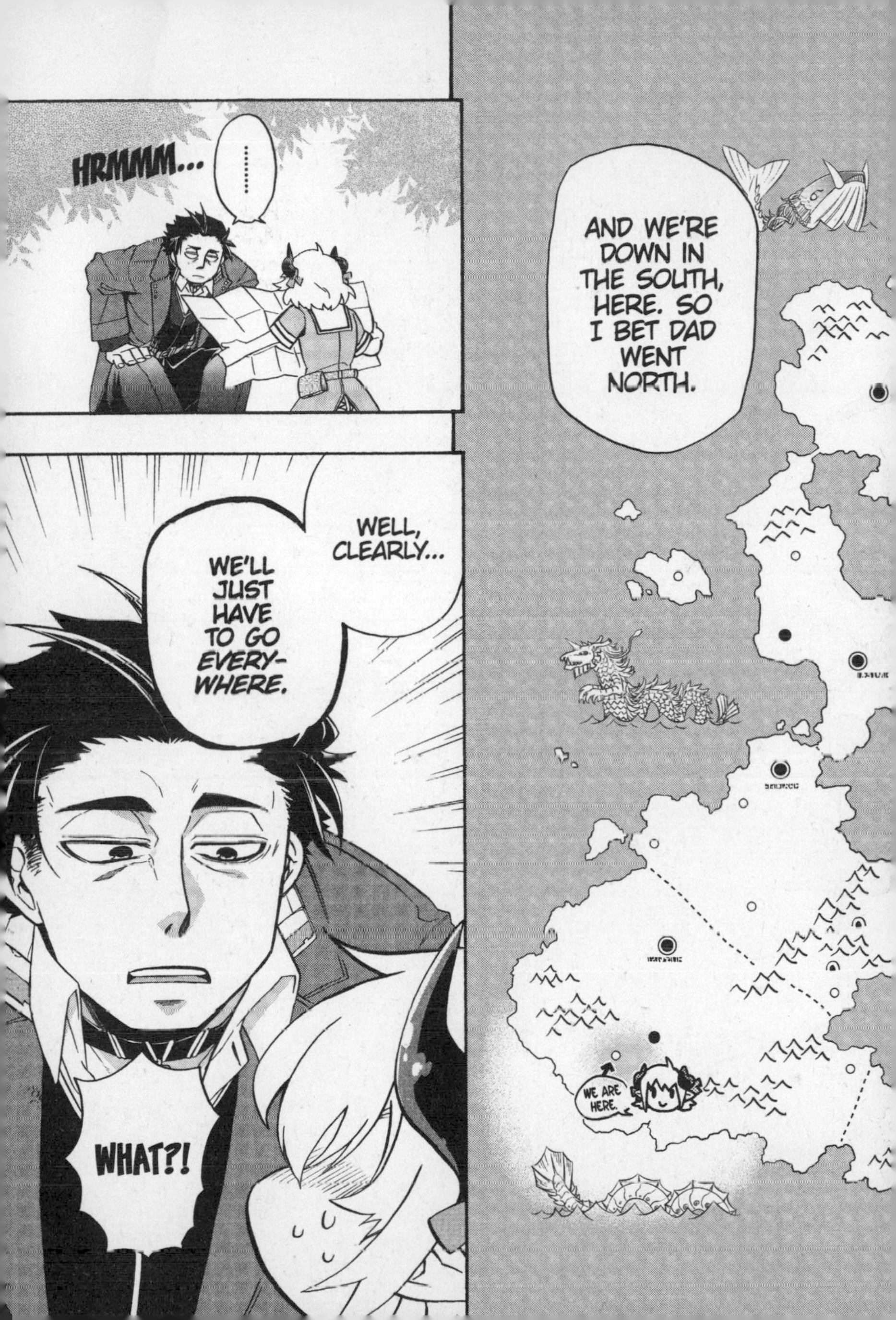
AND WE'RE DOWN IN THE SOUTH, HERE. SO I BET DAD WENT NORTH.
WE ARE HERE.
......
HRMMM...
WELL, CLEARLY...
WE'LL JUST HAVE TO GO EVERY-WHERE.
WHAT?!

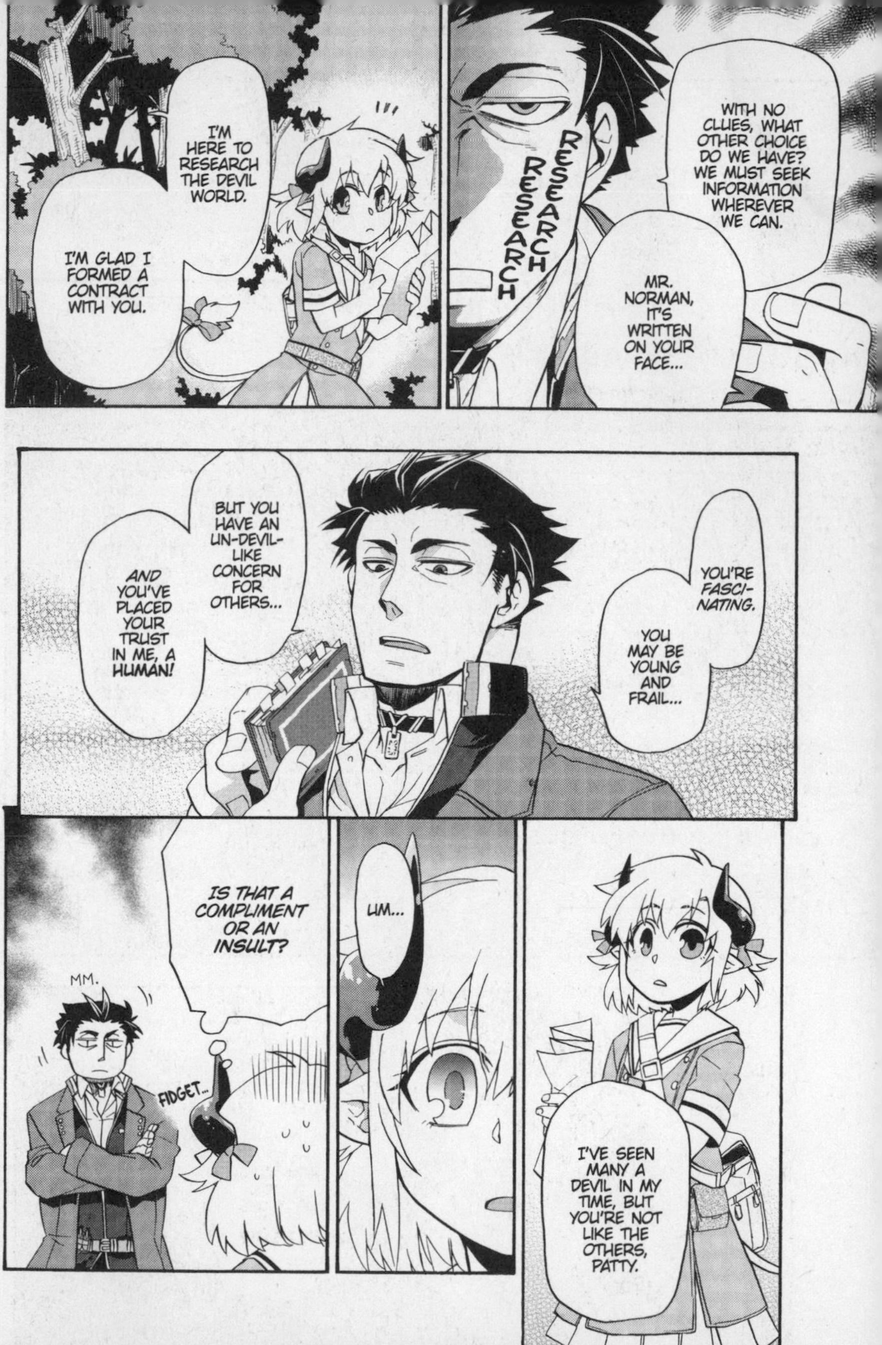
WITH NO CLUES, WHAT OTHER CHOICE DO WE HAVE? WE MUST SEEK INFORMATION WHEREVER WE CAN.
RESEARCH
RESEARCH
MR. NORMAN, IT'S WRITTEN ON YOUR FACE...
I'M HERE TO RESEARCH THE DEVIL WORLD.
I'M GLAD I FORMED A CONTRACT WITH YOU.
YOU'RE FASCINATING.
YOU MAY BE YOUNG AND FRAIL...
BUT YOU HAVE AN UN-DEVIL-LIKE CONCERN FOR OTHERS...
AND YOU'VE PLACED YOUR TRUST IN ME, A HUMAN!
I'VE SEEN MANY A DEVIL IN MY TIME, BUT YOU'RE NOT LIKE THE OTHERS, PATTY.
UM...
IS THAT A COMPLIMENT OR AN INSULT?
MM.
FIDGET...

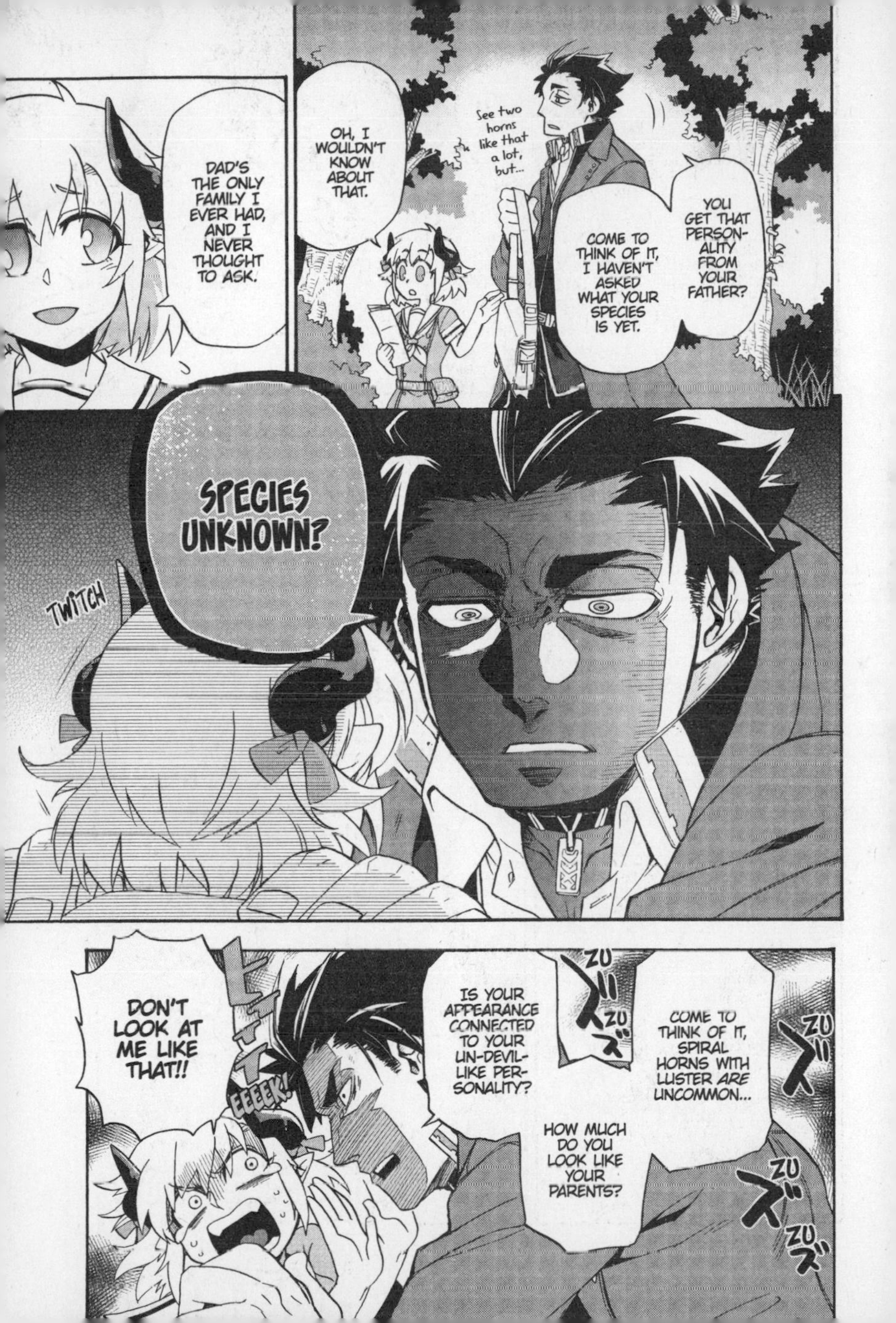
YOU GET THAT PERSON-ALITY FROM YOUR FATHER?
COME TO THINK OF IT, I HAVEN'T ASKED WHAT YOUR SPECIES IS YET.
See two horns like that a lot, but...
OH, I WOULDN'T KNOW ABOUT THAT.
DAD'S THE ONLY FAMILY I EVER HAD, AND I NEVER THOUGHT TO ASK.
SPECIES UNKNOWN?
TWITCH
ZU
COME TO THINK OF IT, SPIRAL HORNS WITH LUSTER *ARE* UNCOMMON...
ZU
ZU
IS YOUR APPEARANCE CONNECTED TO YOUR UN-DEVIL-LIKE PER-SONALITY?
HOW MUCH DO YOU LOOK LIKE YOUR PARENTS?
ZU
ZU
DON'T LOOK AT ME LIKE THAT!!
EEEEK!

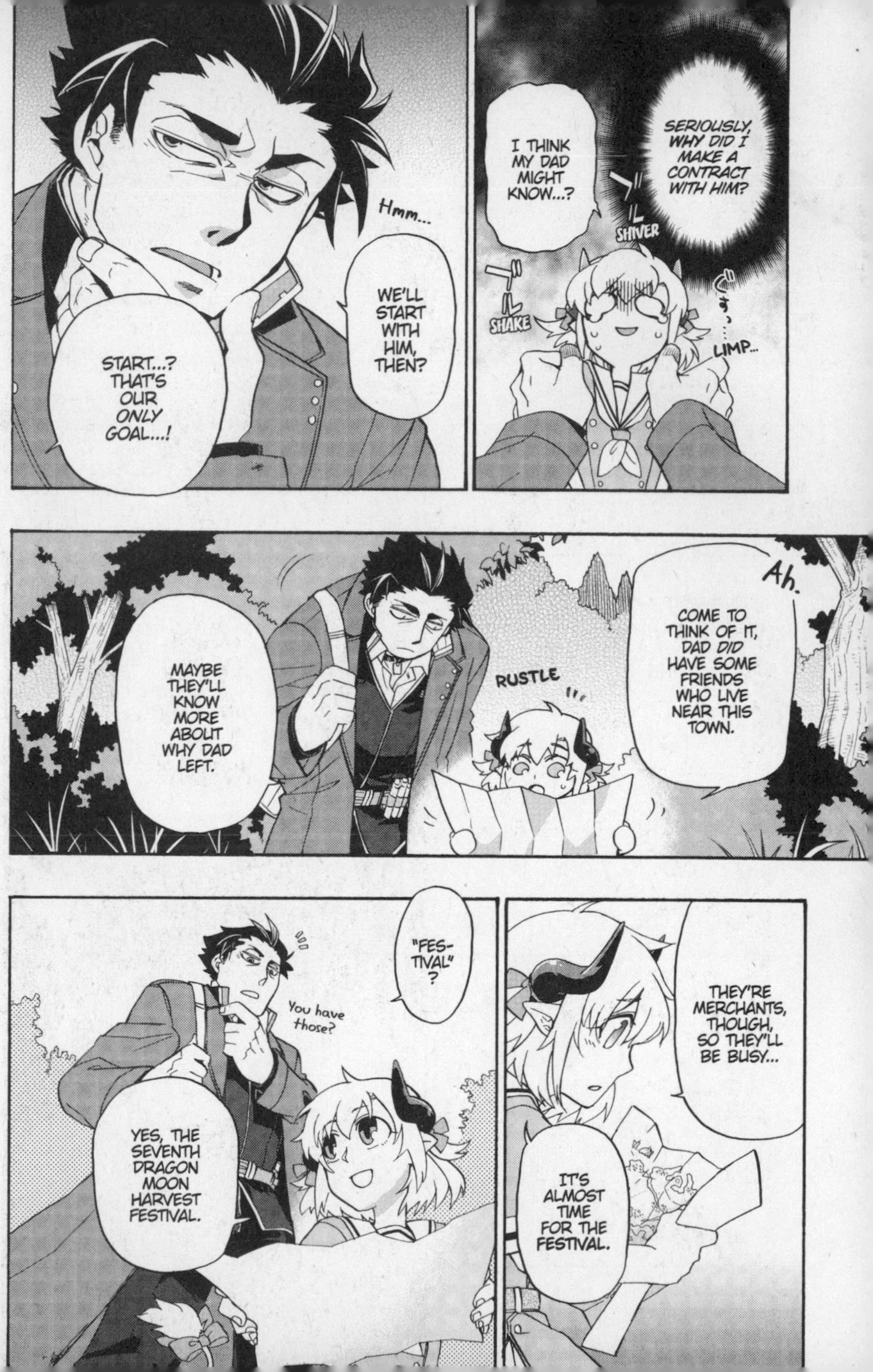
SERIOUSLY, WHY DID I MAKE A CONTRACT WITH HIM?
I THINK MY DAD MIGHT KNOW...?
SHIVER
SHAKE
LIMP...
Hmm...
WE'LL START WITH HIM, THEN?
START...? THAT'S OUR ONLY GOAL...!
Ah.
COME TO THINK OF IT, DAD DID HAVE SOME FRIENDS WHO LIVE NEAR THIS TOWN.
RUSTLE
MAYBE THEY'LL KNOW MORE ABOUT WHY DAD LEFT.
THEY'RE MERCHANTS, THOUGH, SO THEY'LL BE BUSY...
IT'S ALMOST TIME FOR THE FESTIVAL.
"FES-TIVAL"?
You have those?
YES, THE SEVENTH DRAGON MOON HARVEST FESTIVAL.

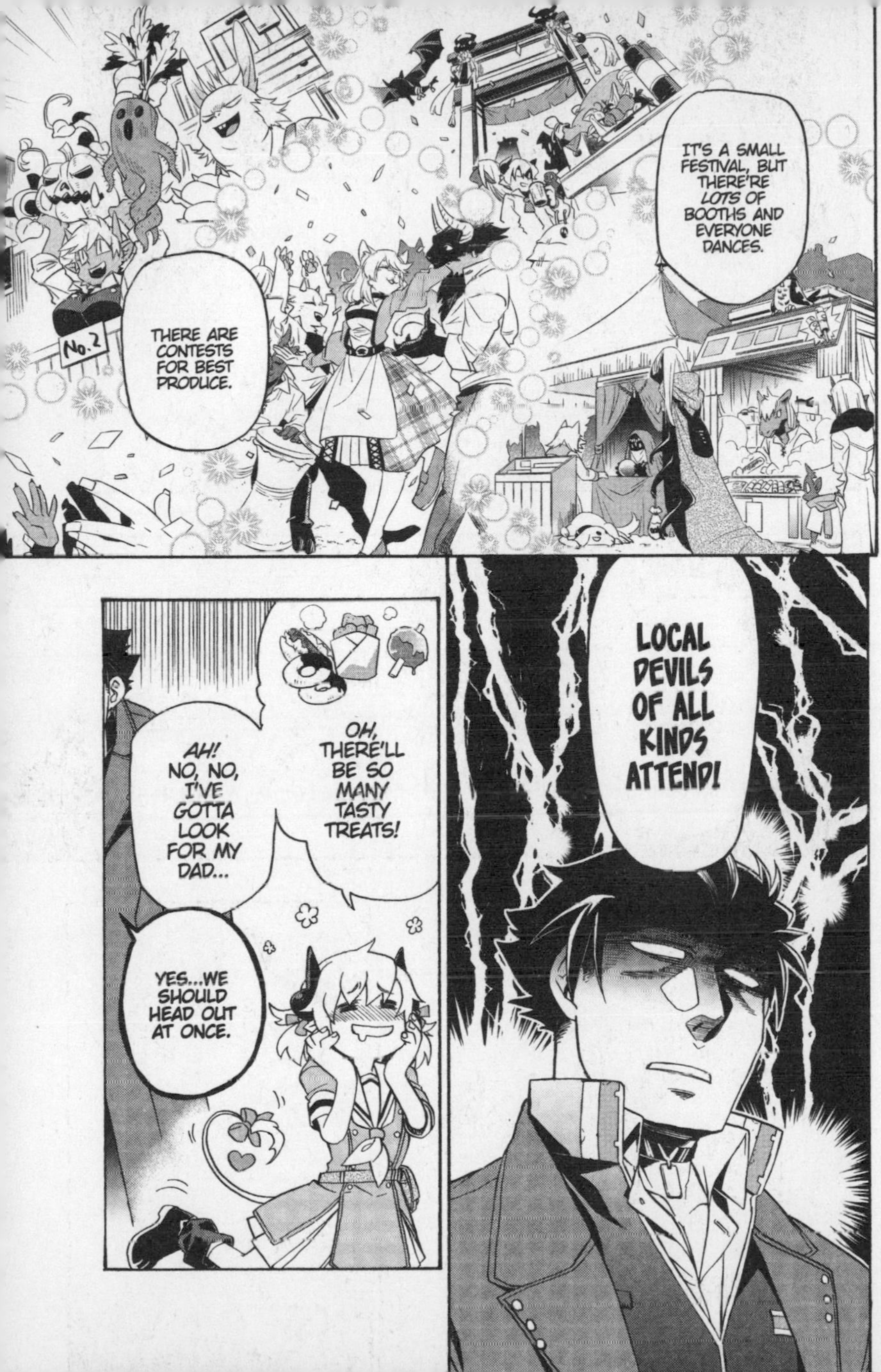
IT'S A SMALL FESTIVAL, BUT THERE'RE *LOTS* OF BOOTHS AND EVERYONE DANCES.
THERE ARE CONTESTS FOR BEST PRODUCE.
No. 2
LOCAL DEVILS OF ALL KINDS ATTEND!
OH, THERE'LL BE SO MANY TASTY TREATS!
AH! NO, NO, I'VE GOTTA LOOK FOR MY DAD...
YES...WE SHOULD HEAD OUT AT ONCE.

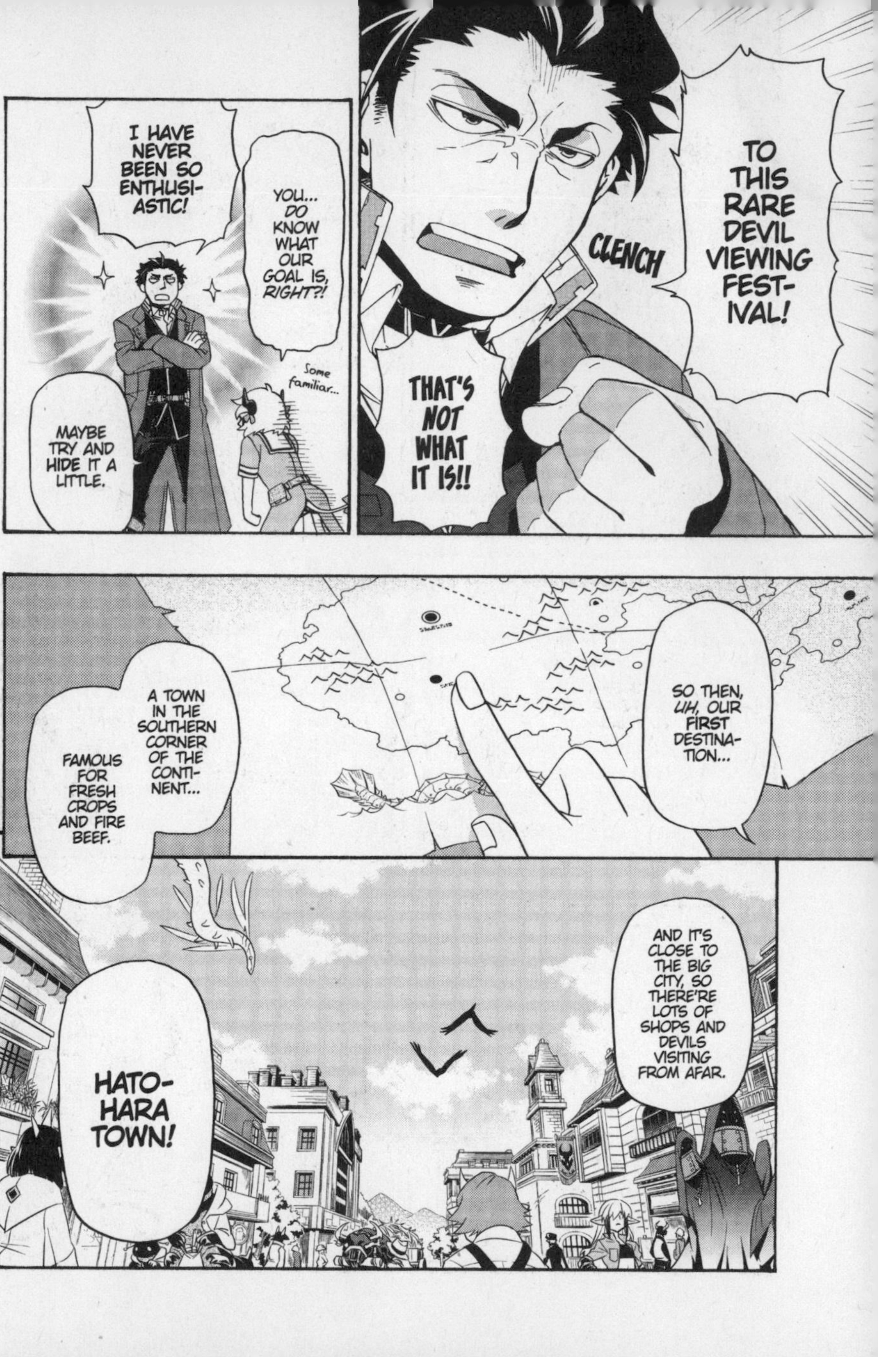
TO THIS RARE DEVIL VIEWING FESTIVAL!
CLENCH
THAT'S NOT WHAT IT IS!!
I HAVE NEVER BEEN SO ENTHUSIASTIC!
YOU... DO KNOW WHAT OUR GOAL IS, RIGHT?!
Some familiar...
MAYBE TRY AND HIDE IT A LITTLE.
SO THEN, UH, OUR FIRST DESTINATION...
A TOWN IN THE SOUTHERN CORNER OF THE CONTINENT...
FAMOUS FOR FRESH CROPS AND FIRE BEEF.
AND IT'S CLOSE TO THE BIG CITY, SO THERE'RE LOTS OF SHOPS AND DEVILS VISITING FROM AFAR.
HATO-HARA TOWN!

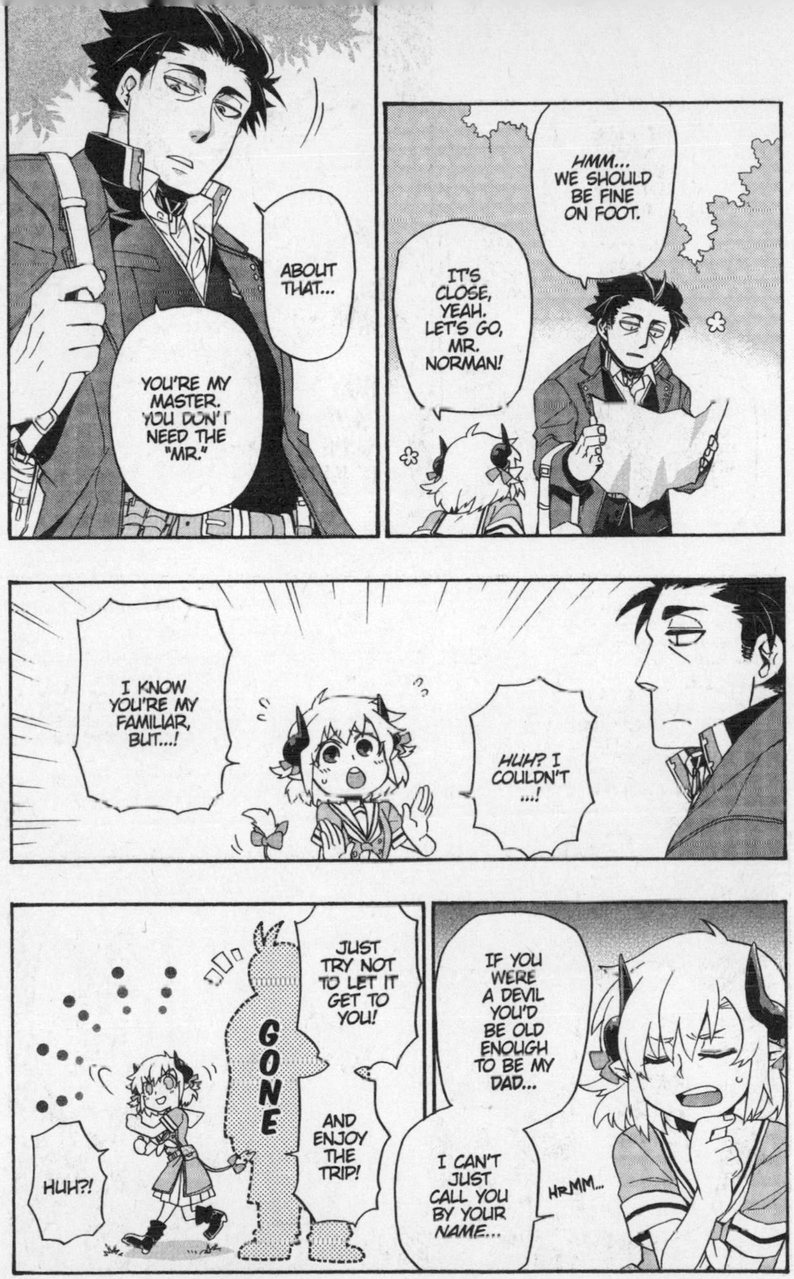
HMM... WE SHOULD BE FINE ON FOOT.
IT'S CLOSE, YEAH. LET'S GO, MR. NORMAN!
ABOUT THAT...
YOU'RE MY MASTER. YOU DON'T NEED THE "MR."
HUH? I COULDN'T ...!
I KNOW YOU'RE MY FAMILIAR, BUT...!
IF YOU WERE A DEVIL YOU'D BE OLD ENOUGH TO BE MY DAD...
HRMM...
I CAN'T JUST CALL YOU BY YOUR NAME...
JUST TRY NOT TO LET IT GET TO YOU!
GONE
AND ENJOY THE TRIP!
HUH?!

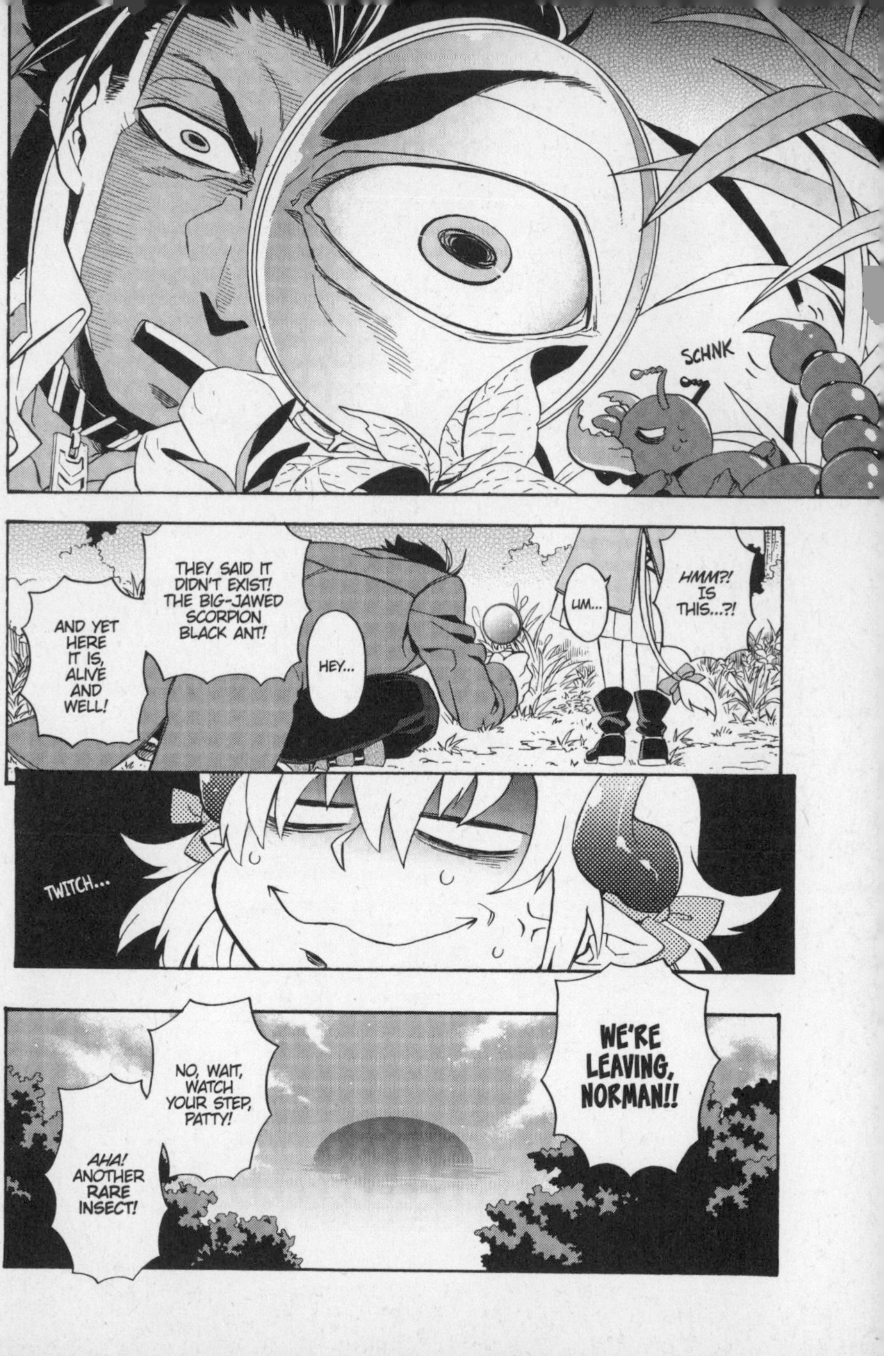
SCHNK
HMM?! IS THIS...?!
UM...
THEY SAID IT DIDN'T EXIST! THE BIG-JAWED SCORPION BLACK ANT!
HEY...
AND YET HERE IT IS, ALIVE AND WELL!
TWITCH...
WE'RE LEAVING, NORMAN!!
NO, WAIT, WATCH YOUR STEP, PATTY!
AHA! ANOTHER RARE INSECT!

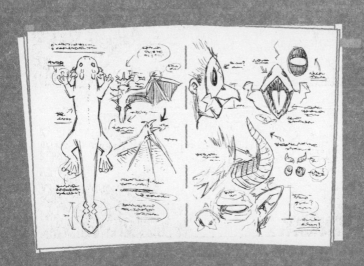

Sorry For My Familiar

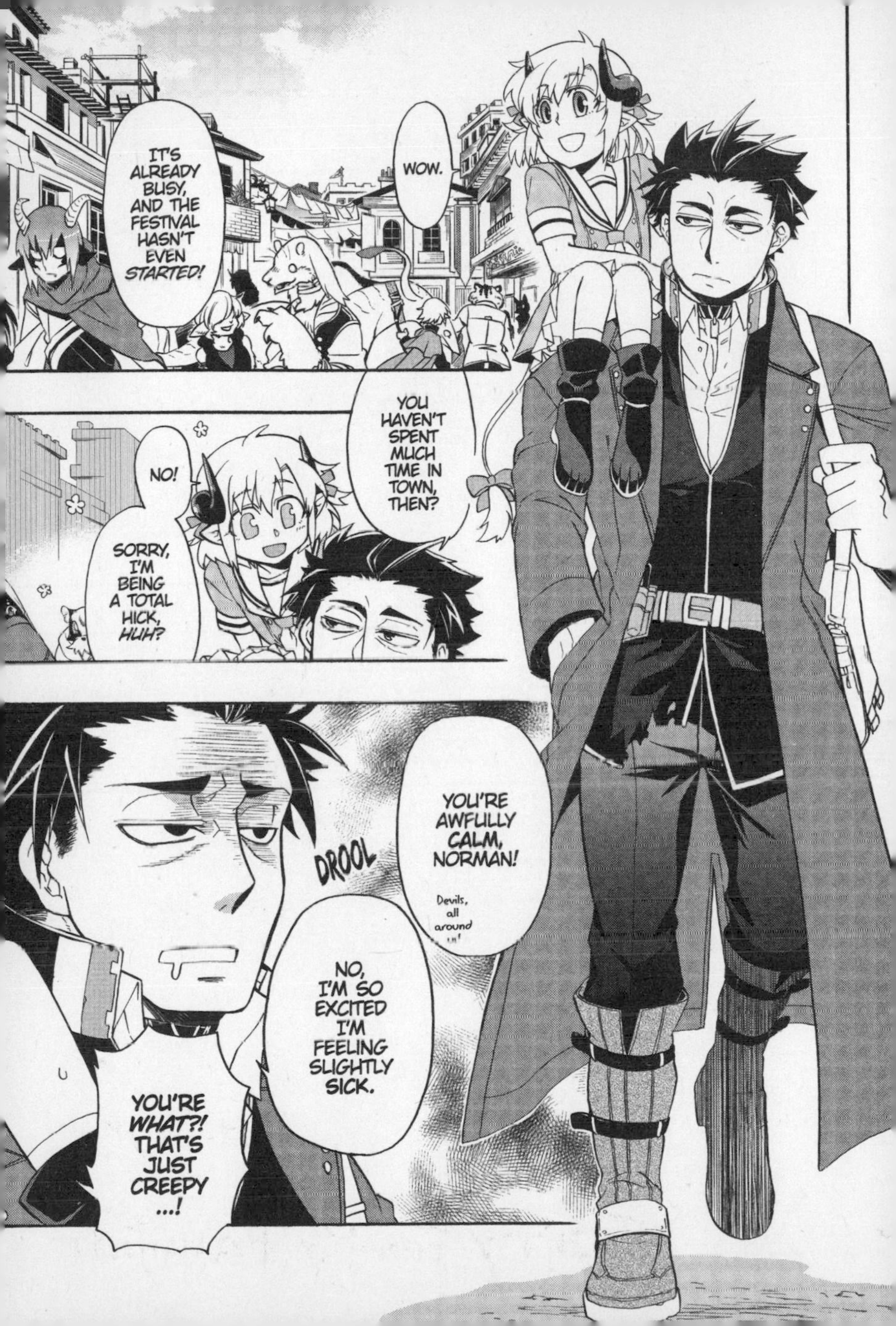
WOW.
IT'S ALREADY BUSY, AND THE FESTIVAL HASN'T EVEN *STARTED!*
YOU HAVEN'T SPENT MUCH TIME IN TOWN, THEN?
NO!
SORRY, I'M BEING A TOTAL HICK, *HUH?*
YOU'RE AWFULLY CALM, NORMAN!
Devils, all around us!
DROOL
NO, I'M SO EXCITED I'M FEELING SLIGHTLY SICK.
YOU'RE *WHAT?!* THAT'S JUST CREEPY ...!

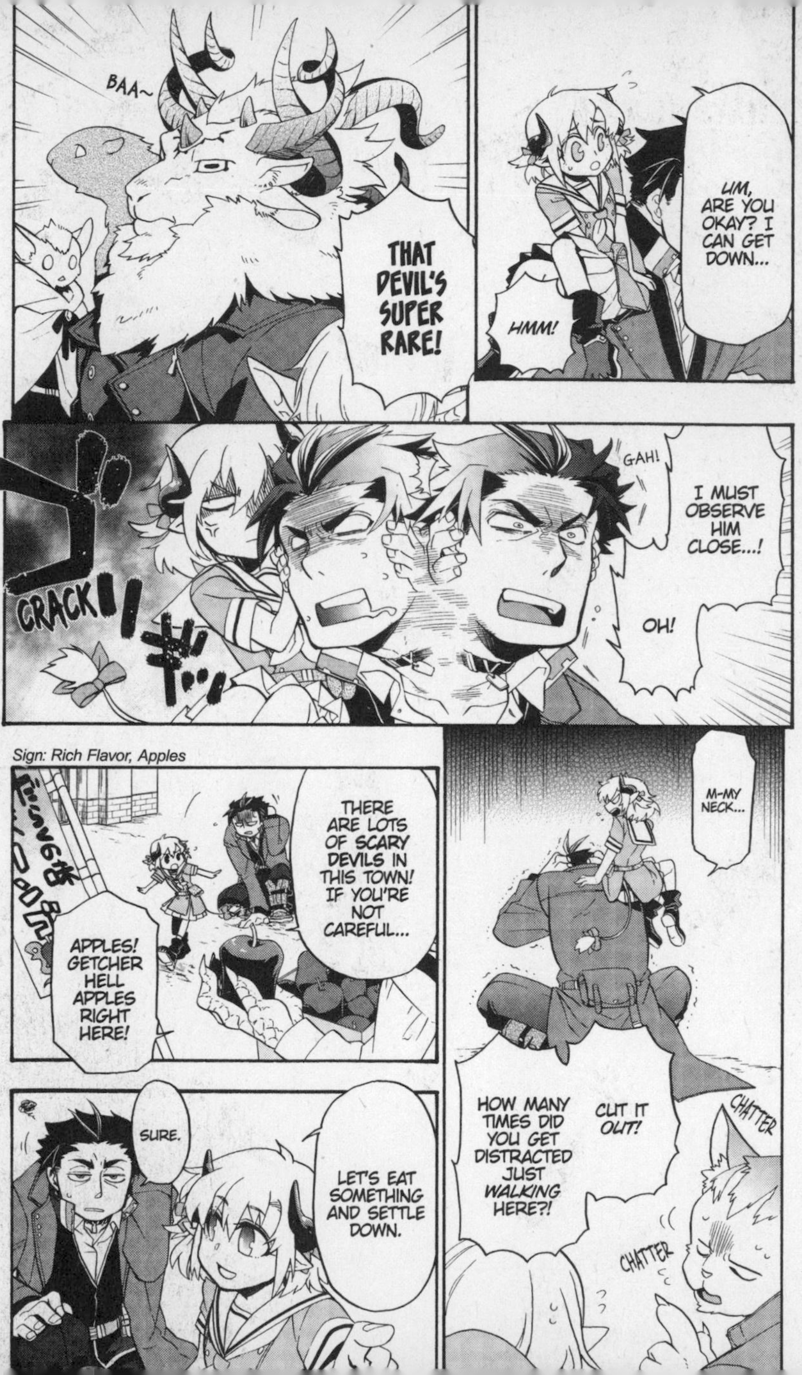
UM, ARE YOU OKAY? I CAN GET DOWN...
HMM!
BAA~
THAT DEVIL'S SUPER RARE!
GAH!
I MUST OBSERVE HIM CLOSE...!
OH!
CRACK
M-MY NECK...
CUT IT OUT!
HOW MANY TIMES DID YOU GET DISTRACTED JUST WALKING HERE?!
CHATTER
CHATTER
Sign: Rich Flavor, Apples
THERE ARE LOTS OF SCARY DEVILS IN THIS TOWN! IF YOU'RE NOT CAREFUL...
APPLES! GETCHER HELL APPLES RIGHT HERE!
LET'S EAT SOMETHING AND SETTLE DOWN.
SURE.

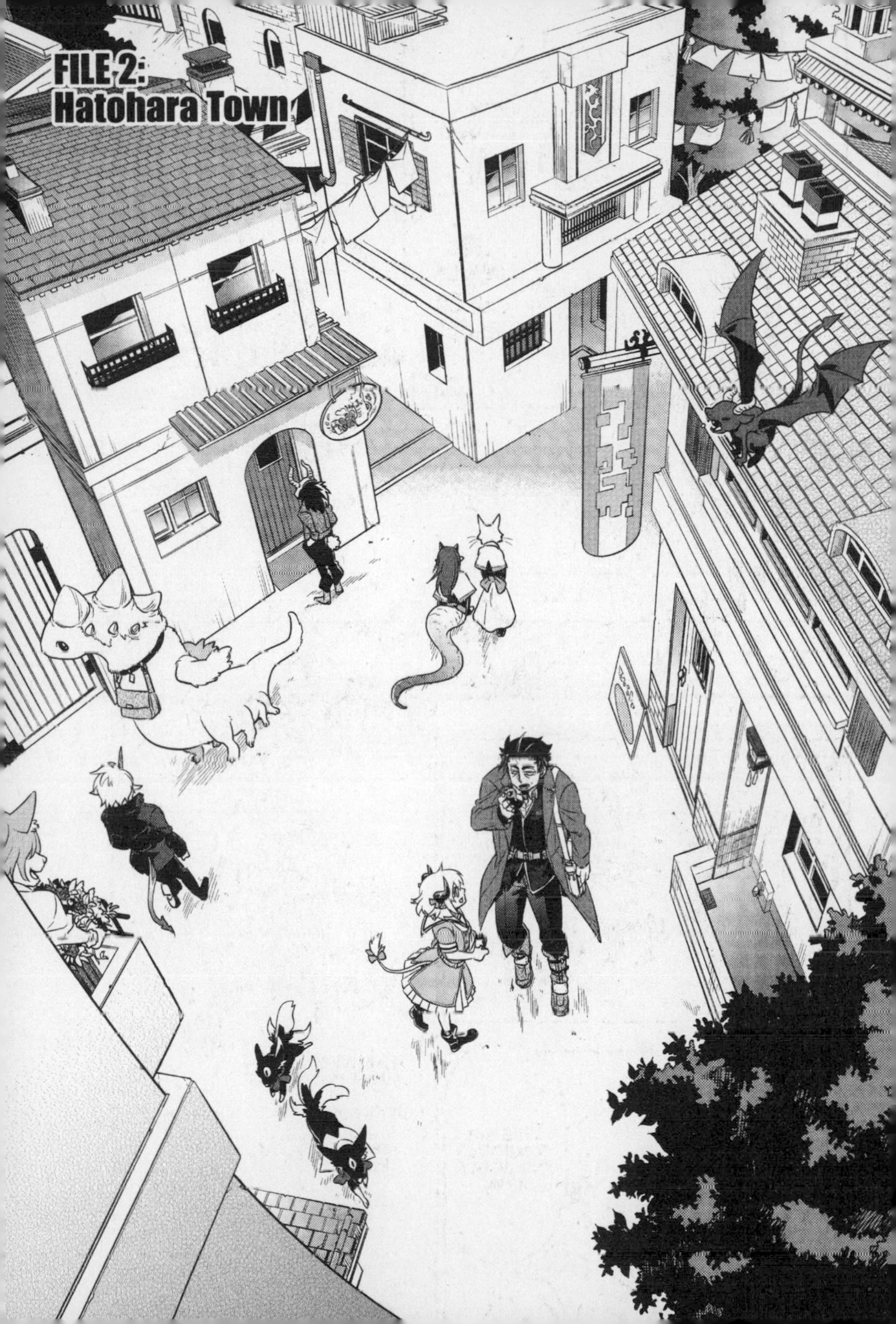
FILE 2:
Hatohara Town

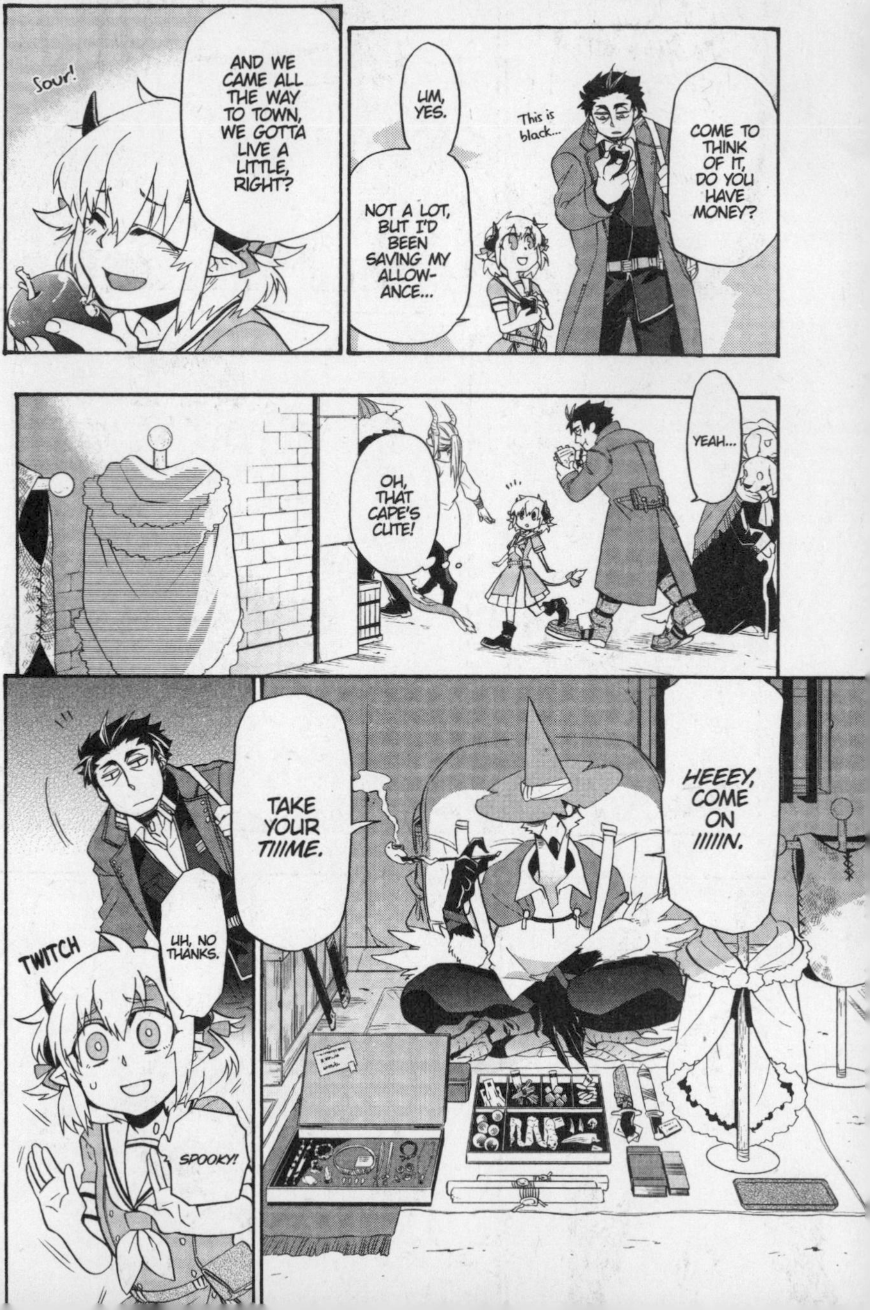
COME TO THINK OF IT, DO YOU HAVE MONEY?
This is black...
UM, YES.
NOT A LOT, BUT I'D BEEN SAVING MY ALLOWANCE...
AND WE CAME ALL THE WAY TO TOWN, WE GOTTA LIVE A LITTLE, RIGHT?
Sour!
YEAH...
OH, THAT CAPE'S CUTE!
HEEEY, COME ON IIIIIN.
TAKE YOUR TIIIME.
UH, NO THANKS.
TWITCH
SPOOKY!

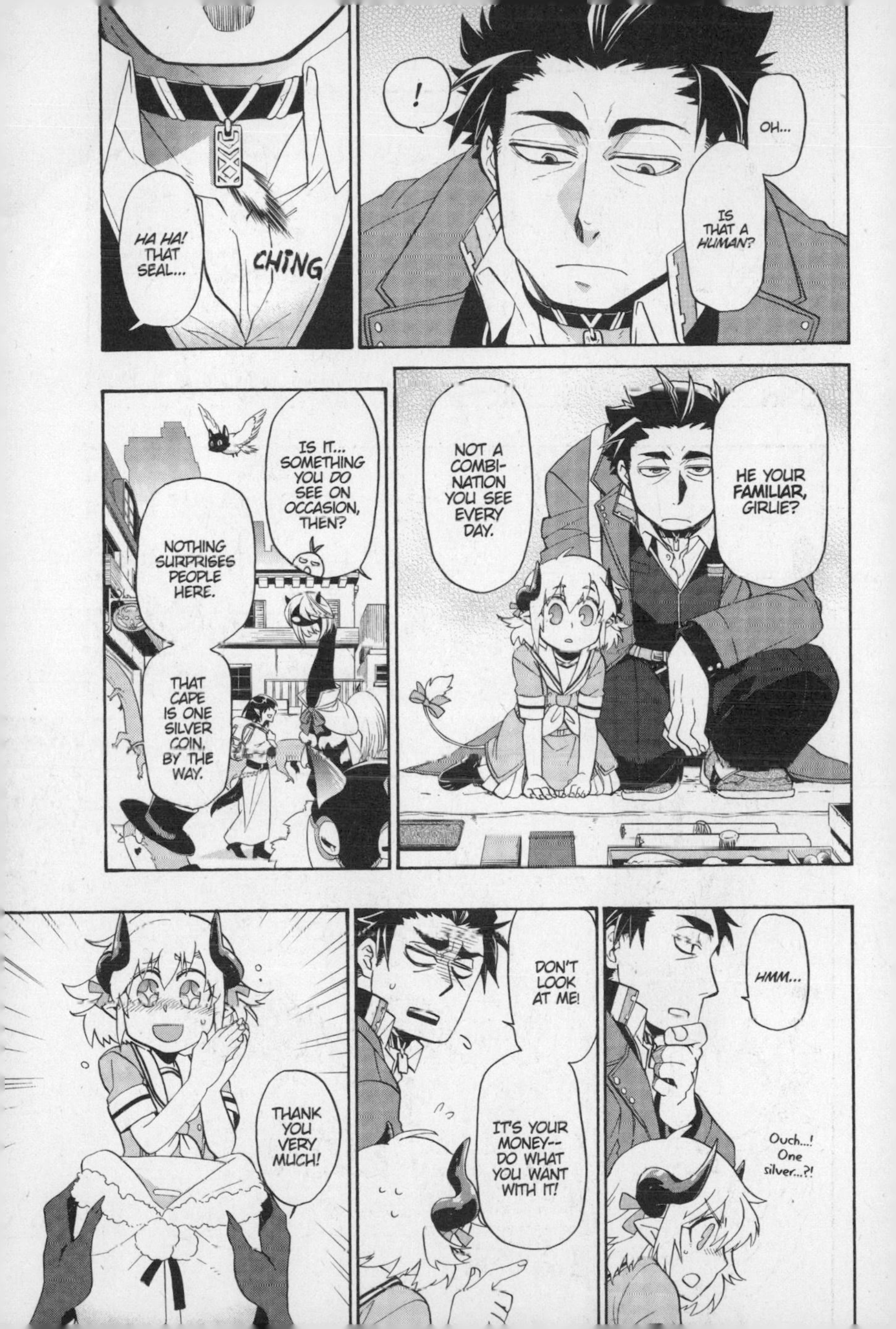
!
OH...
IS THAT A HUMAN?
HA HA! THAT SEAL...
CHING
HE YOUR FAMILIAR, GIRLIE?
NOT A COMBINATION YOU SEE EVERY DAY.
IS IT... SOMETHING YOU DO SEE ON OCCASION, THEN?
NOTHING SURPRISES PEOPLE HERE.
THAT CAPE IS ONE SILVER COIN, BY THE WAY.
HMM...
Ouch...! One silver...?!
DON'T LOOK AT ME!
IT'S YOUR MONEY-- DO WHAT YOU WANT WITH IT!
THANK YOU VERY MUCH!

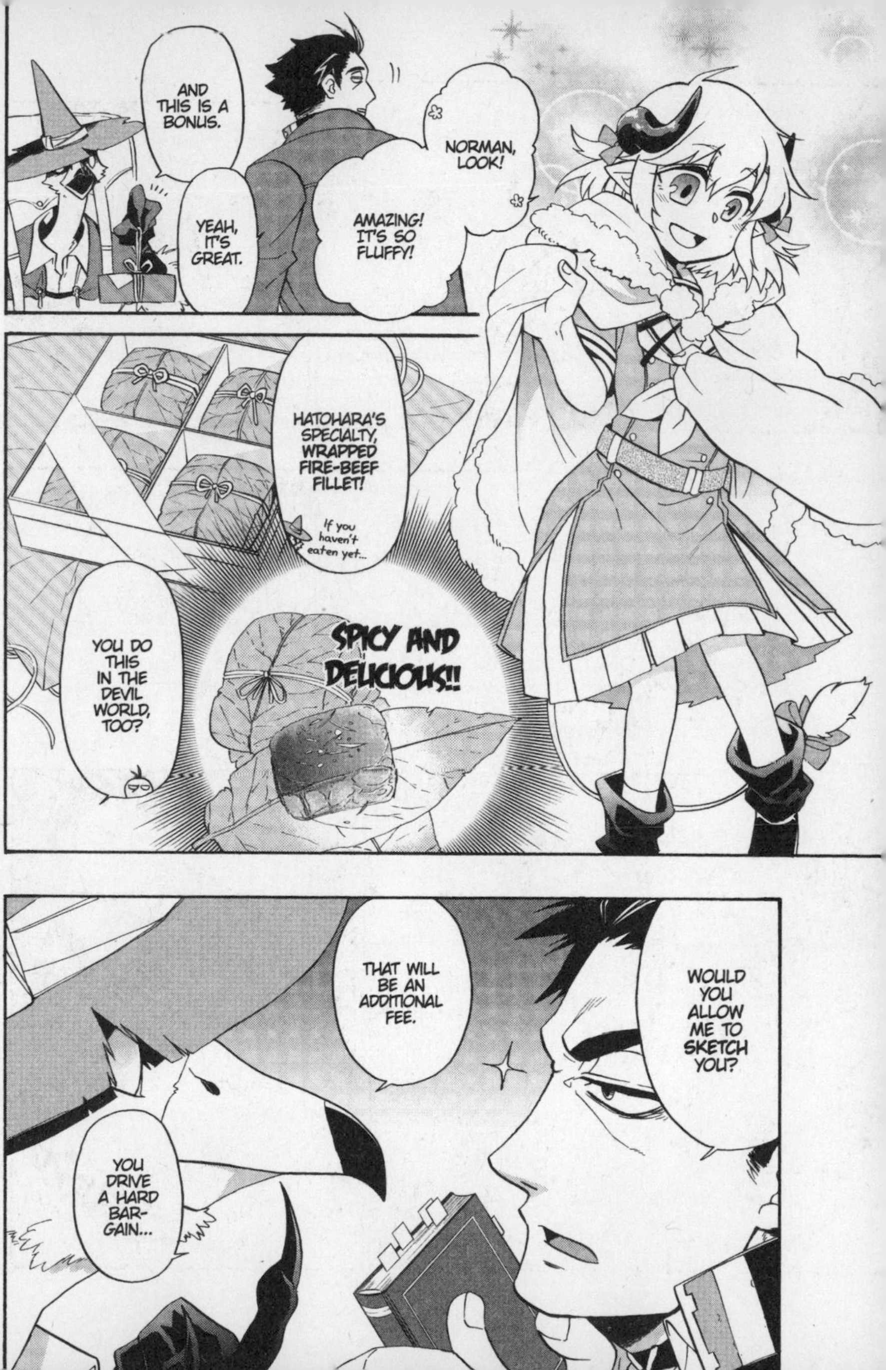
NORMAN, LOOK!
AMAZING! IT'S SO FLUFFY!
YEAH, IT'S GREAT.
AND THIS IS A BONUS.
HATOHARA'S SPECIALTY, WRAPPED FIRE-BEEF FILLET!
If you haven't eaten yet...
SPICY AND DELICIOUS!!
YOU DO THIS IN THE DEVIL WORLD, TOO?
WOULD YOU ALLOW ME TO SKETCH YOU?
THAT WILL BE AN ADDITIONAL FEE.
YOU DRIVE A HARD BAR-GAIN...

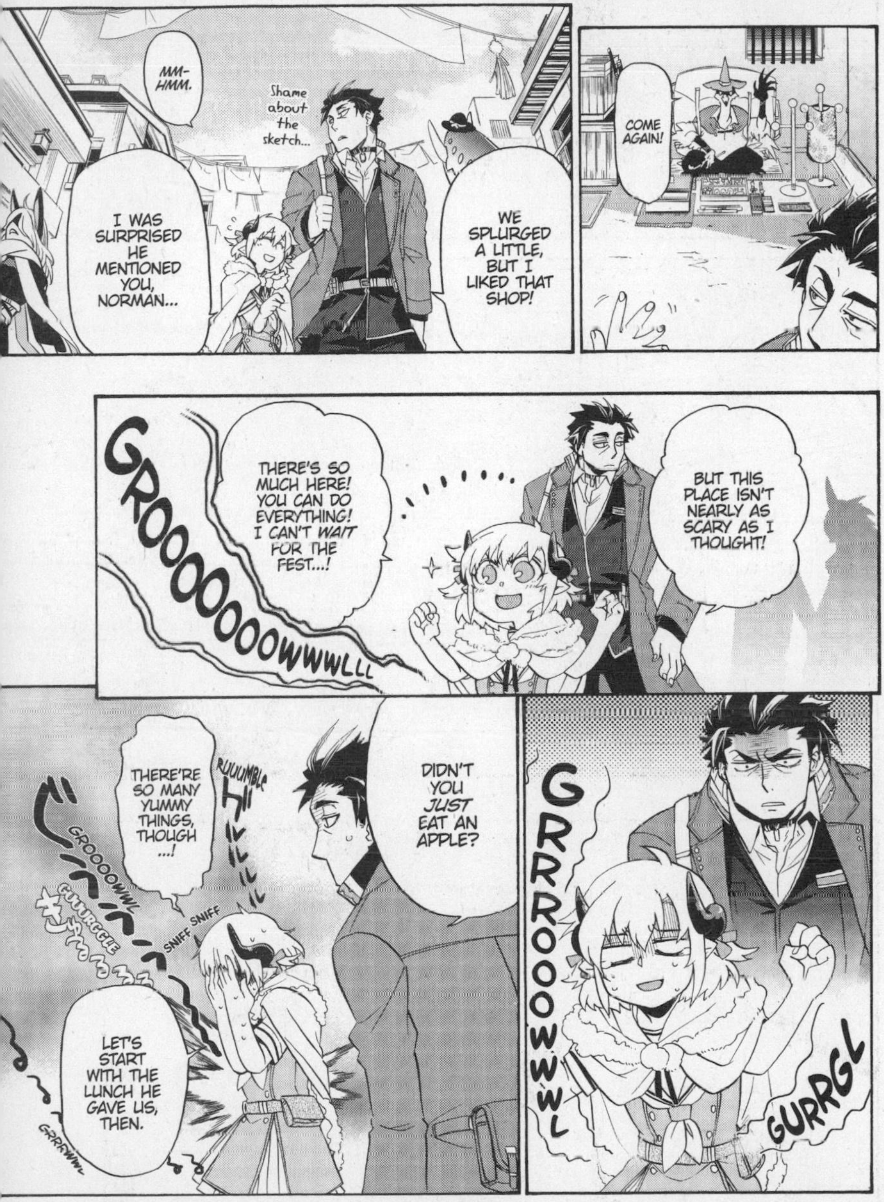
COME AGAIN!
WE SPLURGED A LITTLE, BUT I LIKED THAT SHOP!
Shame about the sketch...
MM-HMM.
I WAS SURPRISED HE MENTIONED YOU, NORMAN...
BUT THIS PLACE ISN'T NEARLY AS SCARY AS I THOUGHT!
......
THERE'S SO MUCH HERE! YOU CAN DO EVERYTHING! I CAN'T WAIT FOR THE FEST...!
GROOOOOOOOOWWWLLL
GRRROOOOWWWL
GURRGL
DIDN'T YOU JUST EAT AN APPLE?
RUUUMBLE
THERE'RE SO MANY YUMMY THINGS, THOUGH...!
GROOOOOWWL
GUUURGGLE
SNIFF SNIFF
LET'S START WITH THE LUNCH HE GAVE US, THEN.
GRRRWWWL

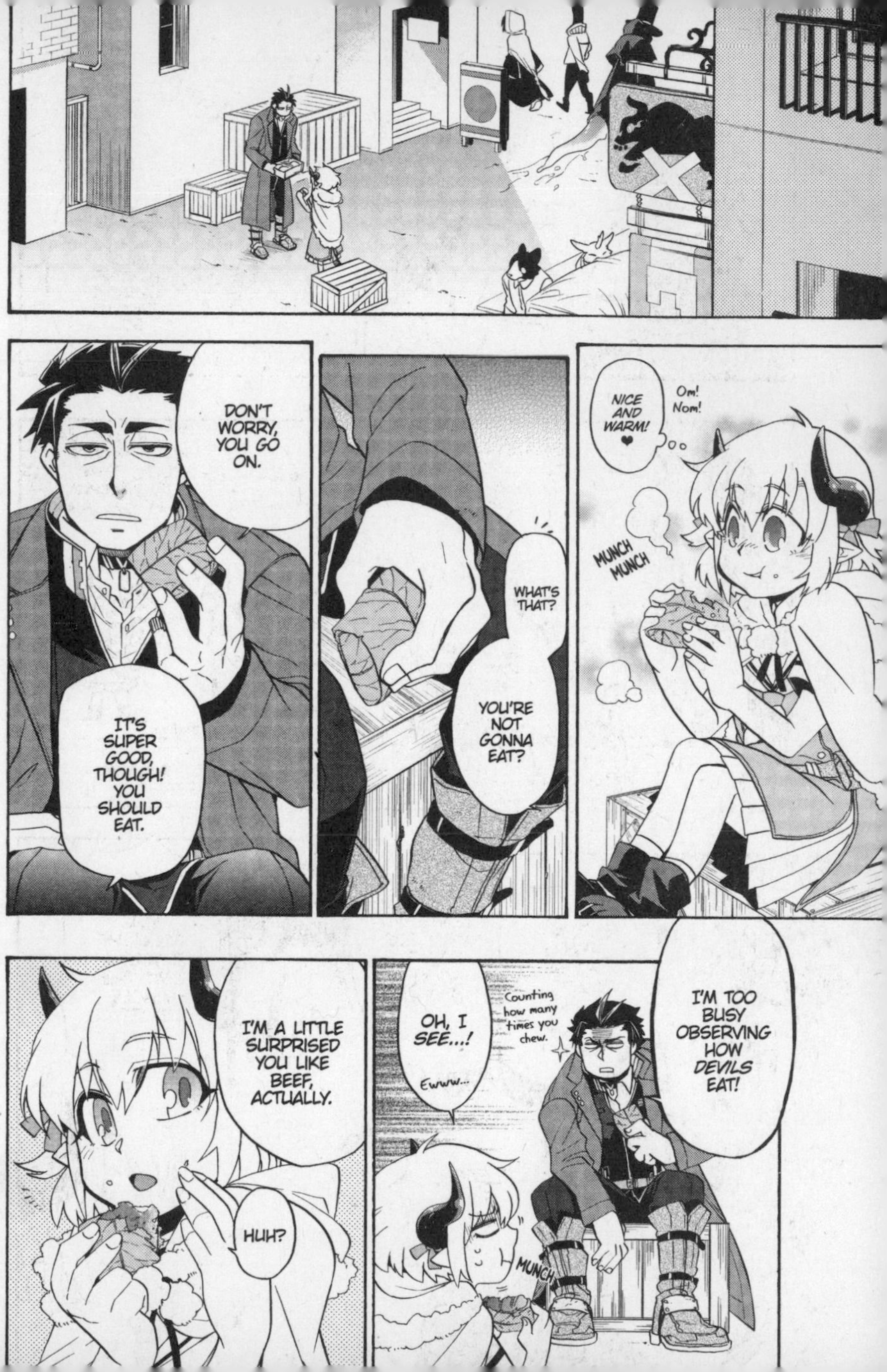
NICE AND WARM! ❤
Om! Nom!
MUNCH MUNCH
WHAT'S THAT?
YOU'RE NOT GONNA EAT?
DON'T WORRY, YOU GO ON.
IT'S SUPER GOOD, THOUGH! YOU SHOULD EAT.
I'M TOO BUSY OBSERVING HOW DEVILS EAT!
Counting how many times you chew.
OH, I SEE...!
Ewww...
MUNCH
I'M A LITTLE SURPRISED YOU LIKE BEEF, ACTUALLY.
HUH?

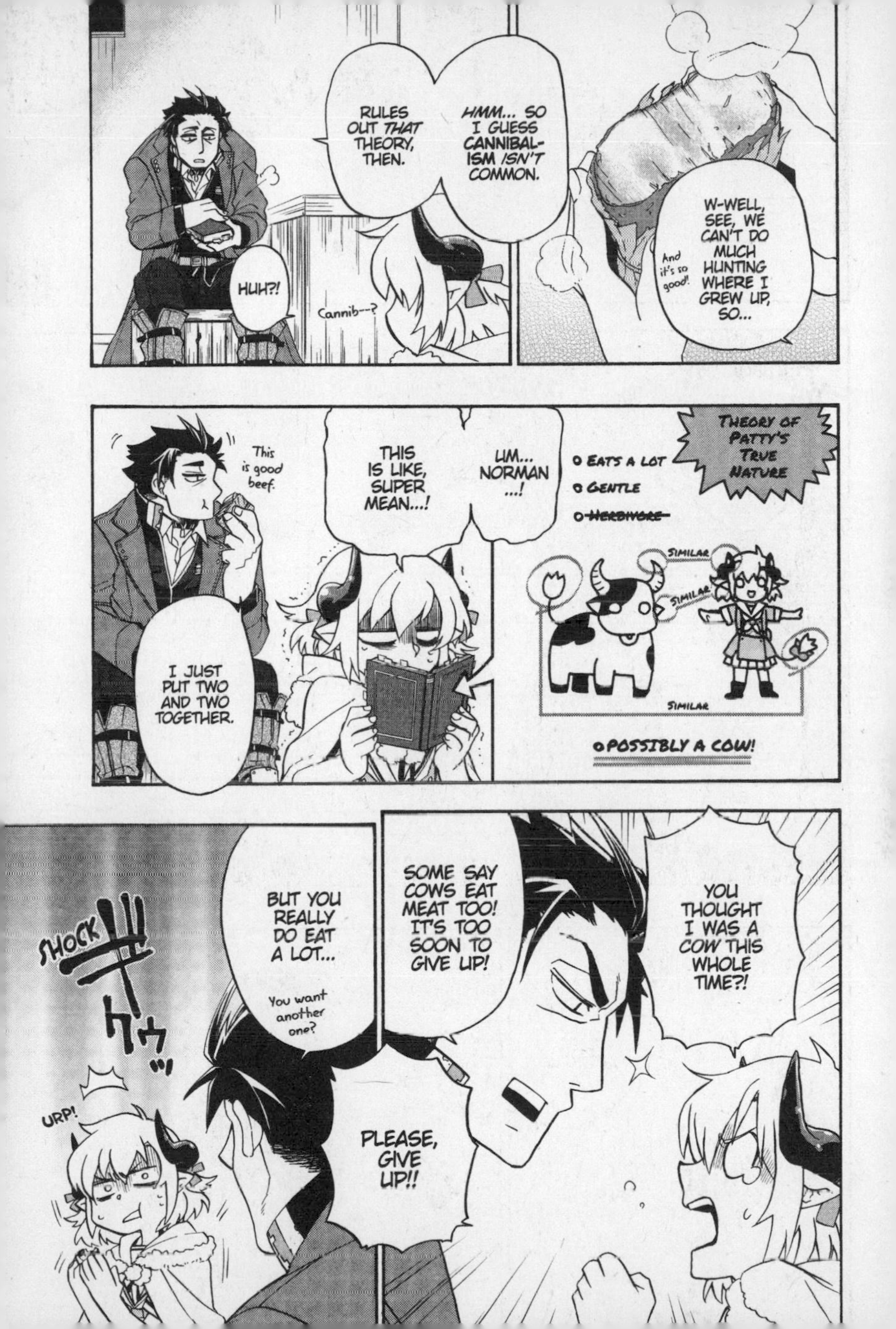
And it's so good!!
W-WELL, SEE, WE CAN'T DO MUCH HUNTING WHERE I GREW UP, SO...
HMM... SO I GUESS CANNIBALISM ISN'T COMMON.
RULES OUT THAT THEORY, THEN.
Cannib--?
HUH?!
THEORY OF PATTY'S TRUE NATURE
Eats a lot
Gentle
~~Herbivore~~
Similar
Similar
Similar
POSSIBLY A COW!
UM... NORMAN...!
THIS IS LIKE, SUPER MEAN...!
This is good beef.
I JUST PUT TWO AND TWO TOGETHER.
YOU THOUGHT I WAS A COW THIS WHOLE TIME?!
SOME SAY COWS EAT MEAT TOO! IT'S TOO SOON TO GIVE UP!
PLEASE, GIVE UP!!
BUT YOU REALLY DO EAT A LOT...
You want another one?
SHOCK
URP!

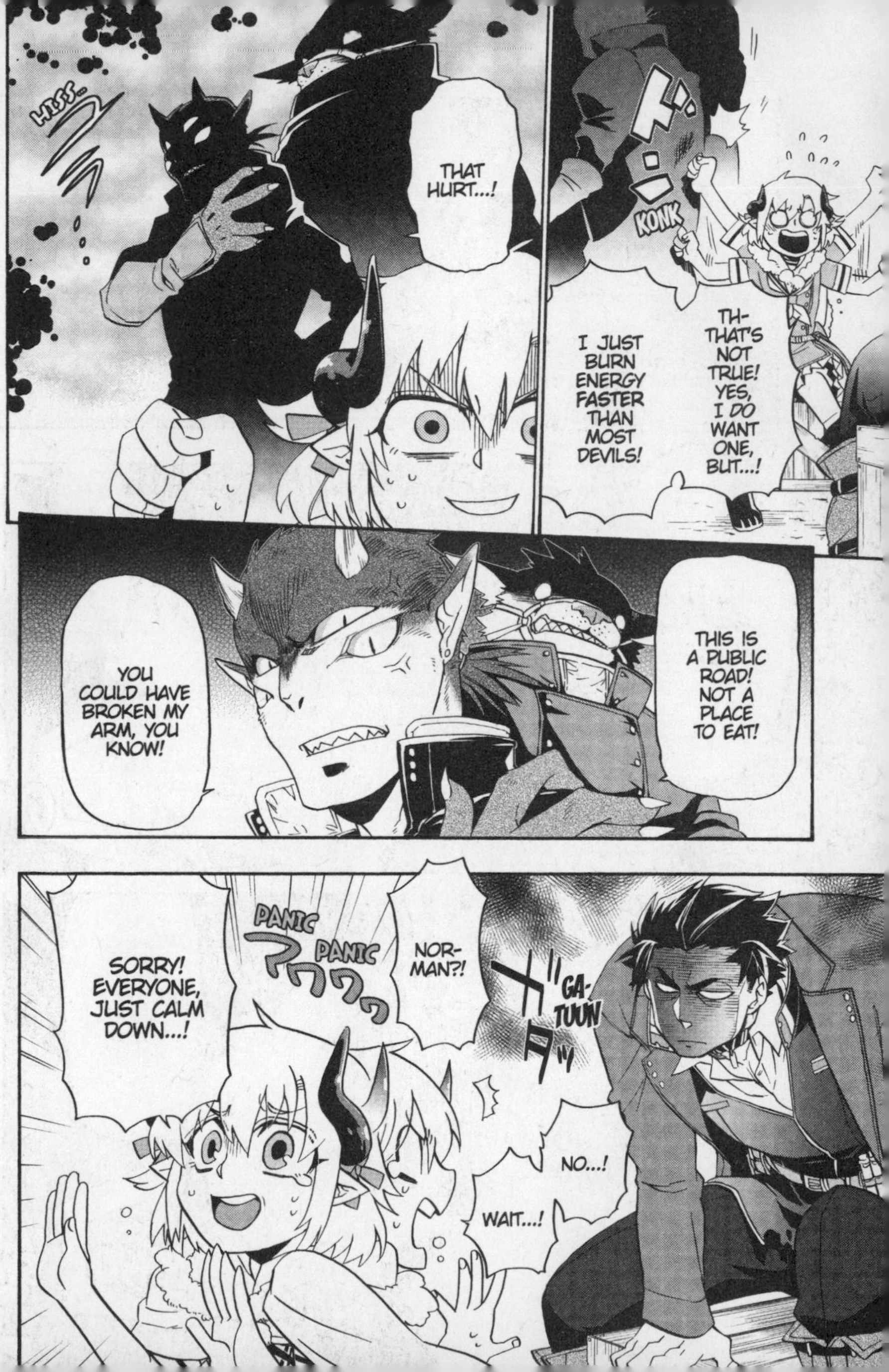
KONK
TH- THAT'S NOT TRUE! YES, I DO WANT ONE, BUT...!
I JUST BURN ENERGY FASTER THAN MOST DEVILS!
THAT HURT...!
HISS...
THIS IS A PUBLIC ROAD! NOT A PLACE TO EAT!
YOU COULD HAVE BROKEN MY ARM, YOU KNOW!
GA-TUUN
NOR-MAN?!
PANIC PANIC
SORRY! EVERYONE, JUST CALM DOWN...!
NO...!
WAIT...!

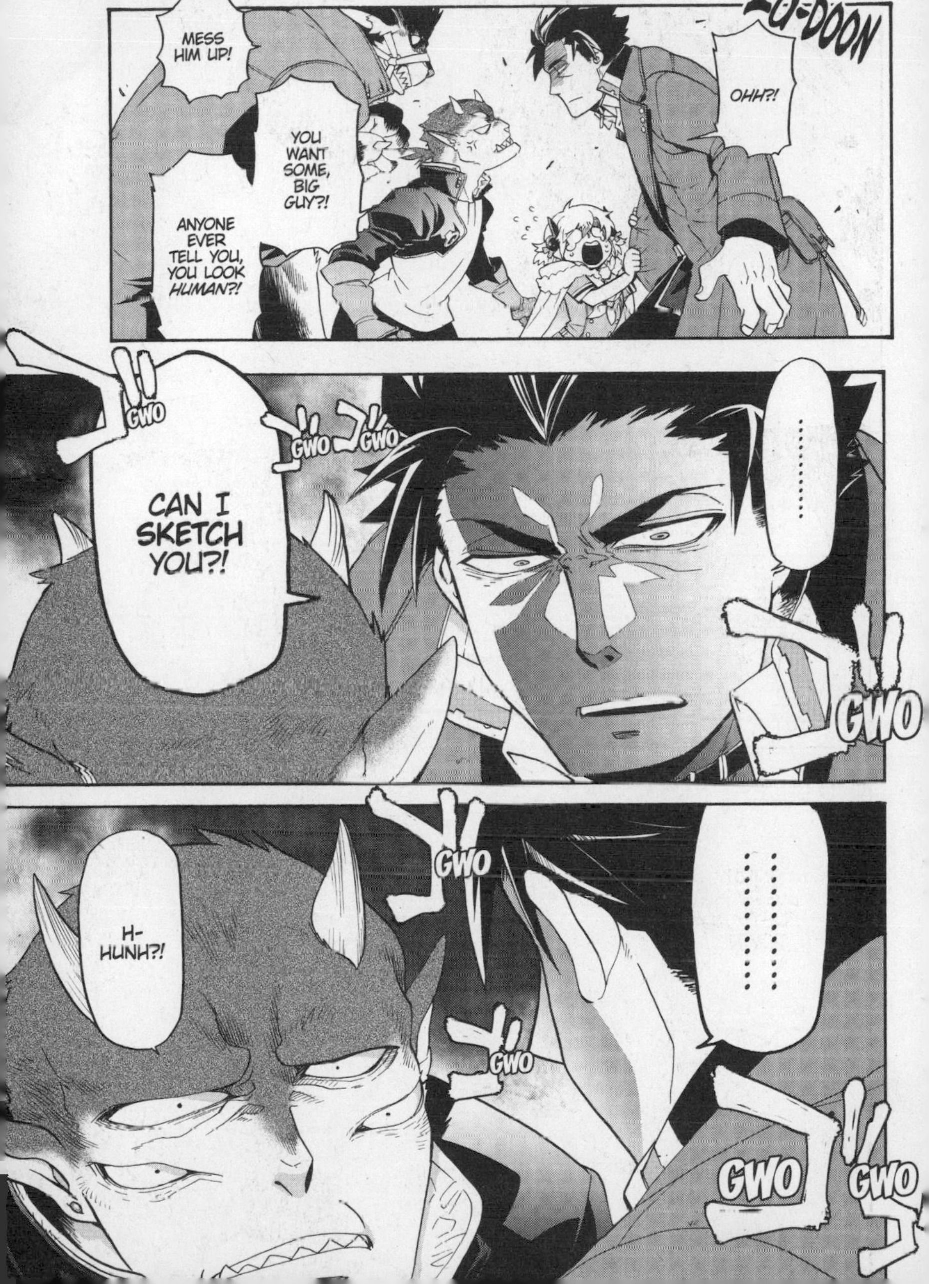
ZU-DOON
OHH?!
MESS HIM UP!
YOU WANT SOME, BIG GUY?!
ANYONE EVER TELL YOU, YOU LOOK *HUMAN?!*
......
GWO GWO GWO
CAN I SKETCH YOU?!
GWO
......
GWO
H-HUNH?!
GWO
GWO GWO

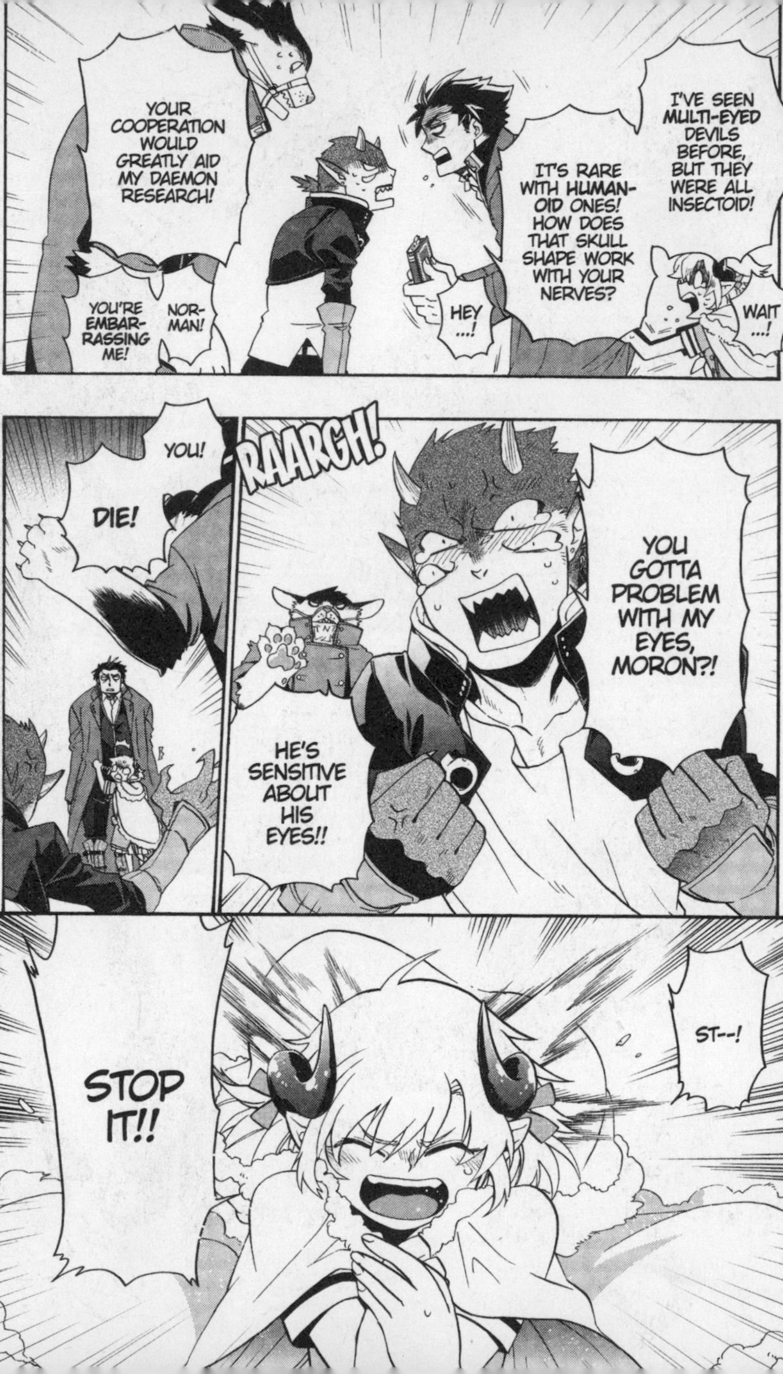
I'VE SEEN MULTI-EYED DEVILS BEFORE, BUT THEY WERE ALL INSECTOID!
WAIT ...!
IT'S RARE WITH HUMAN-OID ONES! HOW DOES THAT SKULL SHAPE WORK WITH YOUR NERVES?
HEY ...!
YOUR COOPERATION WOULD GREATLY AID MY DAEMON RESEARCH!
NOR-MAN!
YOU'RE EMBAR-RASSING ME!
RAAARGH!
YOU GOTTA PROBLEM WITH MY EYES, MORON?!
HE'S SENSITIVE ABOUT HIS EYES!!
YOU!
DIE!
ST--!
STOP IT!!

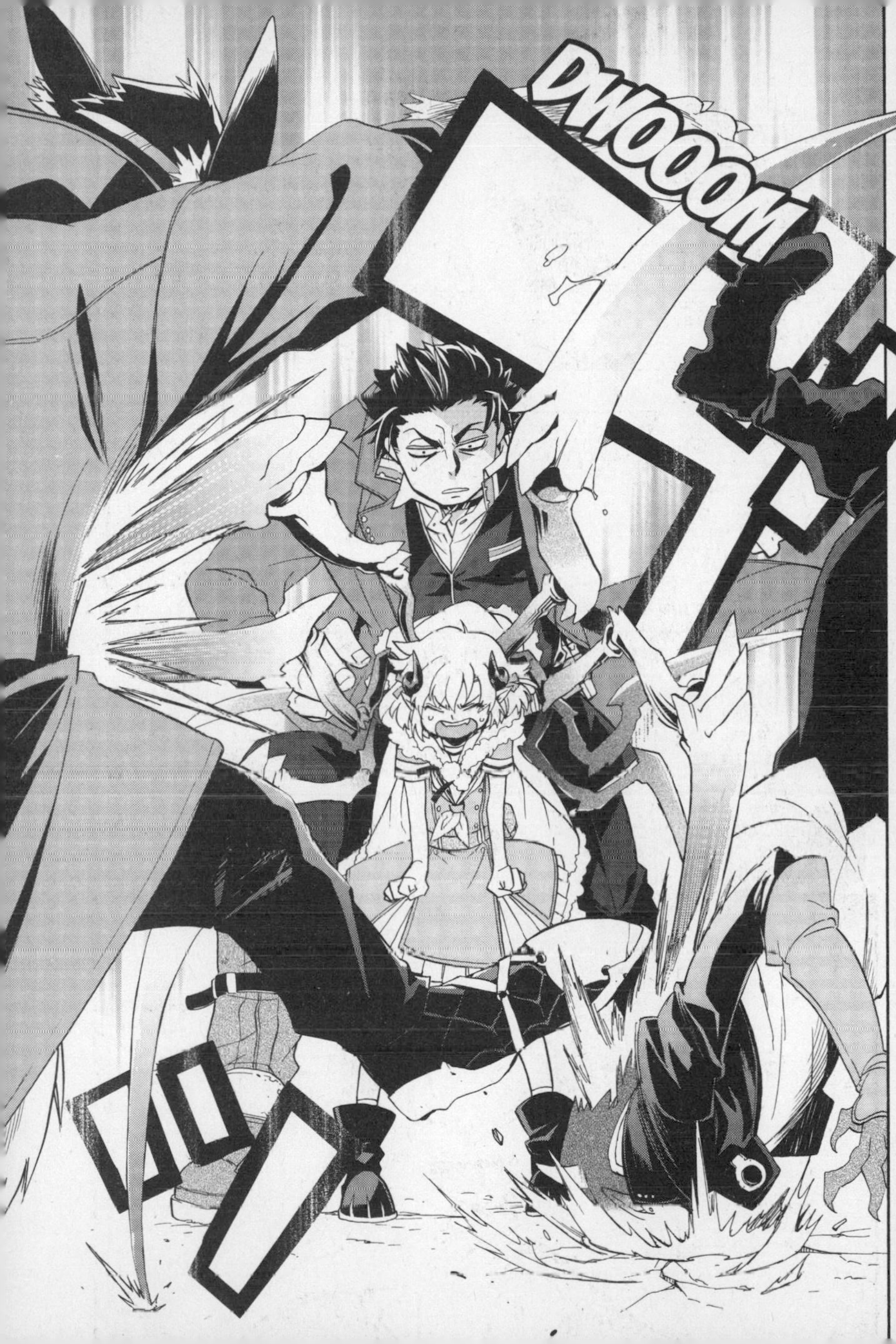
DWOOOM

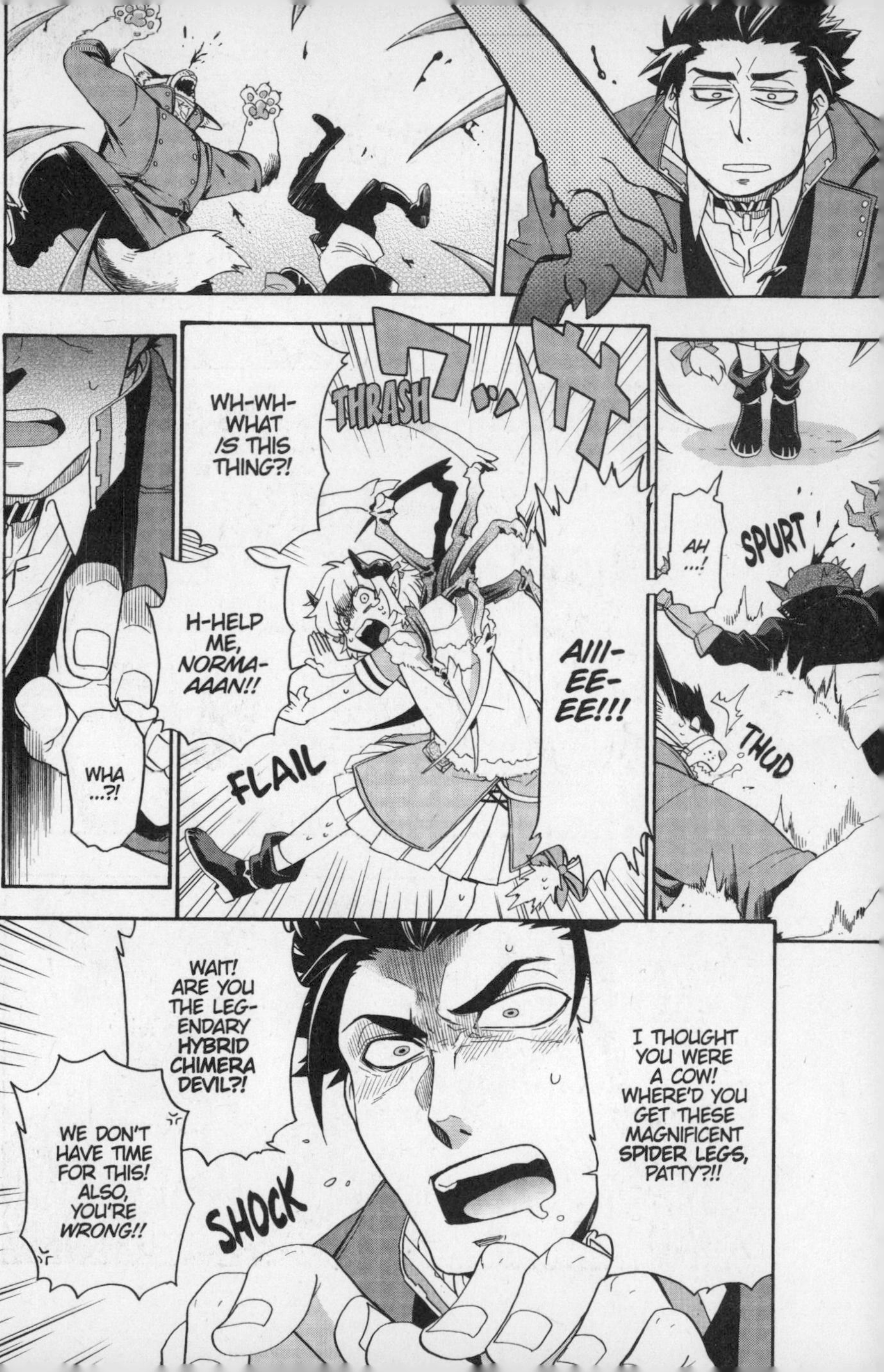
AH ...!
SPURT
THUD
THRASH
WH-WH-WHAT IS THIS THING?!
AIII-EE-EE!!!
H-HELP ME, NORMA-AAAN!!
FLAIL
WHA ...?!
I THOUGHT YOU WERE A COW! WHERE'D YOU GET THESE MAGNIFICENT SPIDER LEGS, PATTY?!!
WAIT! ARE YOU THE LEGENDARY HYBRID CHIMERA DEVIL?!
SHOCK
WE DON'T HAVE TIME FOR THIS! ALSO, YOU'RE WRONG!!

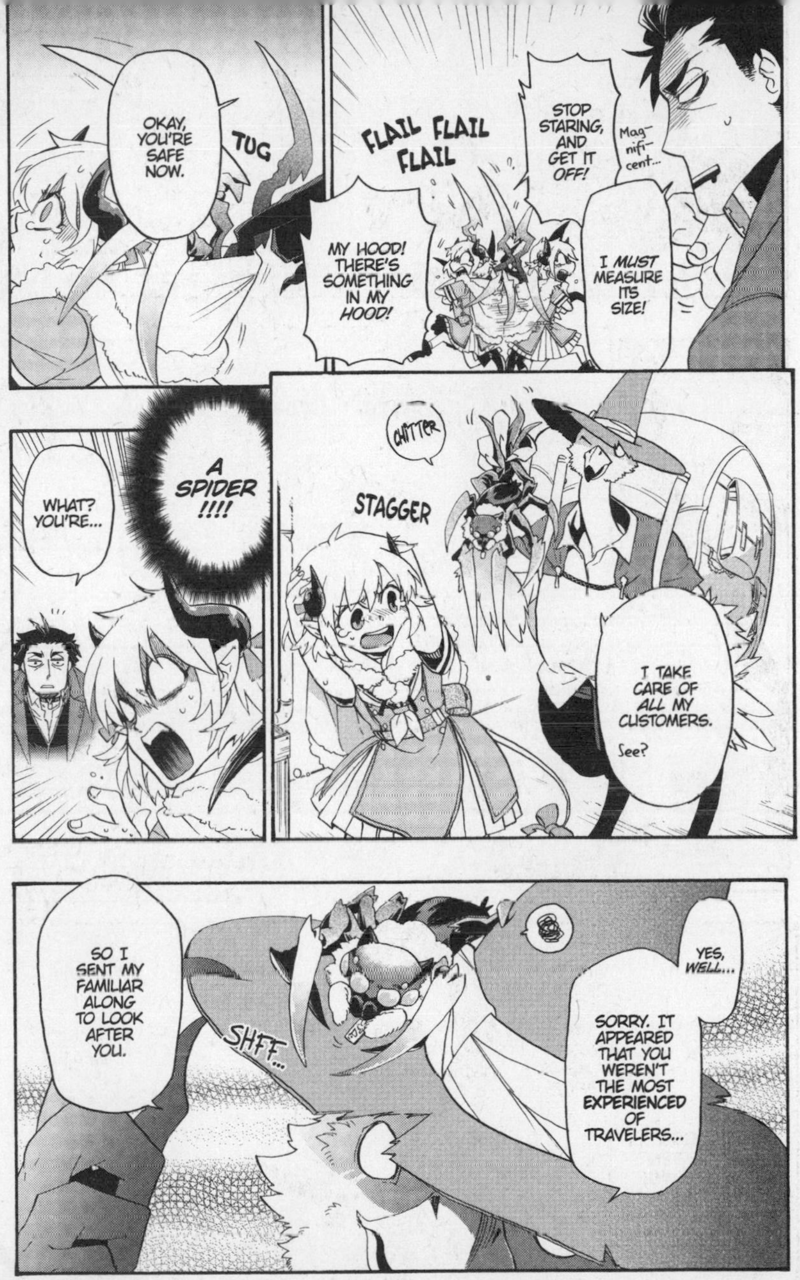
Magnificent...
STOP STARING, AND GET IT OFF!
FLAIL FLAIL FLAIL
I *MUST* MEASURE ITS SIZE!
MY HOOD! THERE'S SOMETHING IN MY *HOOD*!
OKAY, YOU'RE SAFE NOW.
TUG
CHITTER
STAGGER
I TAKE CARE OF *ALL* MY CUSTOMERS.
See?
A SPIDER !!!!
WHAT? YOU'RE...
YES, *WELL*...
SORRY. IT APPEARED THAT YOU WEREN'T THE MOST EXPERIENCED OF TRAVELERS...
SHFF...
SO I SENT MY FAMILIAR ALONG TO LOOK AFTER YOU.

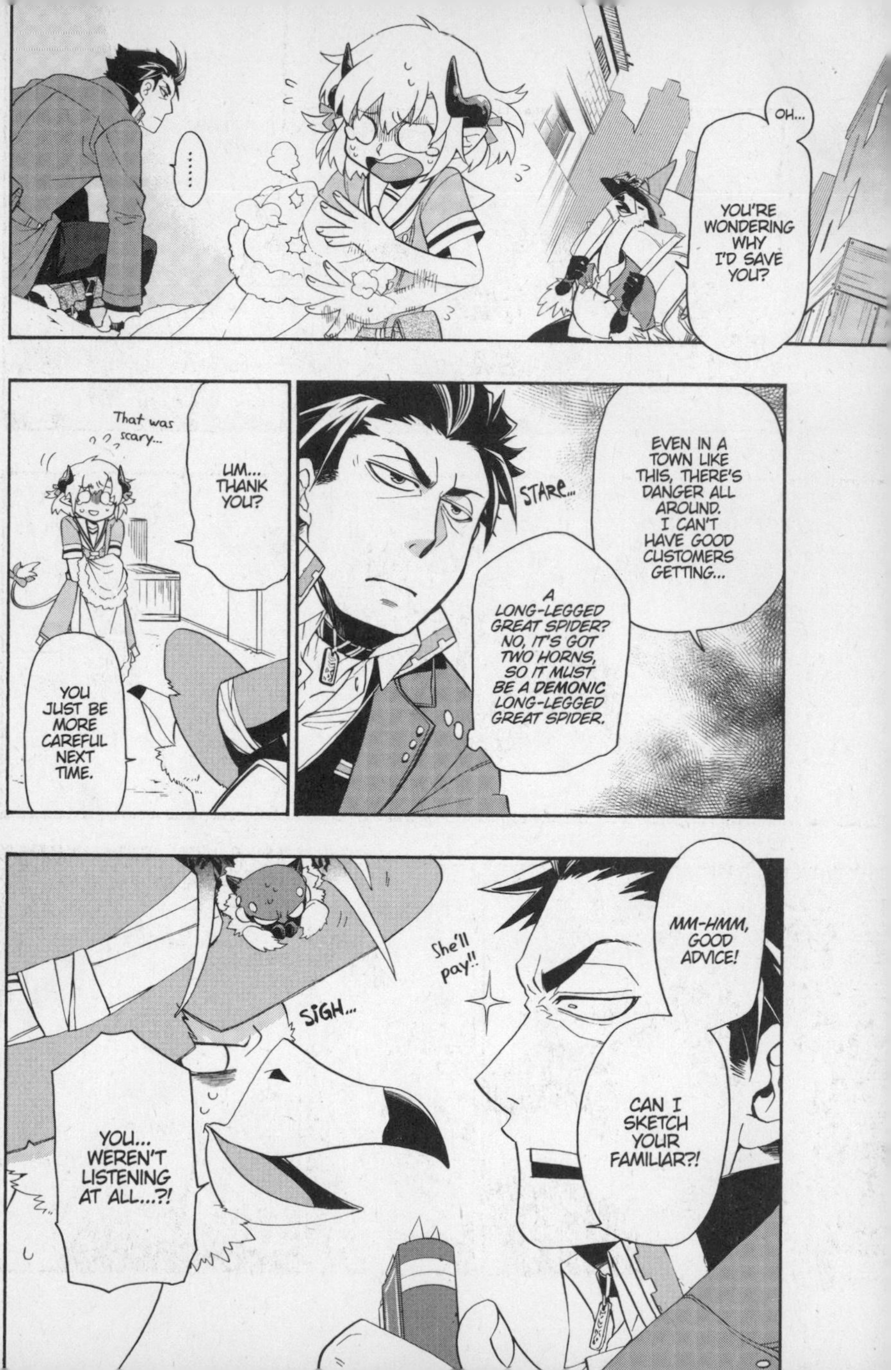
OH...
YOU'RE WONDERING WHY I'D SAVE YOU?
......
EVEN IN A TOWN LIKE THIS, THERE'S DANGER ALL AROUND. I CAN'T HAVE GOOD CUSTOMERS GETTING...
STARE...
A LONG-LEGGED GREAT SPIDER? NO, IT'S GOT TWO HORNS, SO IT MUST BE A DEMONIC LONG-LEGGED GREAT SPIDER.
UM... THANK YOU?
That was scary...
YOU JUST BE MORE CAREFUL NEXT TIME.
MM-HMM, GOOD ADVICE!
CAN I SKETCH YOUR FAMILIAR?!
She'll pay!!
SIGH...
YOU... WEREN'T LISTENING AT ALL...?!

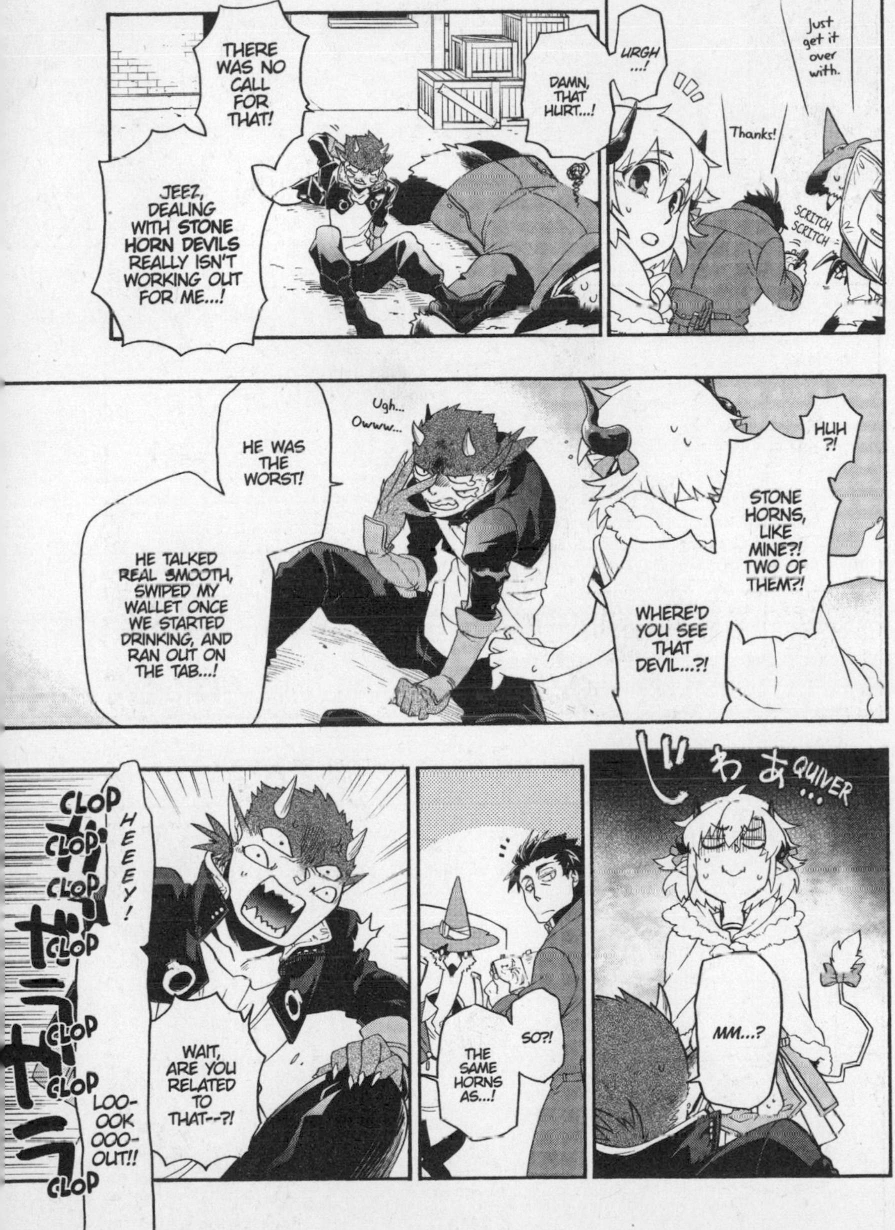
Just get it over with.
URGH ...!
DAMN, THAT HURT...!
Thanks!
SCRITCH SCRITCH
THERE WAS NO CALL FOR THAT!
JEEZ, DEALING WITH STONE HORN DEVILS REALLY ISN'T WORKING OUT FOR ME...!
HUH ?!
STONE HORNS, LIKE MINE?! TWO OF THEM?!
WHERE'D YOU SEE THAT DEVIL...?!
Ugh... Owww...
HE WAS THE WORST!
HE TALKED REAL SMOOTH, SWIPED MY WALLET ONCE WE STARTED DRINKING, AND RAN OUT ON THE TAB...!
じわあ QUIVER...
MM...?
SO?!
THE SAME HORNS AS...!
HEEEY!
WAIT, ARE YOU RELATED TO THAT--?!
LOO-OOK OOO-OUT!!
CLOP CLOP CLOP CLOP CLOP CLOP CLOP

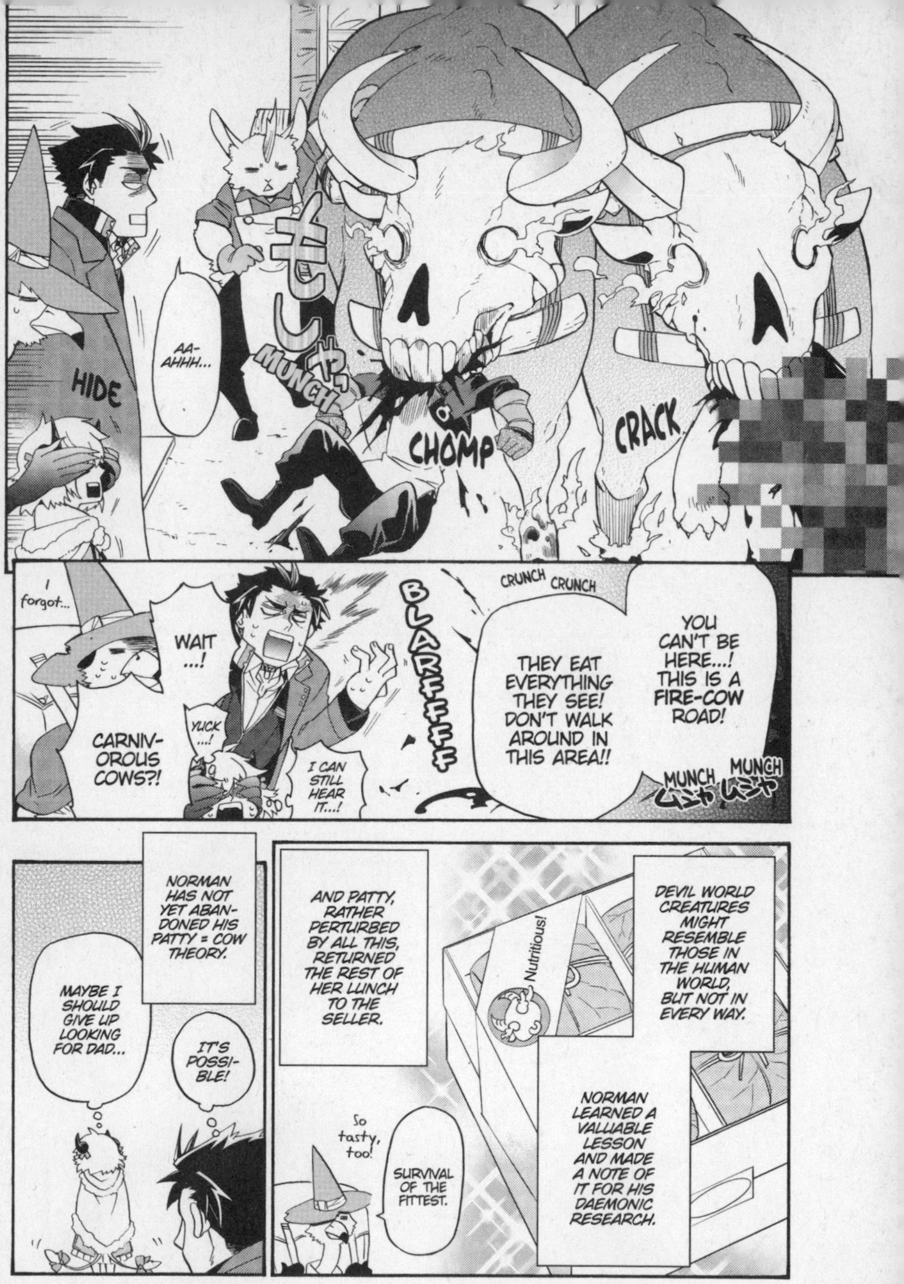
CRACK
CHOMP
MUNCH
もしゃ
AA-AHHH...
HIDE
YOU CAN'T BE HERE...! THIS IS A FIRE-COW ROAD!
MUNCH MUNCH
ムシャムシャ
CRUNCH CRUNCH
THEY EAT EVERYTHING THEY SEE! DON'T WALK AROUND IN THIS AREA!!
BLARFFFFF
WAIT ...!
I forgot...
YUCK ...!
I CAN STILL HEAR IT...!
CARNIV-OROUS COWS?!
DEVIL WORLD CREATURES MIGHT RESEMBLE THOSE IN THE HUMAN WORLD, BUT NOT IN EVERY WAY.
AND PATTY, RATHER PERTURBED BY ALL THIS, RETURNED THE REST OF HER LUNCH TO THE SELLER.
Nutritious!
NORMAN LEARNED A VALUABLE LESSON AND MADE A NOTE OF IT FOR HIS DAEMONIC RESEARCH.
So tasty, too!
SURVIVAL OF THE FITTEST.
NORMAN HAS NOT YET ABAN-DONED HIS PATTY = COW THEORY.
IT'S POSSI-BLE!
MAYBE I SHOULD GIVE UP LOOKING FOR DAD...

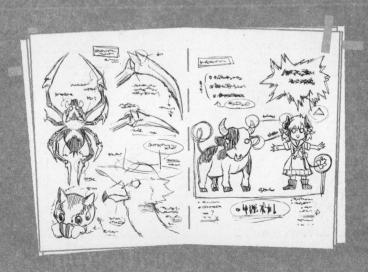

Sorry For My Familiar

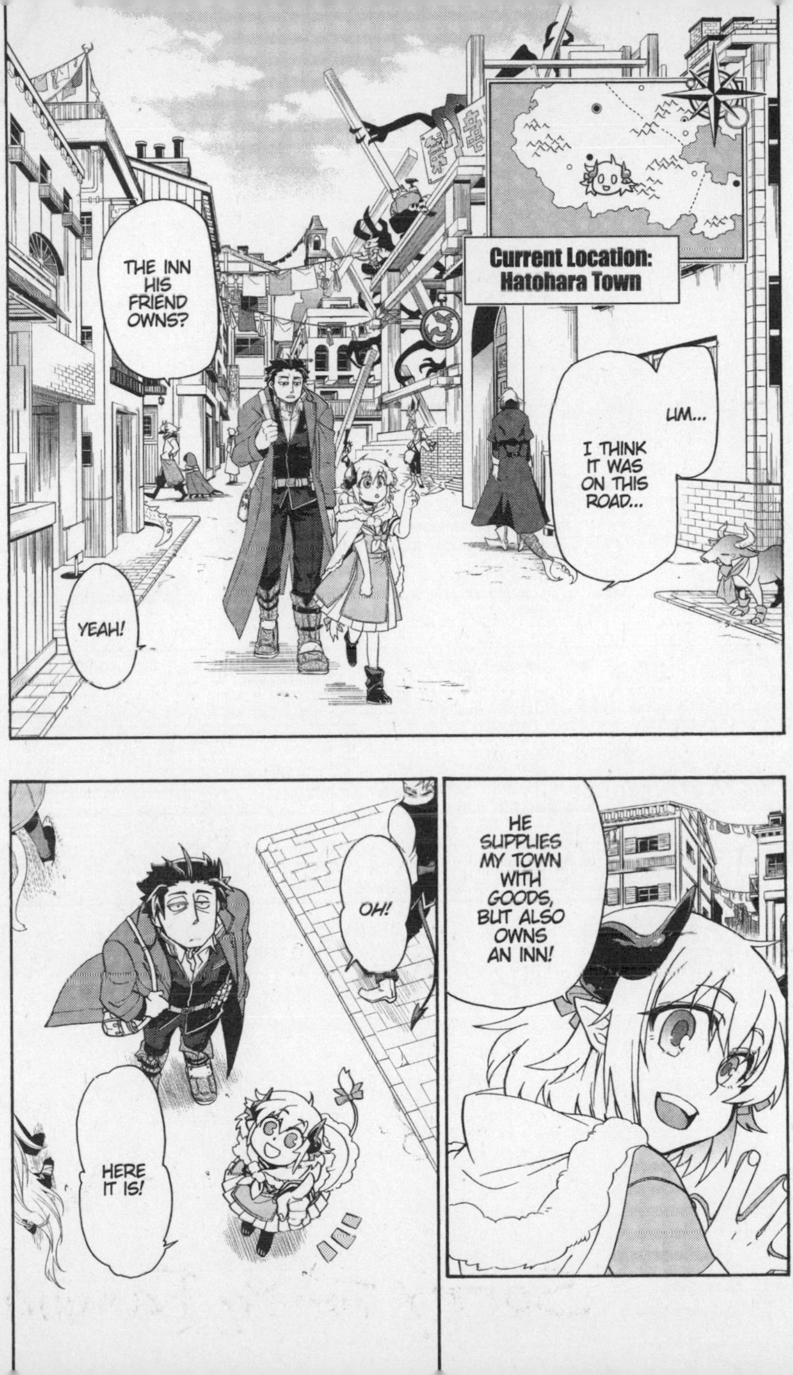
Current Location: Hatohara Town
UM... I THINK IT WAS ON THIS ROAD...
THE INN HIS FRIEND OWNS?
YEAH!
HE SUPPLIES MY TOWN WITH GOODS, BUT ALSO OWNS AN INN!
OH!
HERE IT IS!

FILE 3: Yamaoroshi-tei Inn

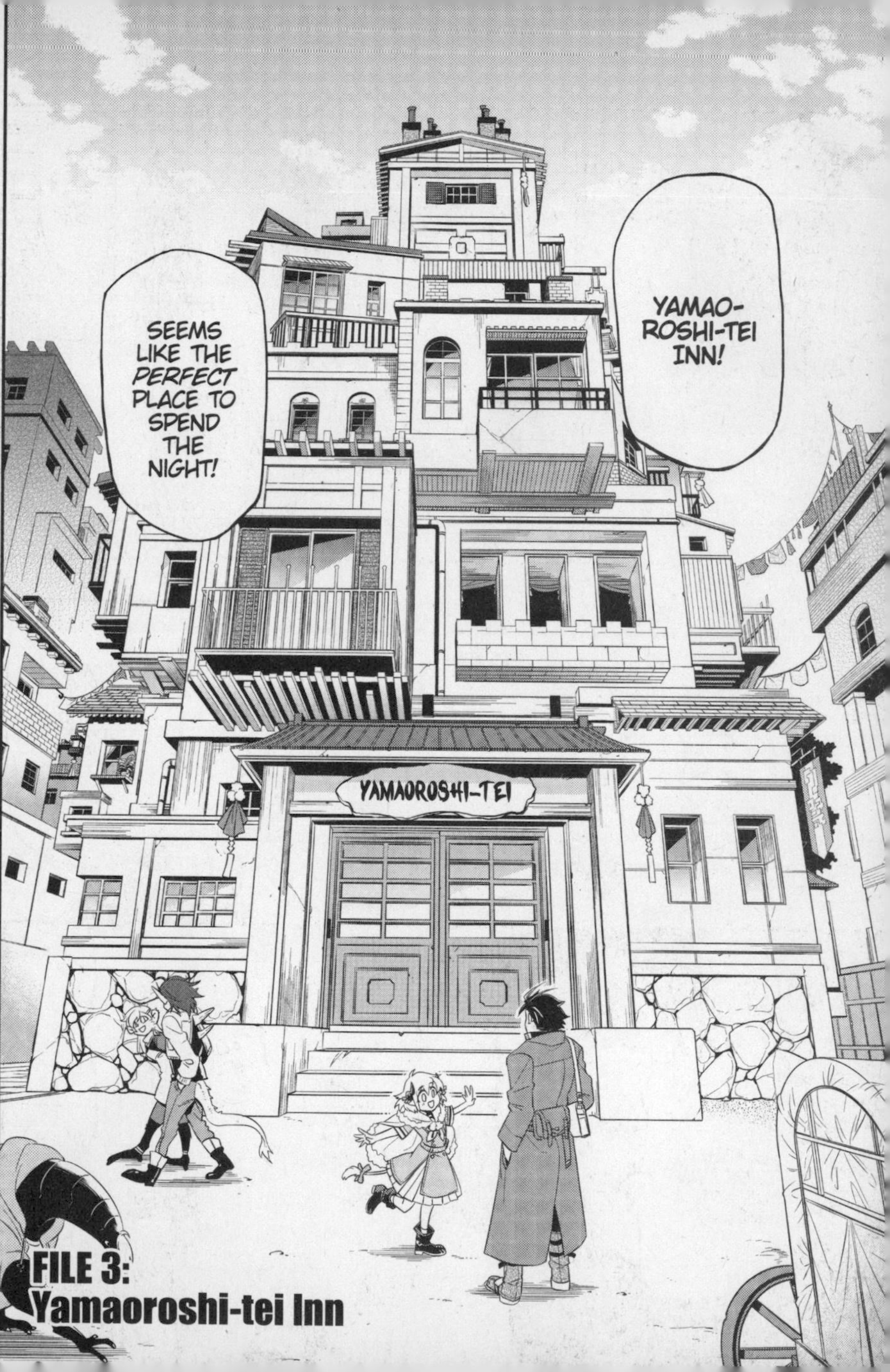
YAMAO-ROSHI-TEI INN!
SEEMS LIKE THE PERFECT PLACE TO SPEND THE NIGHT!
YAMAOROSHI-TEI

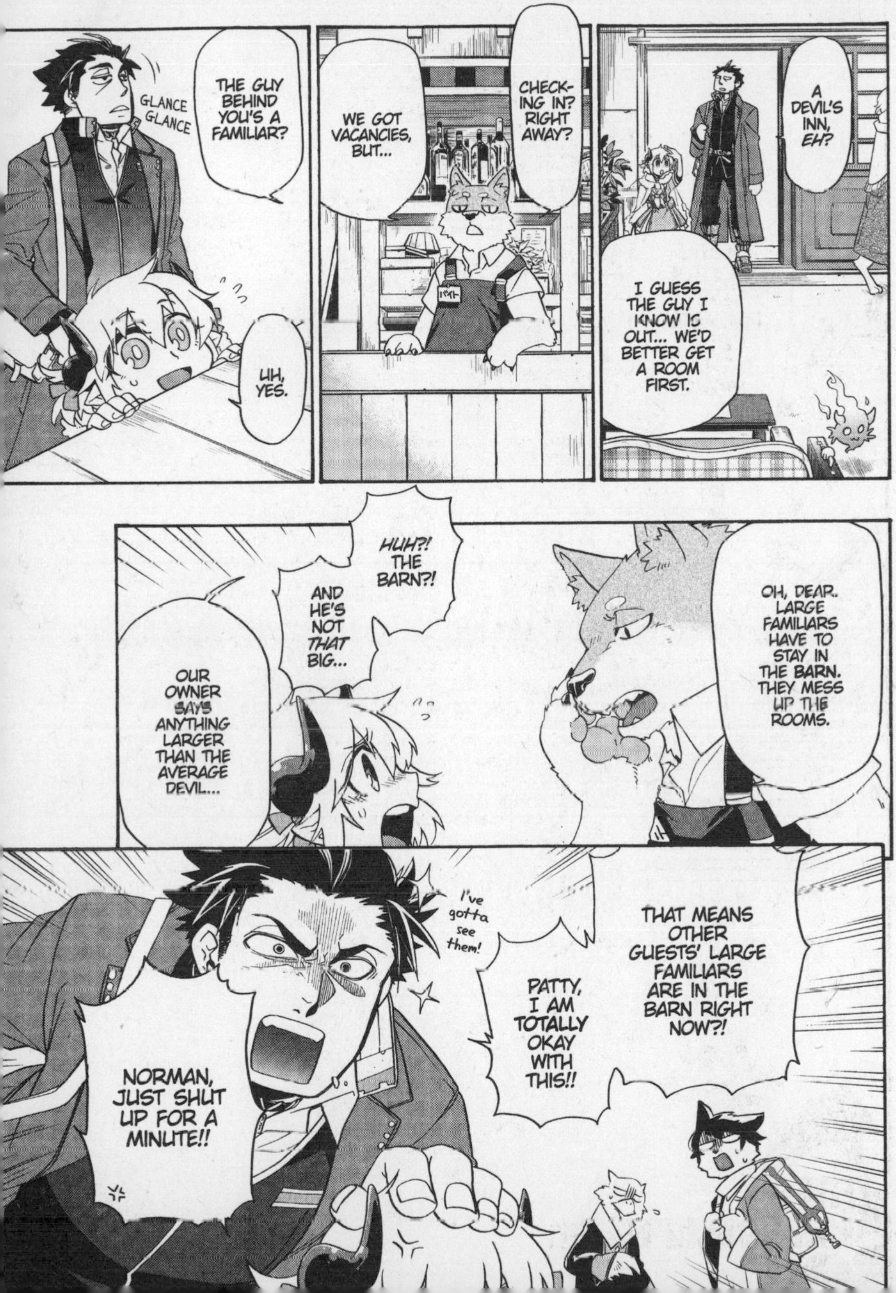
A DEVIL'S INN, *EH?*
I GUESS THE GUY I KNOW IS OUT... WE'D BETTER GET A ROOM FIRST.
CHECKING IN? RIGHT AWAY?
WE GOT VACANCIES, BUT...
THE GUY BEHIND YOU'S A FAMILIAR?
GLANCE GLANCE
UH, YES.
OH, DEAR. LARGE FAMILIARS HAVE TO STAY IN THE BARN. THEY MESS UP THE ROOMS.
HUH?! THE BARN?!
AND HE'S NOT *THAT* BIG...
OUR OWNER SAYS ANYTHING LARGER THAN THE AVERAGE DEVIL...
THAT MEANS OTHER GUESTS' LARGE FAMILIARS ARE IN THE BARN RIGHT NOW?!
I've gotta see them!
PATTY, I AM TOTALLY OKAY WITH THIS!!
NORMAN, JUST SHUT UP FOR A MINUTE!!

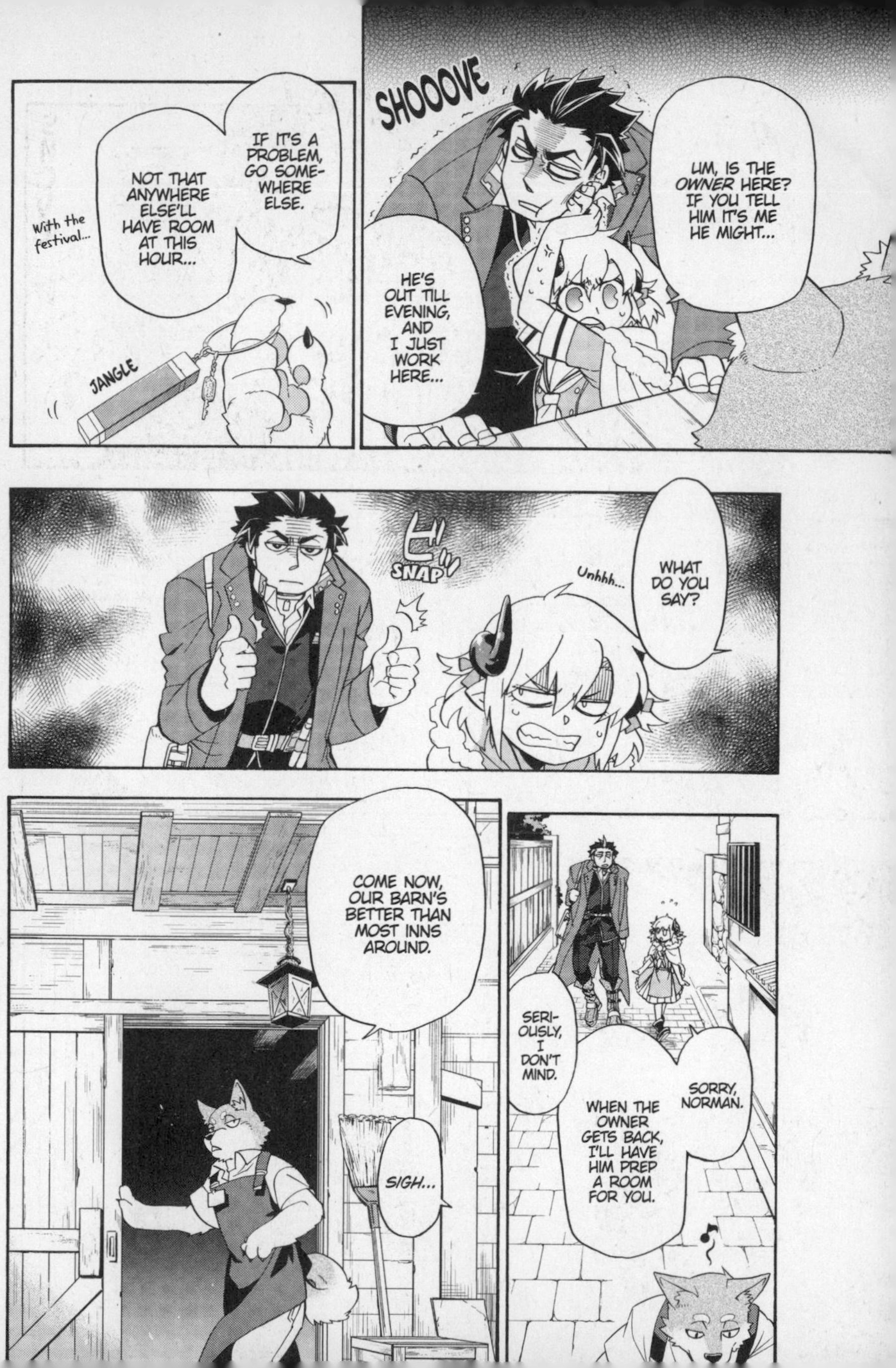
SHOOOVE
UM, IS THE OWNER HERE? IF YOU TELL HIM IT'S ME HE MIGHT...
HE'S OUT TILL EVENING, AND I JUST WORK HERE...
IF IT'S A PROBLEM, GO SOME-WHERE ELSE.
NOT THAT ANYWHERE ELSE'LL HAVE ROOM AT THIS HOUR...
With the festival...
JANGLE
WHAT DO YOU SAY?
Unhhh...
ビッ
SNAP
SORRY, NORMAN.
WHEN THE OWNER GETS BACK, I'LL HAVE HIM PREP A ROOM FOR YOU.
SERI-OUSLY, I DON'T MIND.
COME NOW, OUR BARN'S BETTER THAN MOST INNS AROUND.
SIGH...

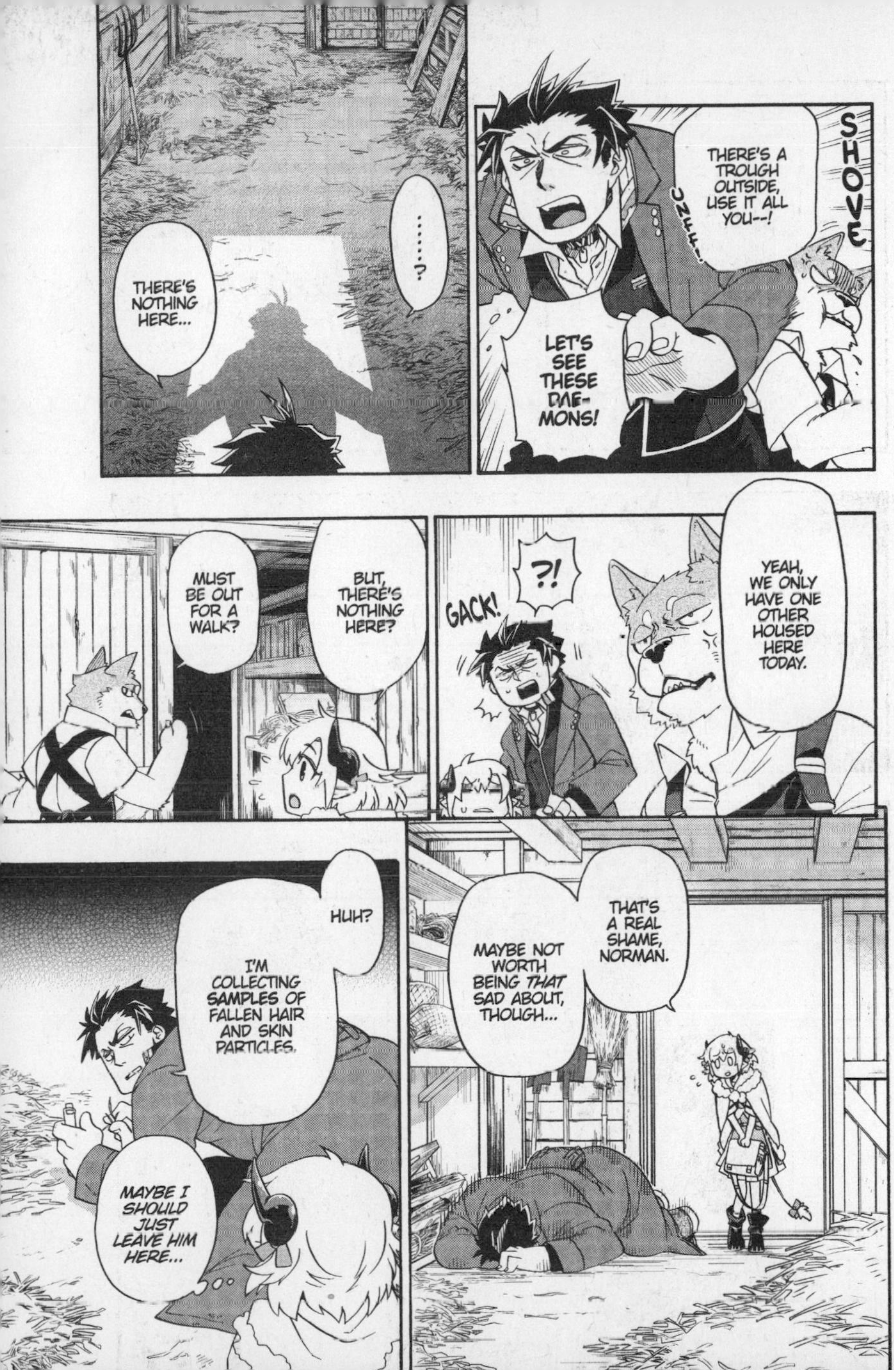
SHOVE
THERE'S A TROUGH OUTSIDE, USE IT ALL YOU--!
UNFF!
LET'S SEE THESE DAE-MONS!
......?
THERE'S NOTHING HERE...
YEAH, WE ONLY HAVE ONE OTHER HOUSED HERE TODAY.
?!
GACK!
BUT, THERE'S NOTHING HERE?
MUST BE OUT FOR A WALK?
THAT'S A REAL SHAME, NORMAN.
MAYBE NOT WORTH BEING *THAT* SAD ABOUT, THOUGH...
HUH?
I'M COLLECTING SAMPLES OF FALLEN HAIR AND SKIN PARTICLES.
MAYBE I SHOULD JUST LEAVE HIM HERE...

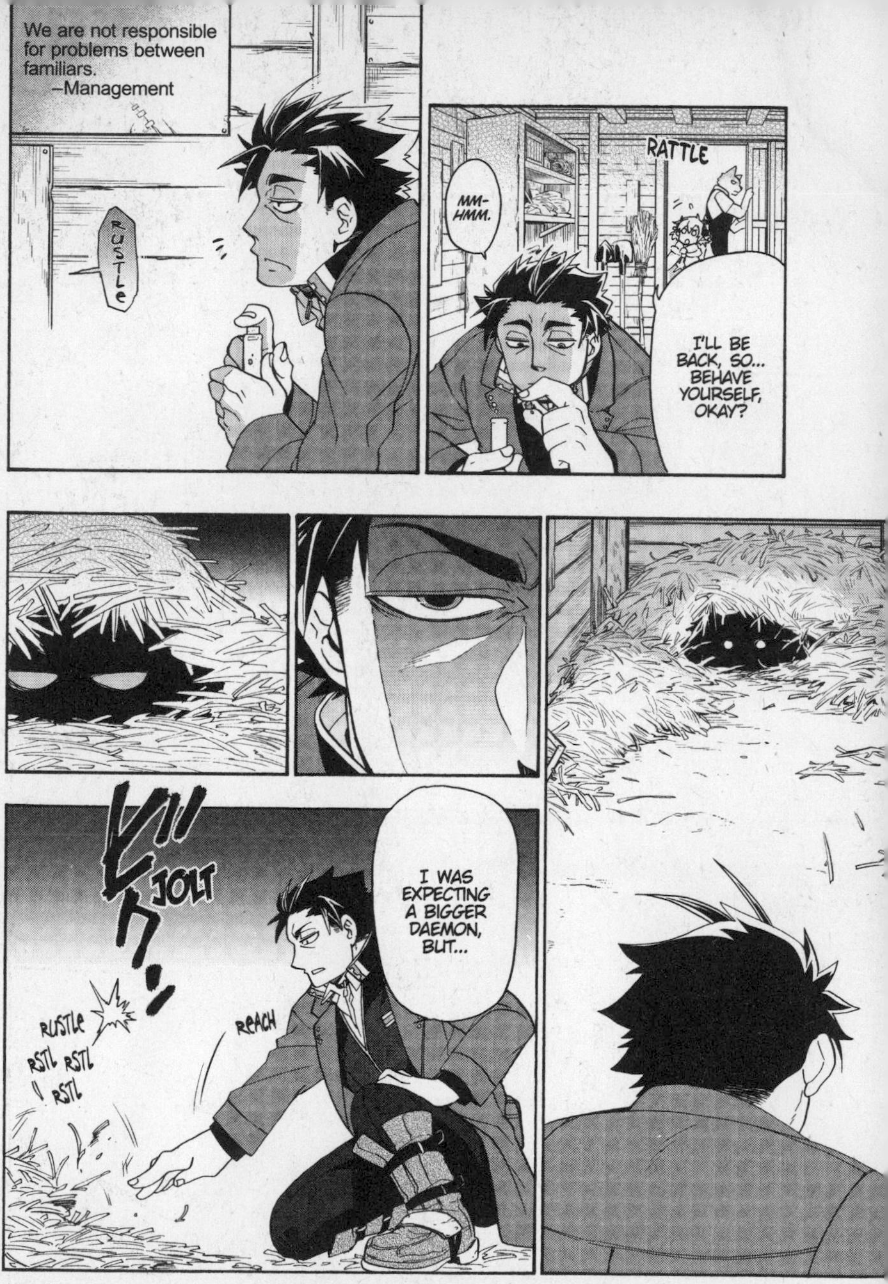

RATTLE
I'LL BE BACK, SO... BEHAVE YOURSELF, OKAY?
MM-HMM.
We are not responsible for problems between familiars.
–Management
RUSTLE
I WAS EXPECTING A BIGGER DAEMON, BUT...
JOLT
REACH
RUSTLE
RSTL RSTL
RSTL

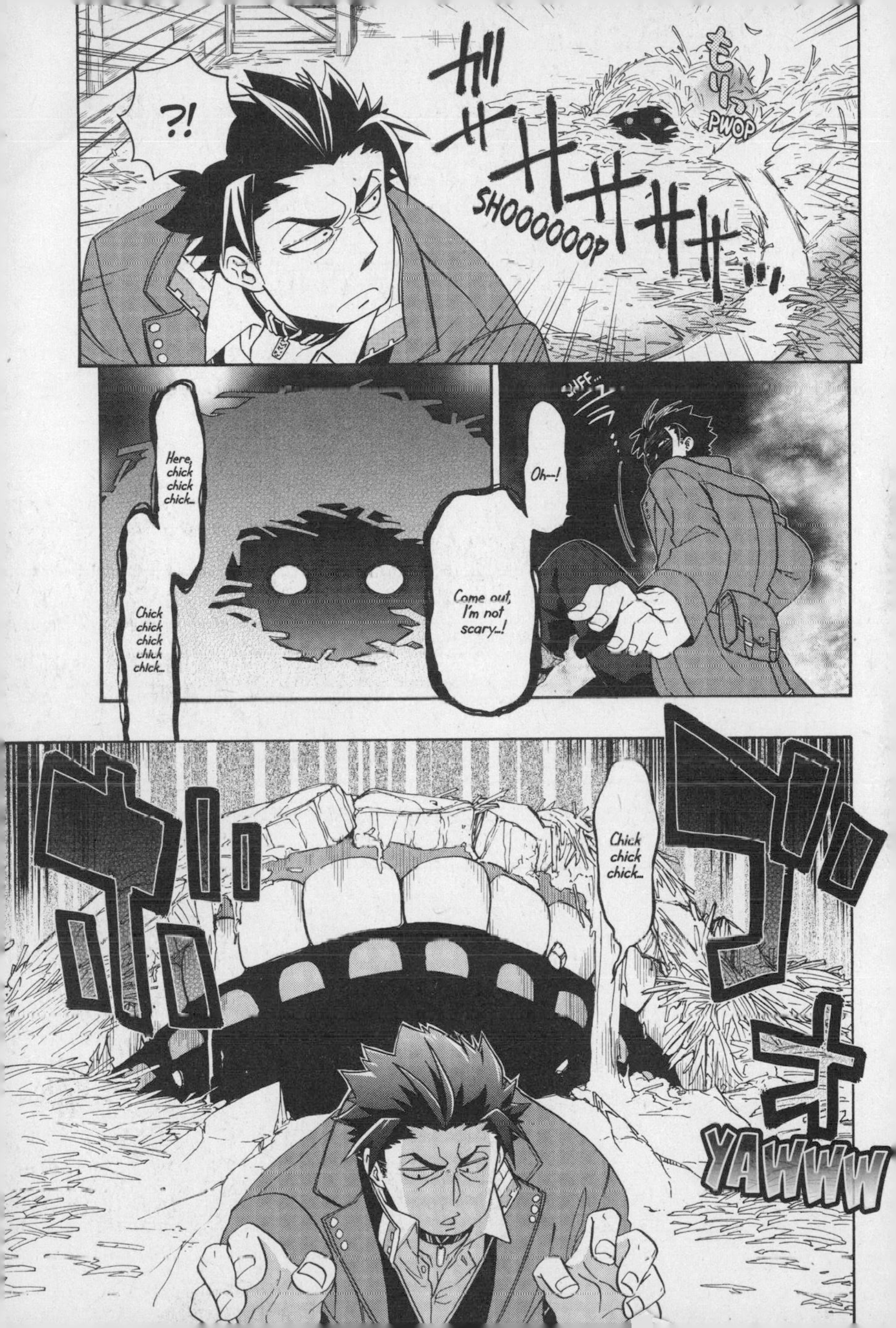
PWOP
SHOOOOOOP
?!
SNIFF...
Oh—!
Come out, I'm not scary...!
Here, chick chick chick...
Chick chick chick chick chick...
YAWWW
Chick chick chick...

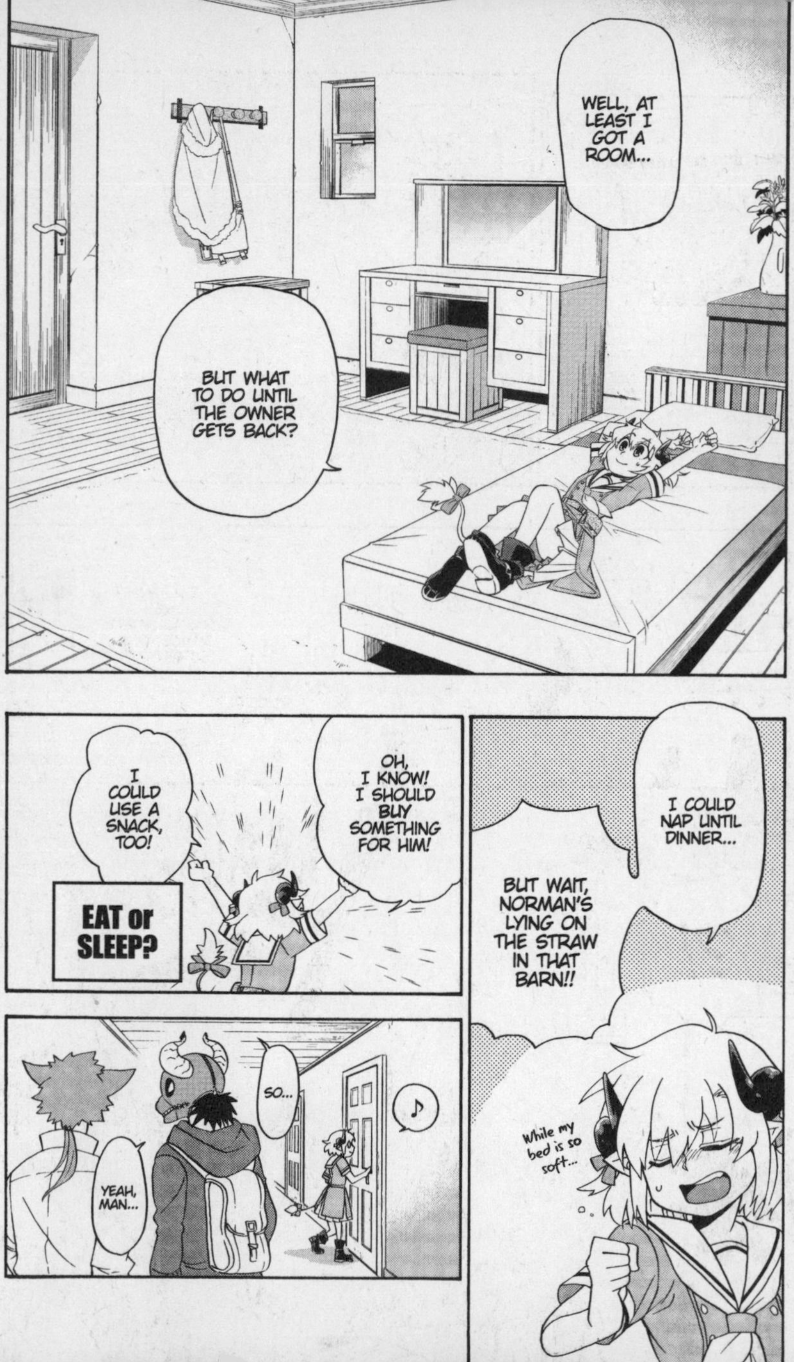
WELL, AT LEAST I GOT A ROOM...
BUT WHAT TO DO UNTIL THE OWNER GETS BACK?
I COULD NAP UNTIL DINNER...
BUT WAIT, NORMAN'S LYING ON THE STRAW IN THAT BARN!!
While my bed is so soft...
OH, I KNOW! I SHOULD BUY SOMETHING FOR HIM!
I COULD USE A SNACK, TOO!
EAT or SLEEP?
SO...
♪
YEAH, MAN...

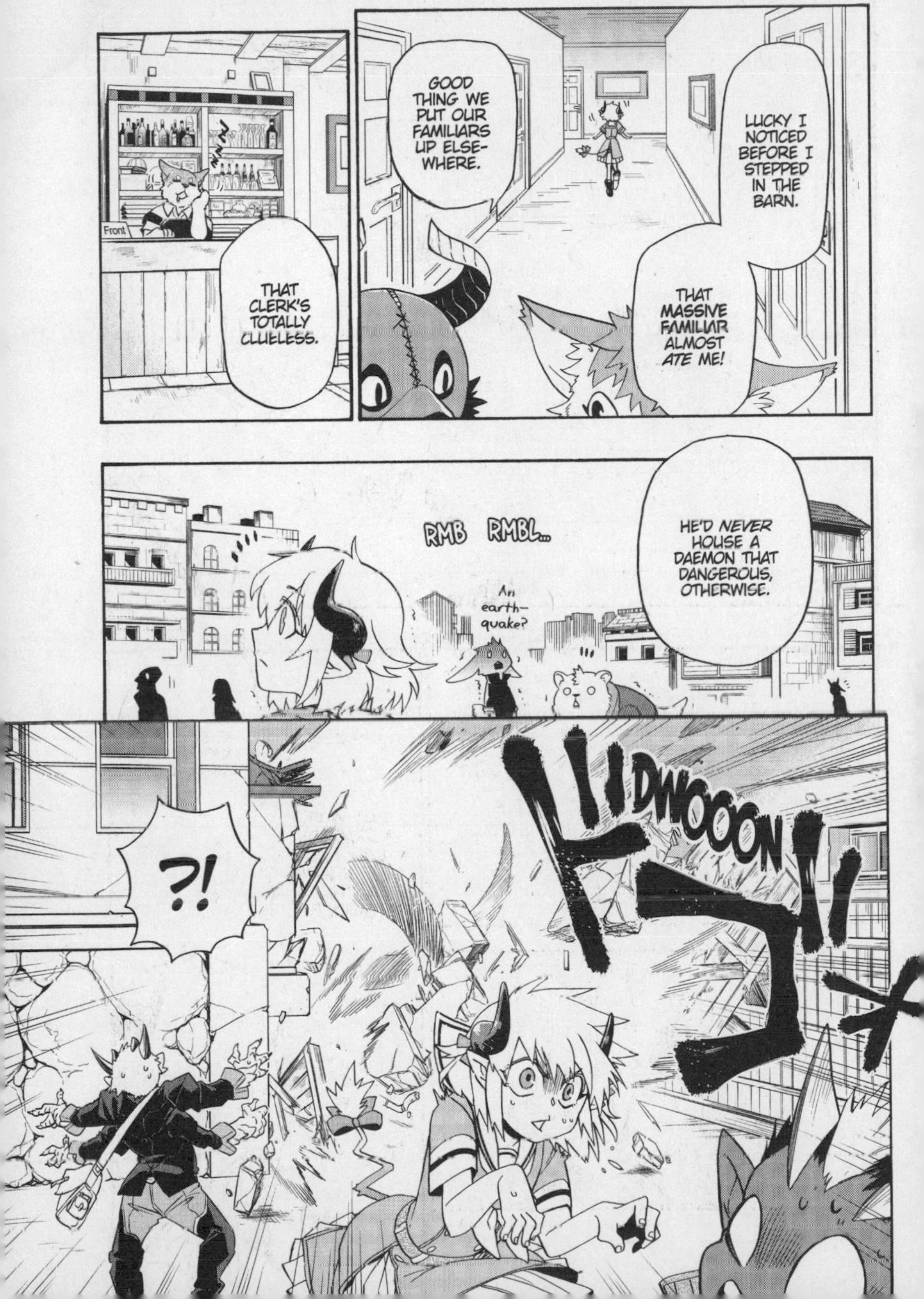

LUCKY I NOTICED BEFORE I STEPPED IN THE BARN.
THAT MASSIVE FAMILIAR ALMOST ATE ME!
GOOD THING WE PUT OUR FAMILIARS UP ELSEWHERE.
MNN
Front
THAT CLERK'S TOTALLY CLUELESS.
HE'D NEVER HOUSE A DAEMON THAT DANGEROUS, OTHERWISE.
RMB RMBL...
An earthquake?
DWOOOON!!
?!

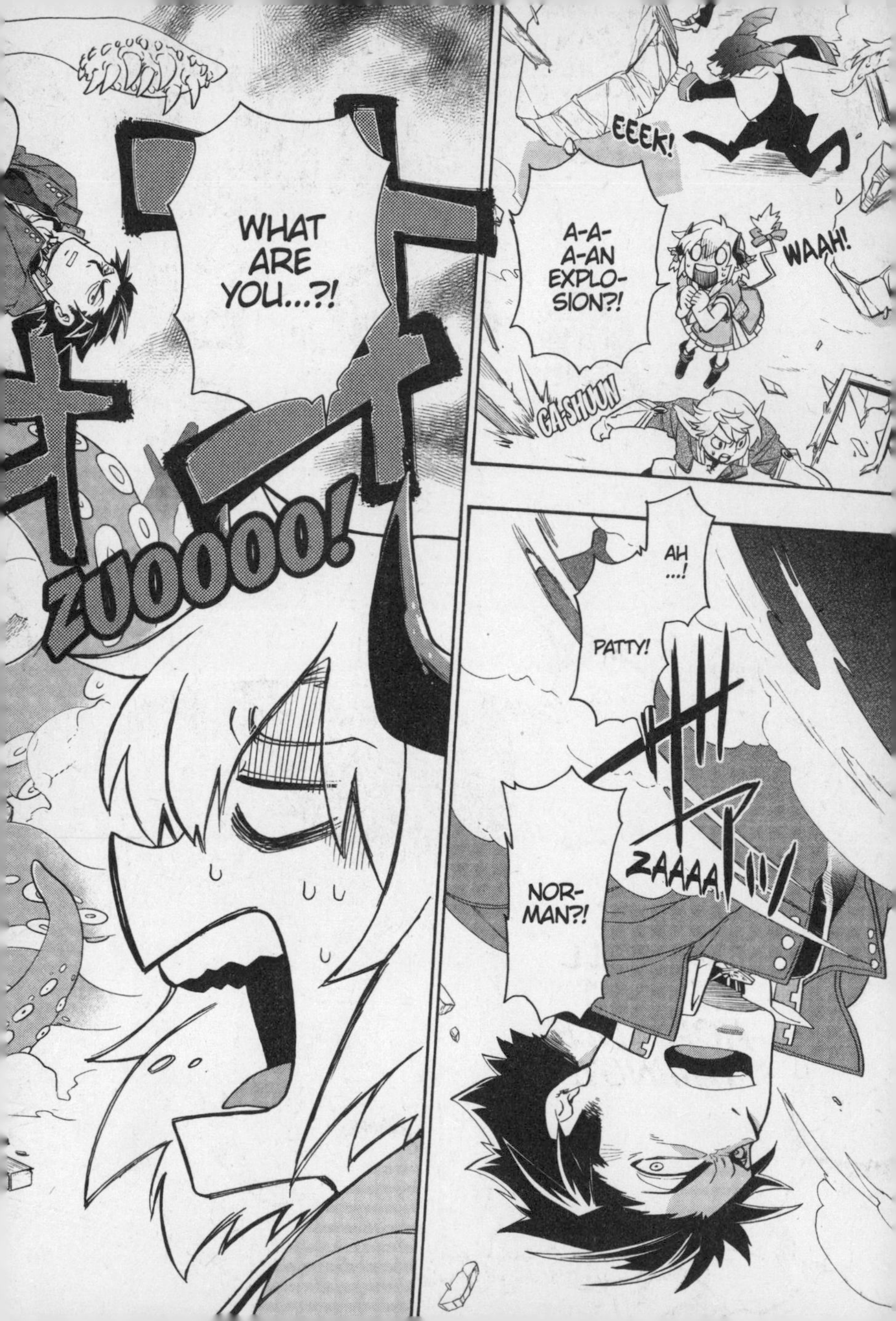
EEEK!
WAAH!
A-A-A-AN EXPLOSION?!
GA-SHOUN
AH ...!
PATTY!
ZAAAA
NOR-MAN?!
WHAT ARE YOU...?!
ZUOOOO!

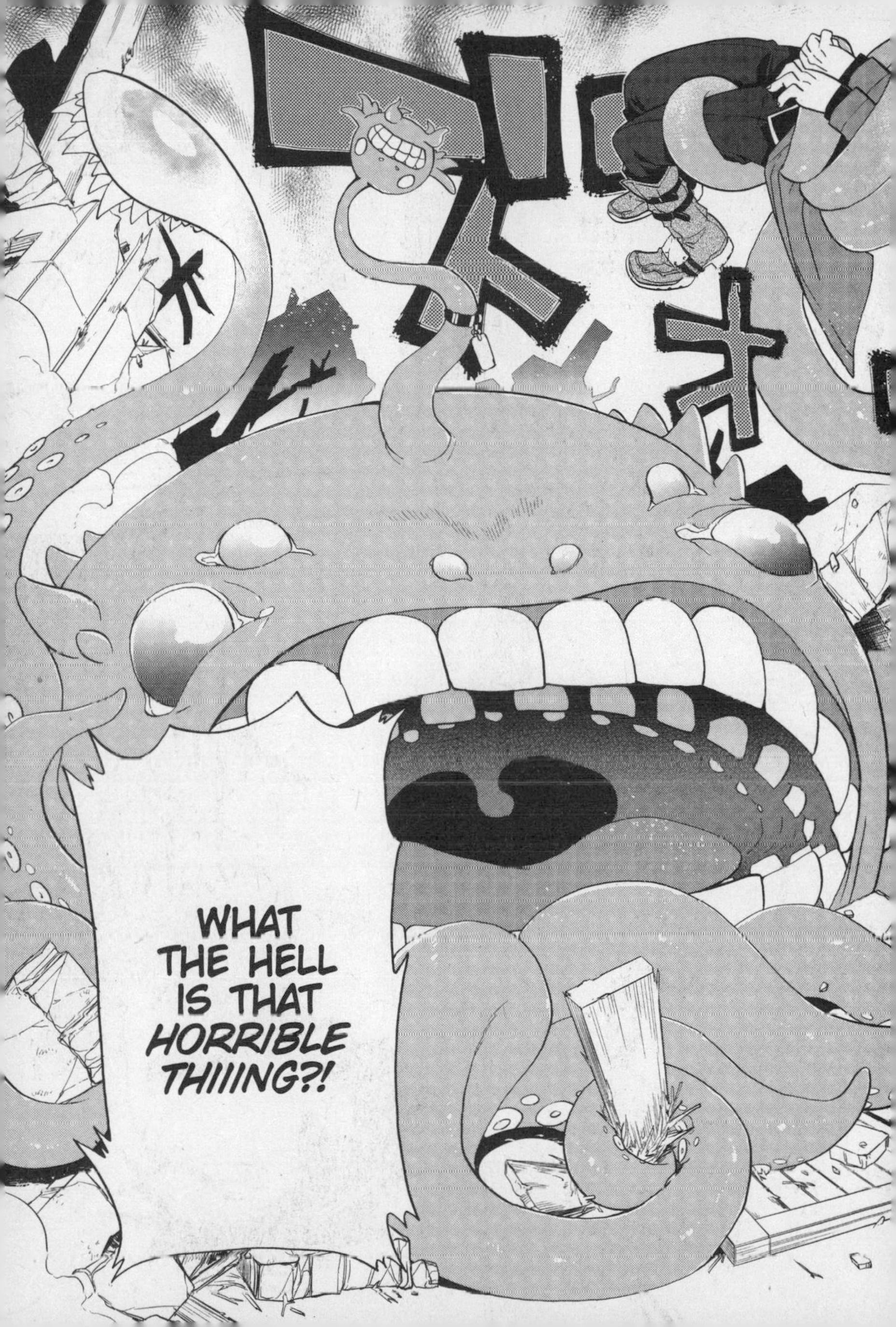
WHAT THE HELL IS THAT HORRIBLE THIIING?!

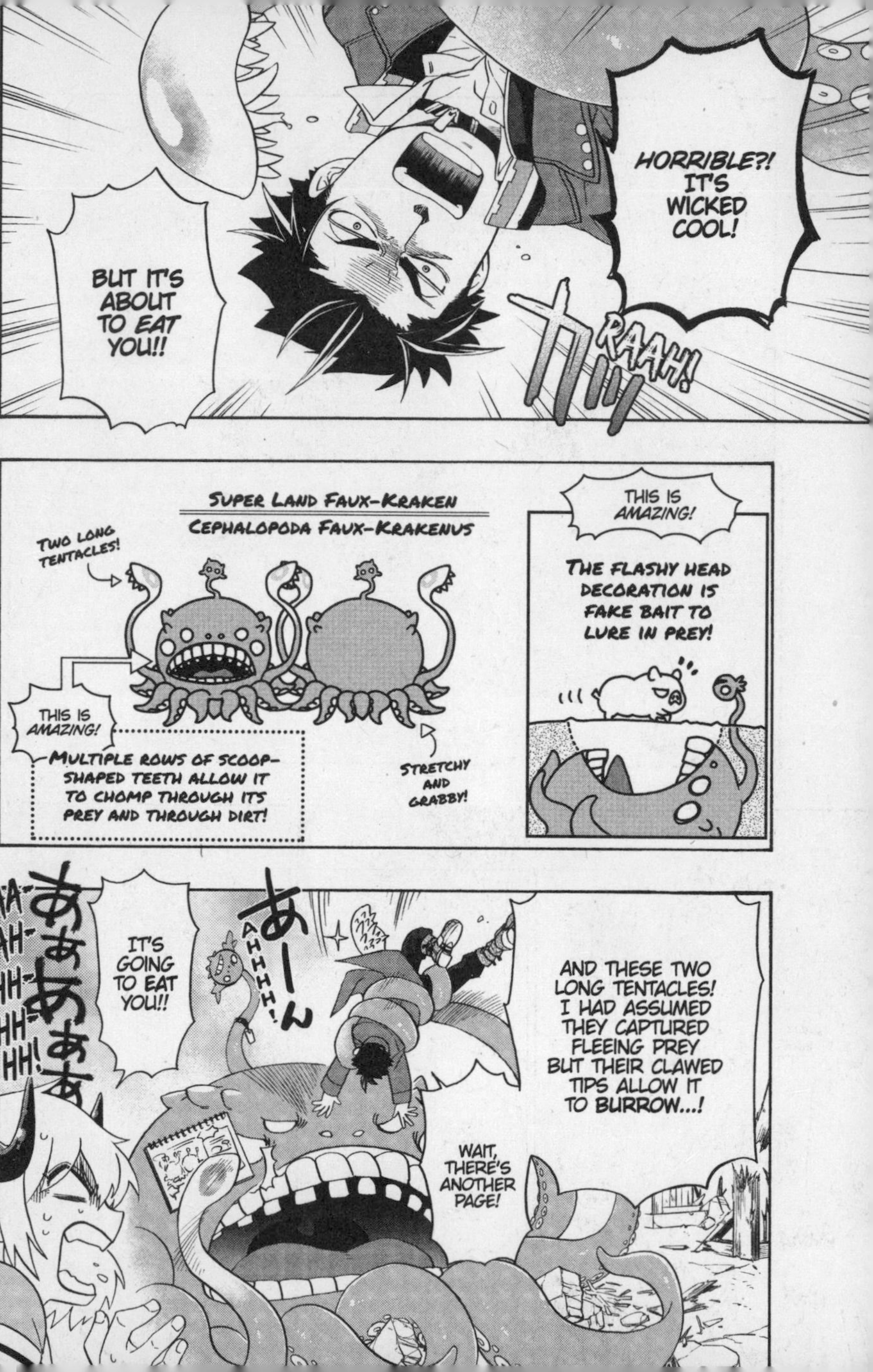
HORRIBLE?! IT'S WICKED COOL!
RAAH!
BUT IT'S ABOUT TO EAT YOU!!
THIS IS AMAZING!
THE FLASHY HEAD DECORATION IS FAKE BAIT TO LURE IN PREY!
SUPER LAND FAUX-KRAKEN
CEPHALOPODA FAUX-KRAKENUS
TWO LONG TENTACLES!
THIS IS AMAZING!
MULTIPLE ROWS OF SCOOP-SHAPED TEETH ALLOW IT TO CHOMP THROUGH ITS PREY AND THROUGH DIRT!
STRETCHY AND GRABBY!
AND THESE TWO LONG TENTACLES! I HAD ASSUMED THEY CAPTURED FLEEING PREY BUT THEIR CLAWED TIPS ALLOW IT TO BURROW...!
WAIT, THERE'S ANOTHER PAGE!
あーん
AHHHH!
IT'S GOING TO EAT YOU!!
あああぁ
AA-AH-HH-HH-HH!

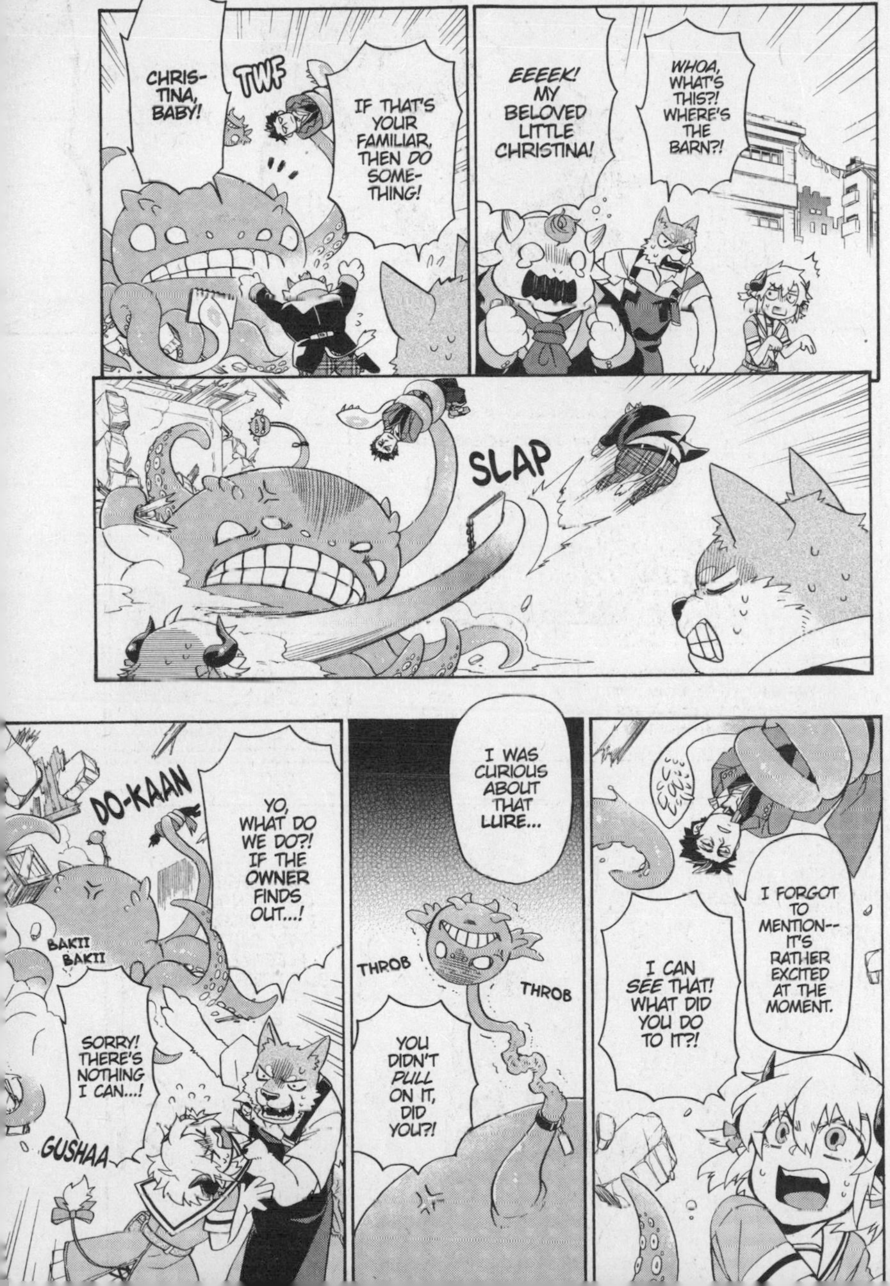
WHOA, WHAT'S THIS?! WHERE'S THE BARN?!
EEEEK! MY BELOVED LITTLE CHRISTINA!
IF THAT'S YOUR FAMILIAR, THEN *DO* SOME-THING!
TWF
CHRIS-TINA, BABY!
SLAP
I FORGOT TO MENTION-- IT'S RATHER EXCITED AT THE MOMENT.
I CAN *SEE* THAT! WHAT DID YOU DO TO IT?!
I WAS CURIOUS ABOUT THAT LURE...
THROB
THROB
YOU DIDN'T *PULL* ON IT, DID YOU?!
YO, WHAT DO WE DO?! IF THE OWNER FINDS OUT...!
DO-KAAN
BAKII BAKII
SORRY! THERE'S NOTHING I CAN...!
GUSHAA

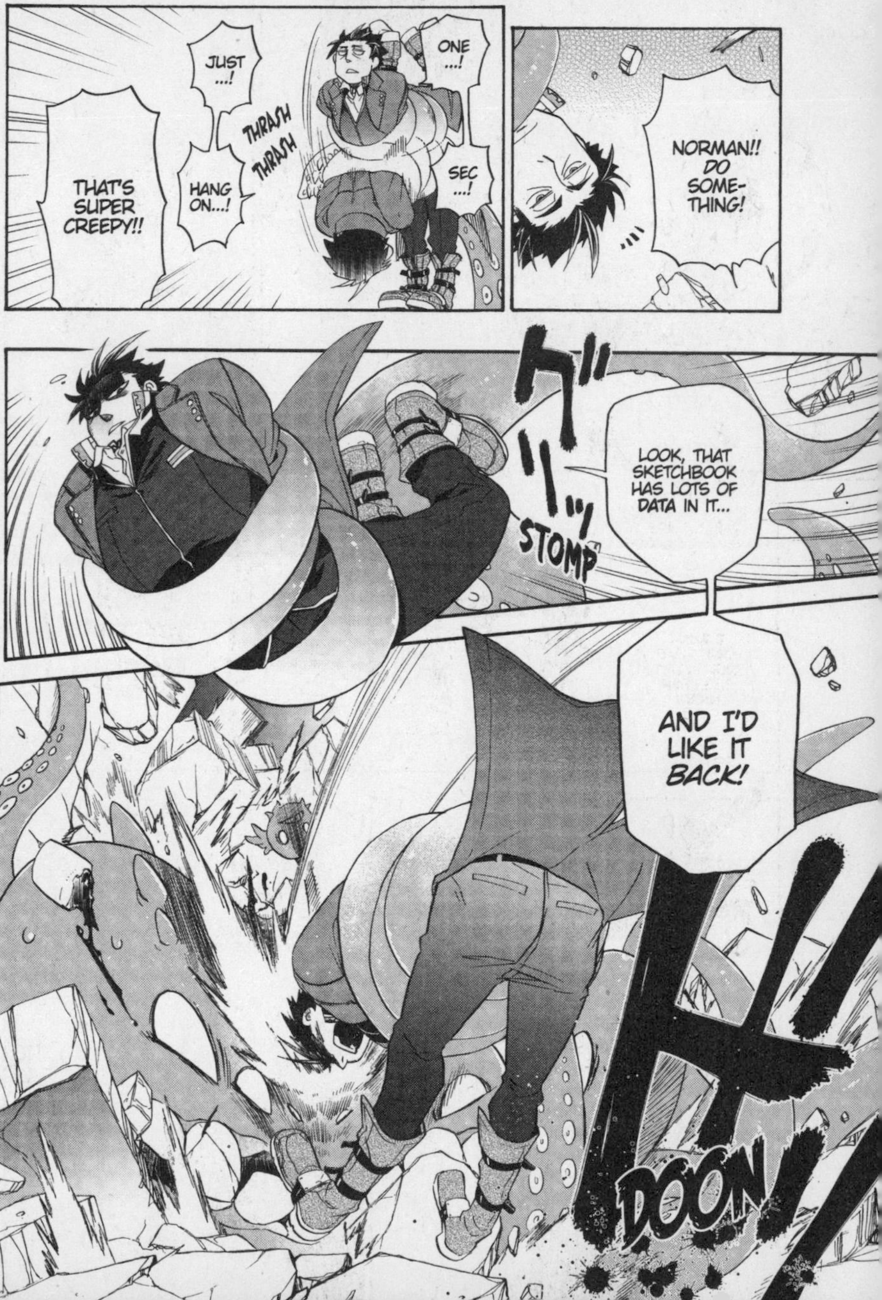
NORMAN!! DO SOME-THING!
ONE ...! SEC ...!
JUST ...! HANG ON...!
THRASH THRASH
THAT'S SUPER CREEPY!!
STOMP
LOOK, THAT SKETCHBOOK HAS LOTS OF DATA IN IT...
AND I'D LIKE IT *BACK!*
DOON

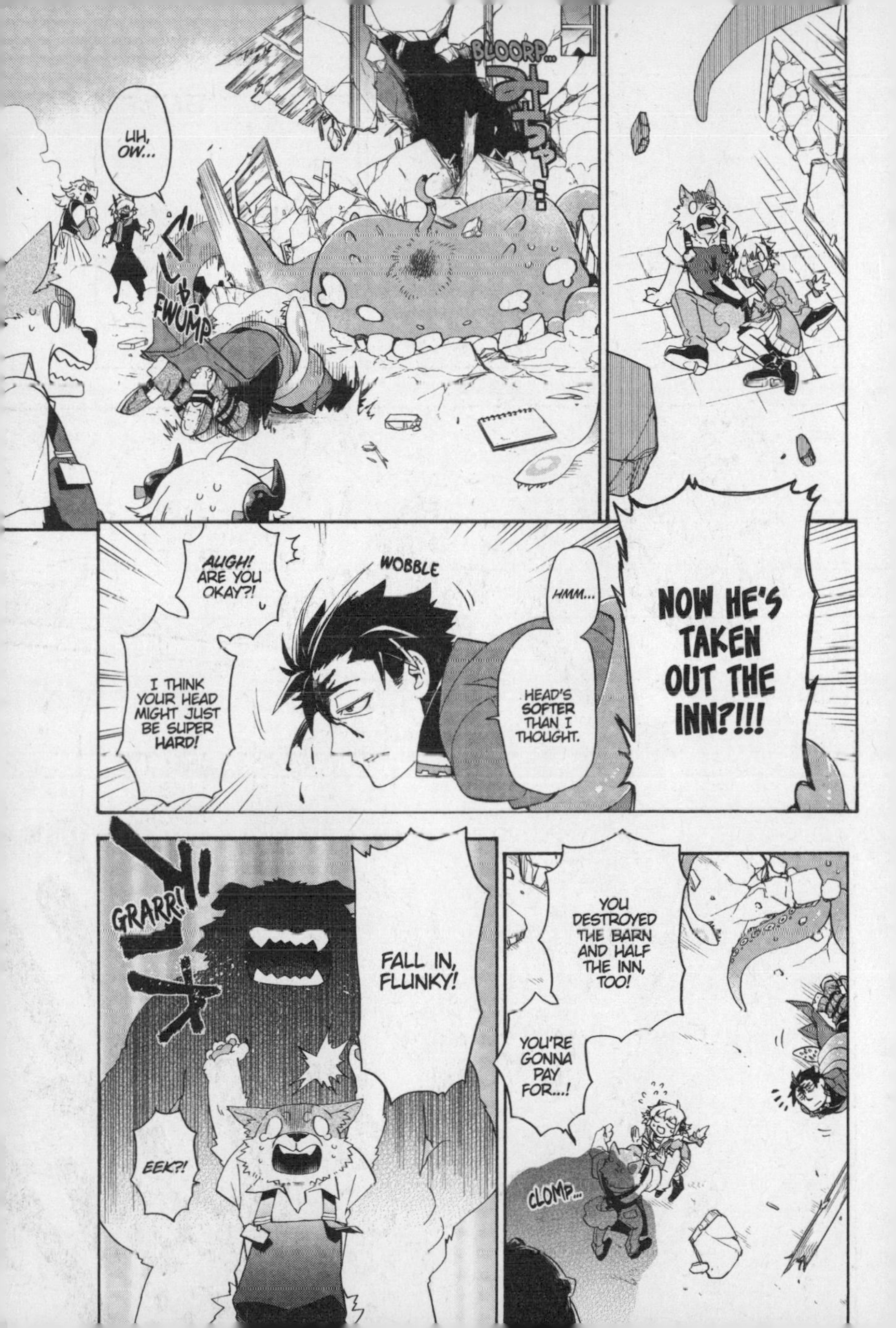
BLOORP...
UH, OW...
FWUMP
NOW HE'S TAKEN OUT THE INN?!!!
HMM...
HEAD'S SOFTER THAN I THOUGHT.
WOBBLE
AUGH! ARE YOU OKAY?!
I THINK YOUR HEAD MIGHT JUST BE SUPER HARD!
YOU DESTROYED THE BARN AND HALF THE INN, TOO!
YOU'RE GONNA PAY FOR...!
CLOMP...
FALL IN, FLUNKY!
GRARR?!
EEK?!

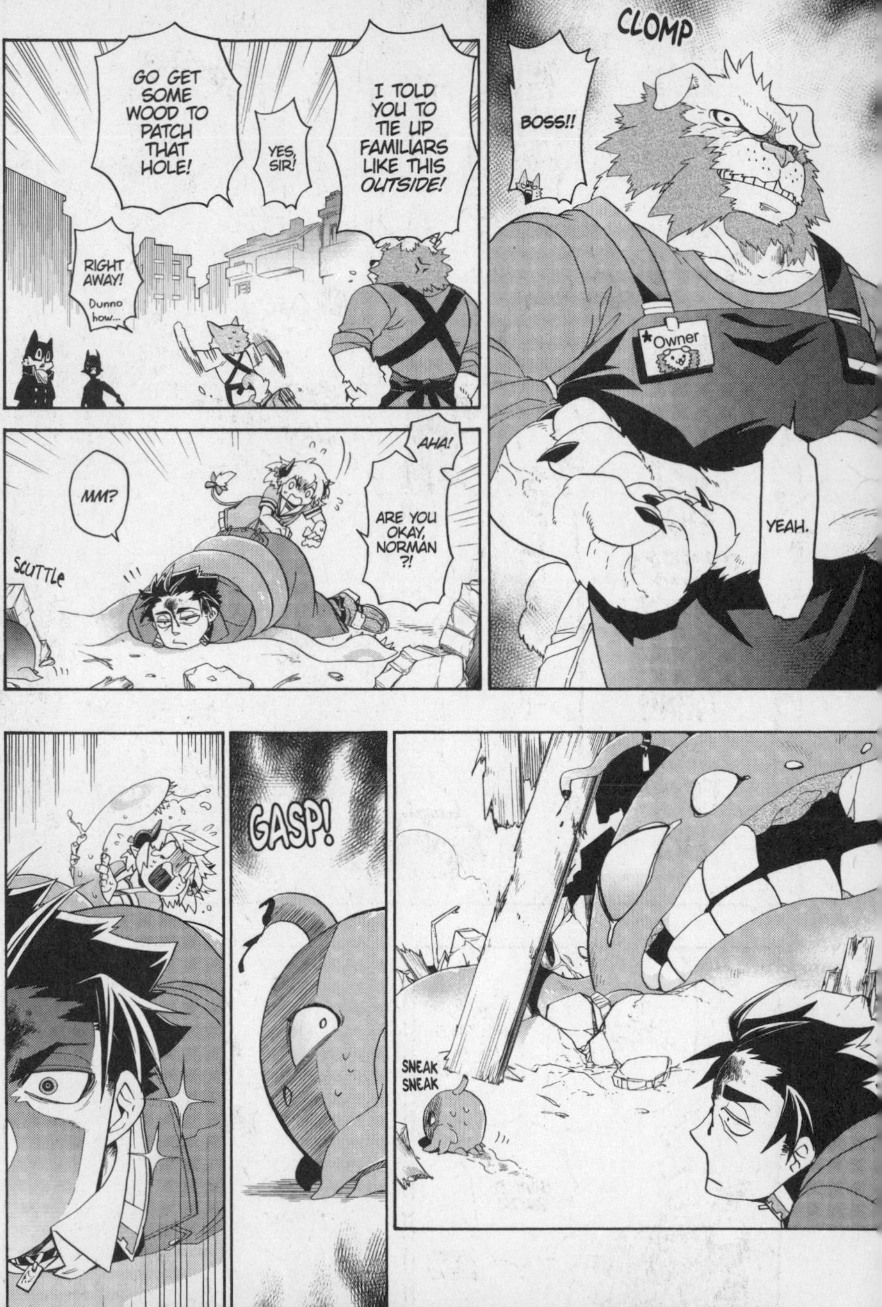
CLOMP
BOSS!!
YEAH.
I TOLD YOU TO TIE UP FAMILIARS LIKE THIS OUTSIDE!
YES, SIR!
GO GET SOME WOOD TO PATCH THAT HOLE!
RIGHT AWAY!
Dunno how...
AHA!
ARE YOU OKAY, NORMAN?!
MM?
SCUTTLE
SNEAK SNEAK
GASP!

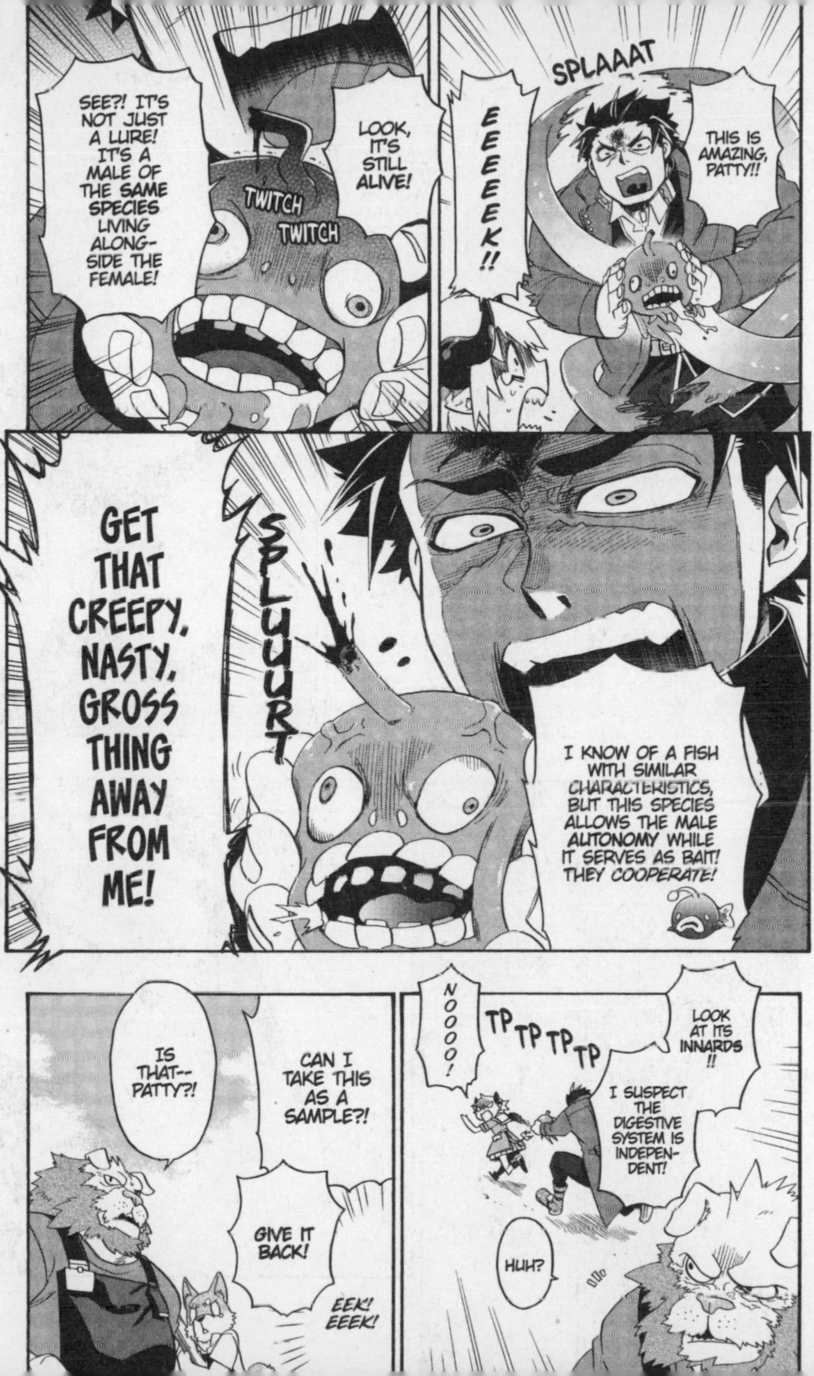
SPLAAAT
THIS IS AMAZING, PATTY!!
EEEEEEK!!
LOOK, IT'S STILL ALIVE!
SEE?! IT'S NOT JUST A LURE! IT'S A MALE OF THE SAME SPECIES LIVING ALONG-SIDE THE FEMALE!
TWITCH
TWITCH
I KNOW OF A FISH WITH SIMILAR CHARACTERISTICS, BUT THIS SPECIES ALLOWS THE MALE AUTONOMY WHILE IT SERVES AS BAIT! THEY *COOPERATE*!
SPLUUURT
GET THAT CREEPY, NASTY, GROSS THING AWAY FROM ME!
LOOK AT ITS INNARDS!!
I SUSPECT THE DIGESTIVE SYSTEM IS INDEPEN-DENT!
TP TP TP TP
NOOOOO!
HUH?
CAN I TAKE THIS AS A SAMPLE?!
IS THAT-- PATTY?!
GIVE IT BACK!
EEK! EEEK!

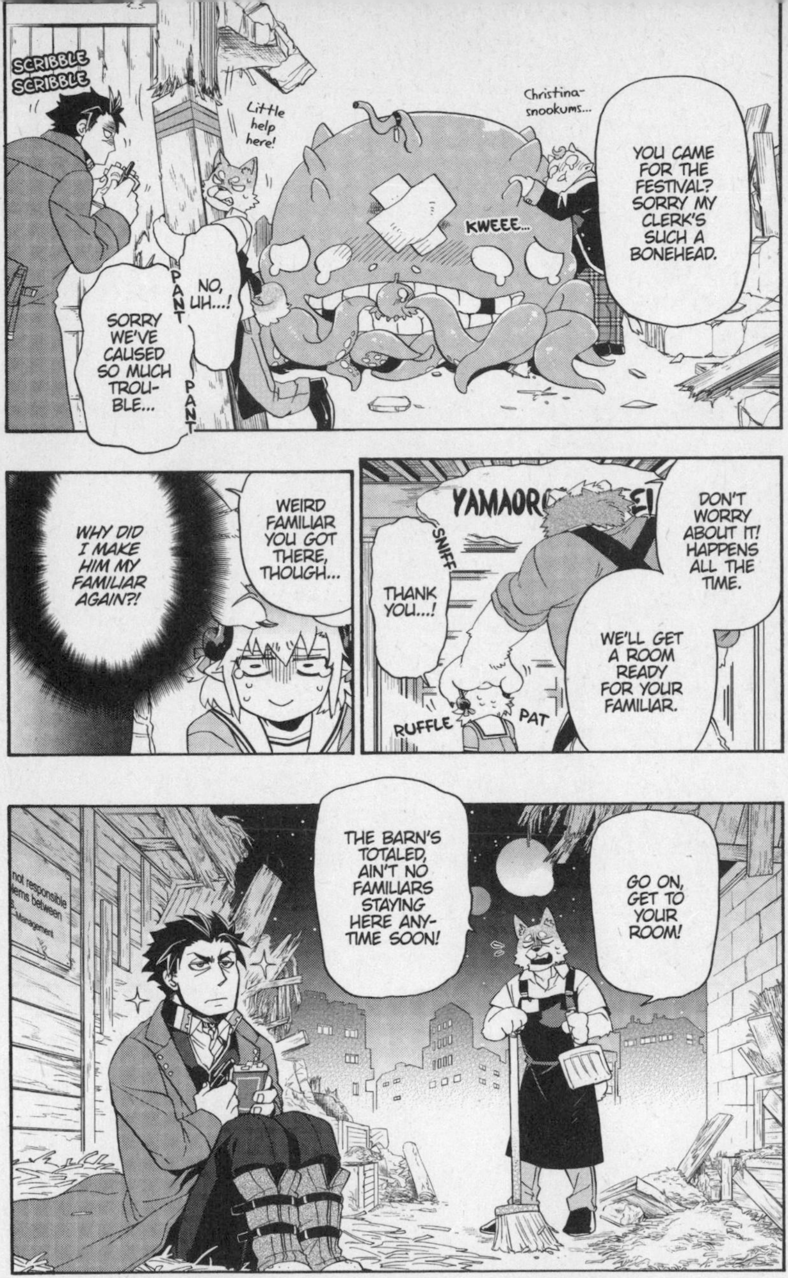
Christina-snookums...
YOU CAME FOR THE FESTIVAL? SORRY MY CLERK'S SUCH A BONEHEAD.
KWEEE...
Little help here!
SCRIBBLE SCRIBBLE
NO, UH...!
PANT PANT
SORRY WE'VE CAUSED SO MUCH TROUBLE...
YAMAORO
DON'T WORRY ABOUT IT! HAPPENS ALL THE TIME.
WE'LL GET A ROOM READY FOR YOUR FAMILIAR.
SNIFF
THANK YOU...!
PAT
RUFFLE
WEIRD FAMILIAR YOU GOT THERE, THOUGH...
WHY DID I MAKE HIM MY FAMILIAR AGAIN?!
GO ON, GET TO YOUR ROOM!
THE BARN'S TOTALED, AIN'T NO FAMILIARS STAYING HERE ANYTIME SOON!

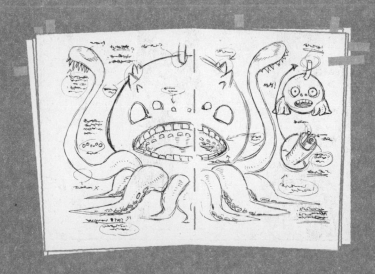

Sorry For My Familiar

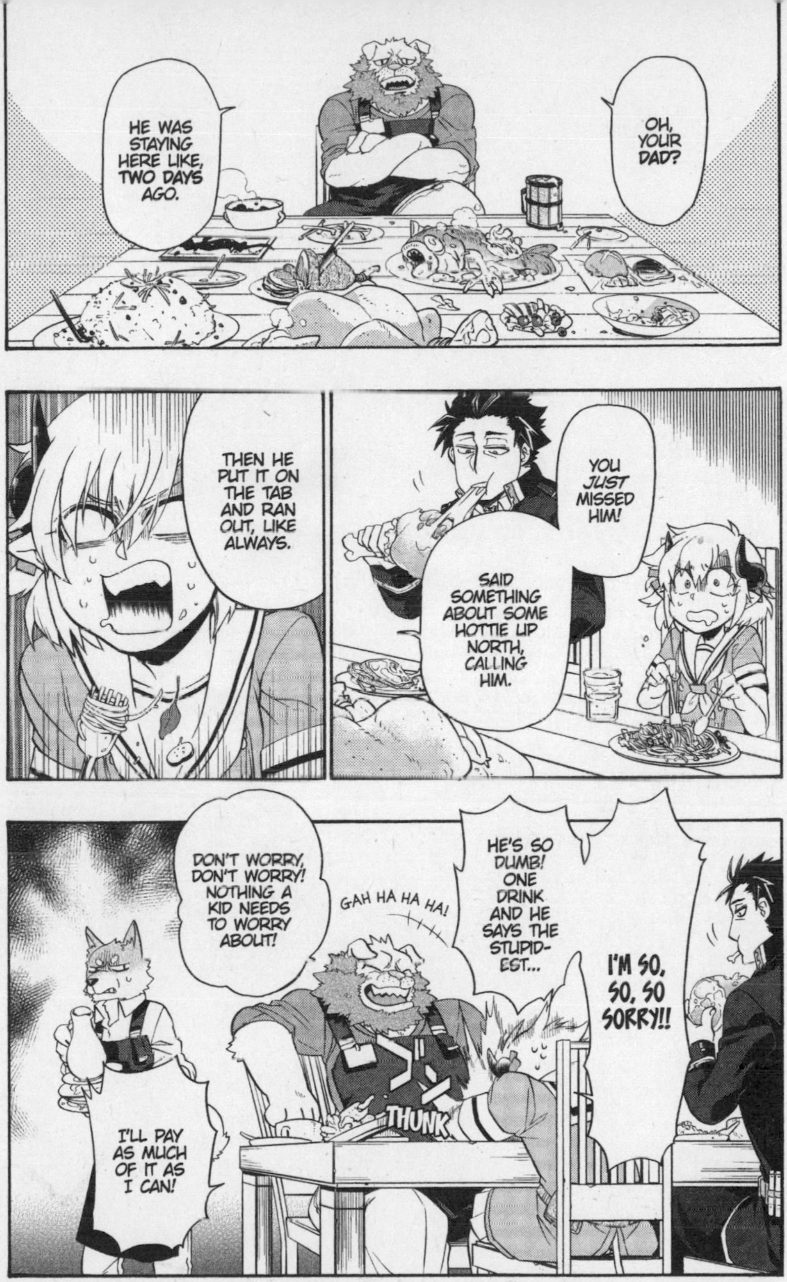
OH, YOUR DAD?
HE WAS STAYING HERE LIKE, TWO DAYS AGO.
YOU JUST MISSED HIM!
SAID SOMETHING ABOUT SOME HOTTIE UP NORTH, CALLING HIM.
THEN HE PUT IT ON THE TAB AND RAN OUT, LIKE ALWAYS.
I'M SO, SO, SO SORRY!!
HE'S SO DUMB! ONE DRINK AND HE SAYS THE STUPID-EST...
GAH HA HA HA!
THUNK
DON'T WORRY, DON'T WORRY! NOTHING A KID NEEDS TO WORRY ABOUT!
I'LL PAY AS MUCH OF IT AS I CAN!

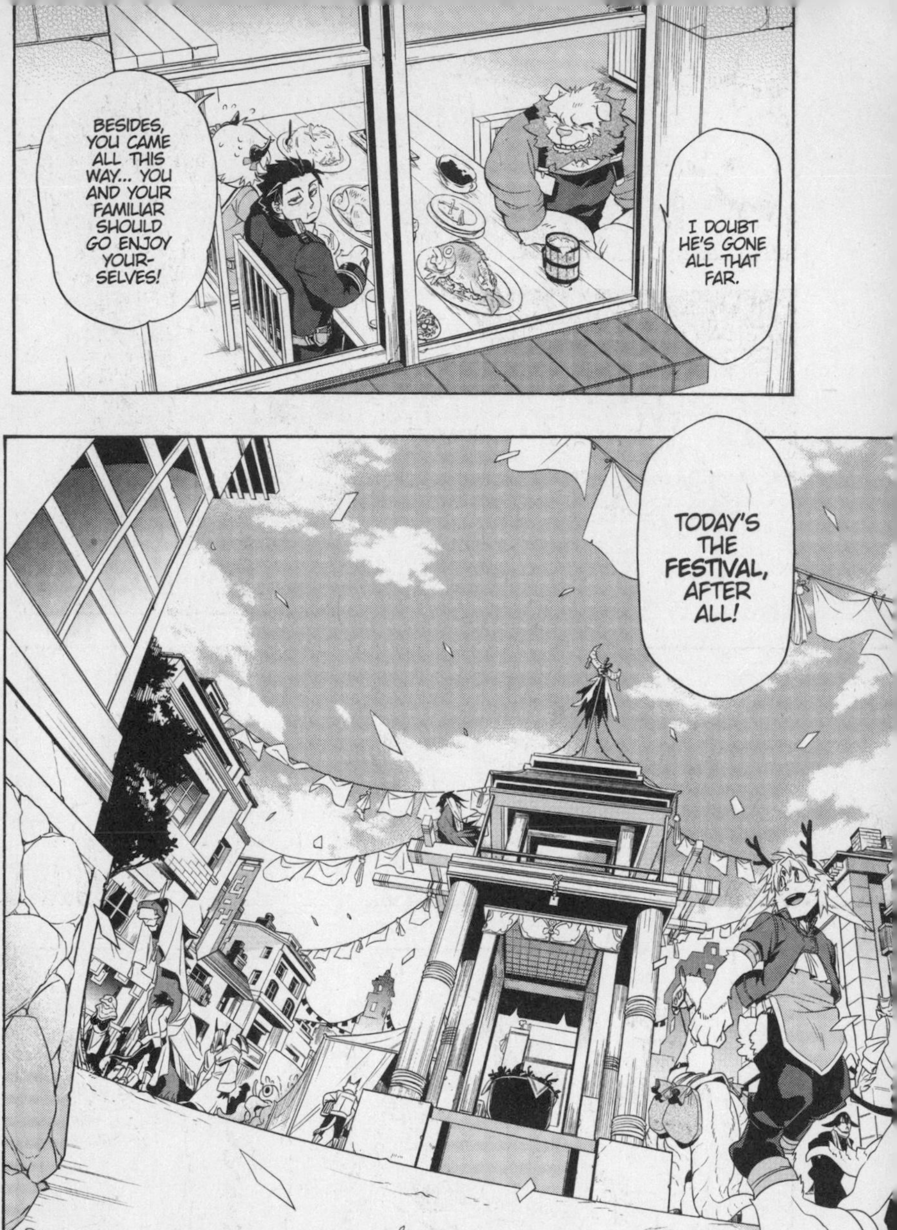
I DOUBT HE'S GONE ALL THAT FAR.
BESIDES, YOU CAME ALL THIS WAY... YOU AND YOUR FAMILIAR SHOULD GO ENJOY YOUR-SELVES!
TODAY'S THE FESTIVAL, AFTER ALL!

FILE 4:
7th Dragon Moon Harvest Festival ①

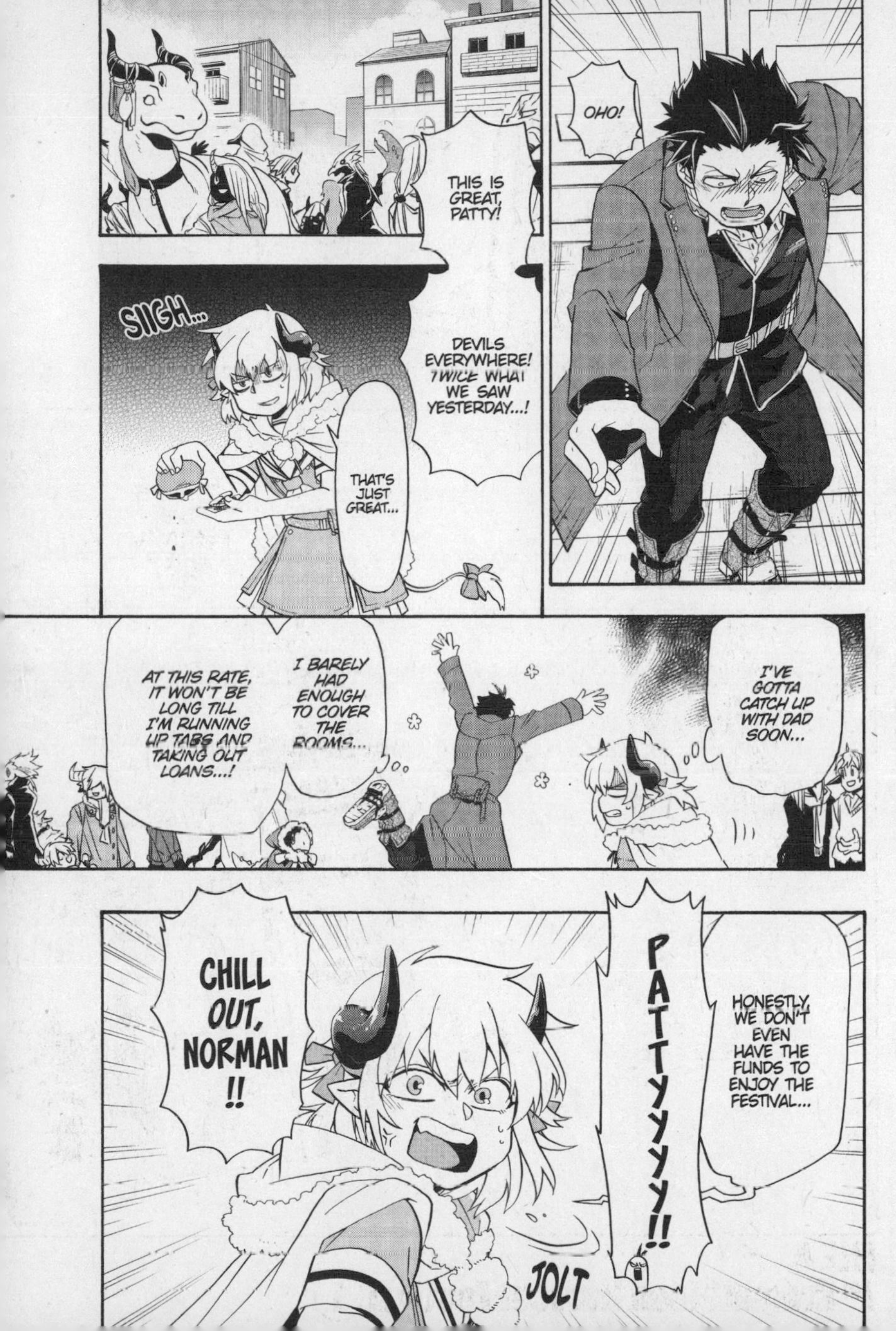
OHO!
THIS IS GREAT, PATTY!
DEVILS EVERYWHERE! TWICE WHAT WE SAW YESTERDAY...!
SIIGH...
THAT'S JUST GREAT...
I'VE GOTTA CATCH UP WITH DAD SOON...
I BARELY HAD ENOUGH TO COVER THE ROOMS...
AT THIS RATE, IT WON'T BE LONG TILL I'M RUNNING UP TABS AND TAKING OUT LOANS...!
HONESTLY, WE DON'T EVEN HAVE THE FUNDS TO ENJOY THE FESTIVAL...
PATTYYYYY!!
CHILL OUT, NORMAN!!
JOLT

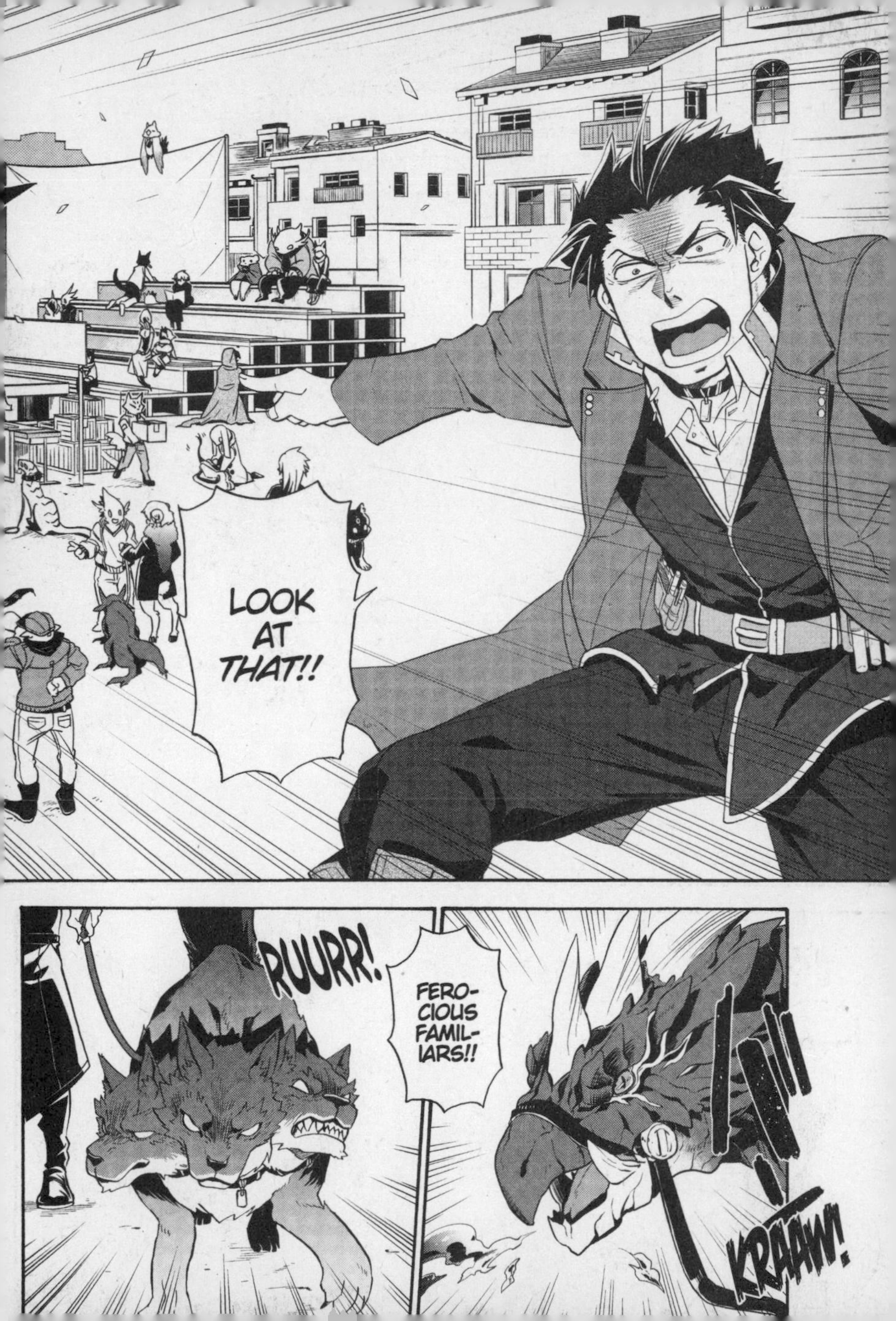
LOOK AT THAT!!
KRAAW!
FERO-CIOUS FAMIL-IARS!!
RUURR!

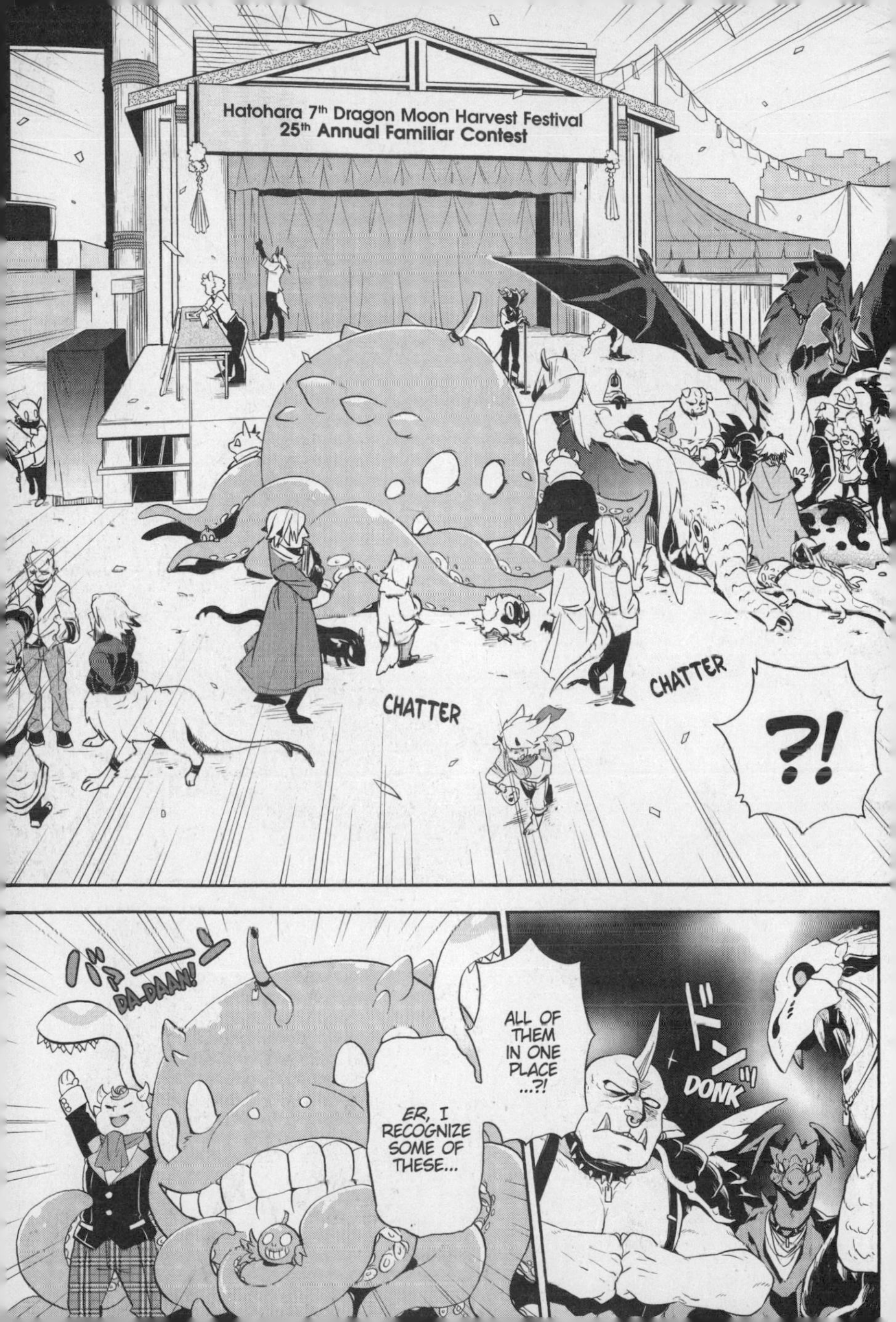
Hatohara 7th Dragon Moon Harvest Festival
25th Annual Familiar Contest
CHATTER
CHATTER
?!
DONK
ALL OF THEM IN ONE PLACE ...?!
DA-DAAN!
ER, I RECOGNIZE SOME OF THESE...

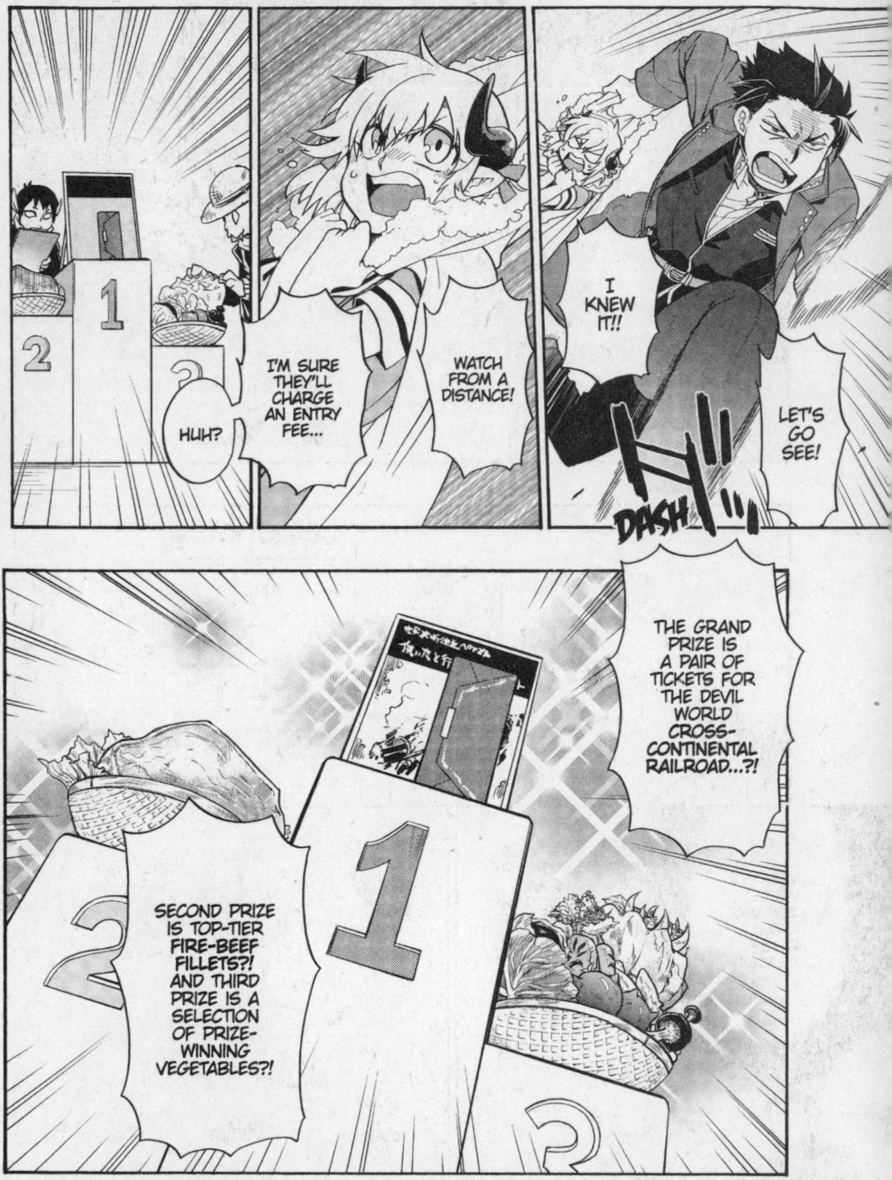
I KNEW IT!!
LET'S GO SEE!
DASH
WATCH FROM A DISTANCE!
I'M SURE THEY'LL CHARGE AN ENTRY FEE...
HUH?
THE GRAND PRIZE IS A PAIR OF TICKETS FOR THE DEVIL WORLD CROSS-CONTINENTAL RAILROAD...?!
SECOND PRIZE IS TOP-TIER FIRE-BEEF FILLETS?! AND THIRD PRIZE IS A SELECTION OF PRIZE-WINNING VEGETABLES?!

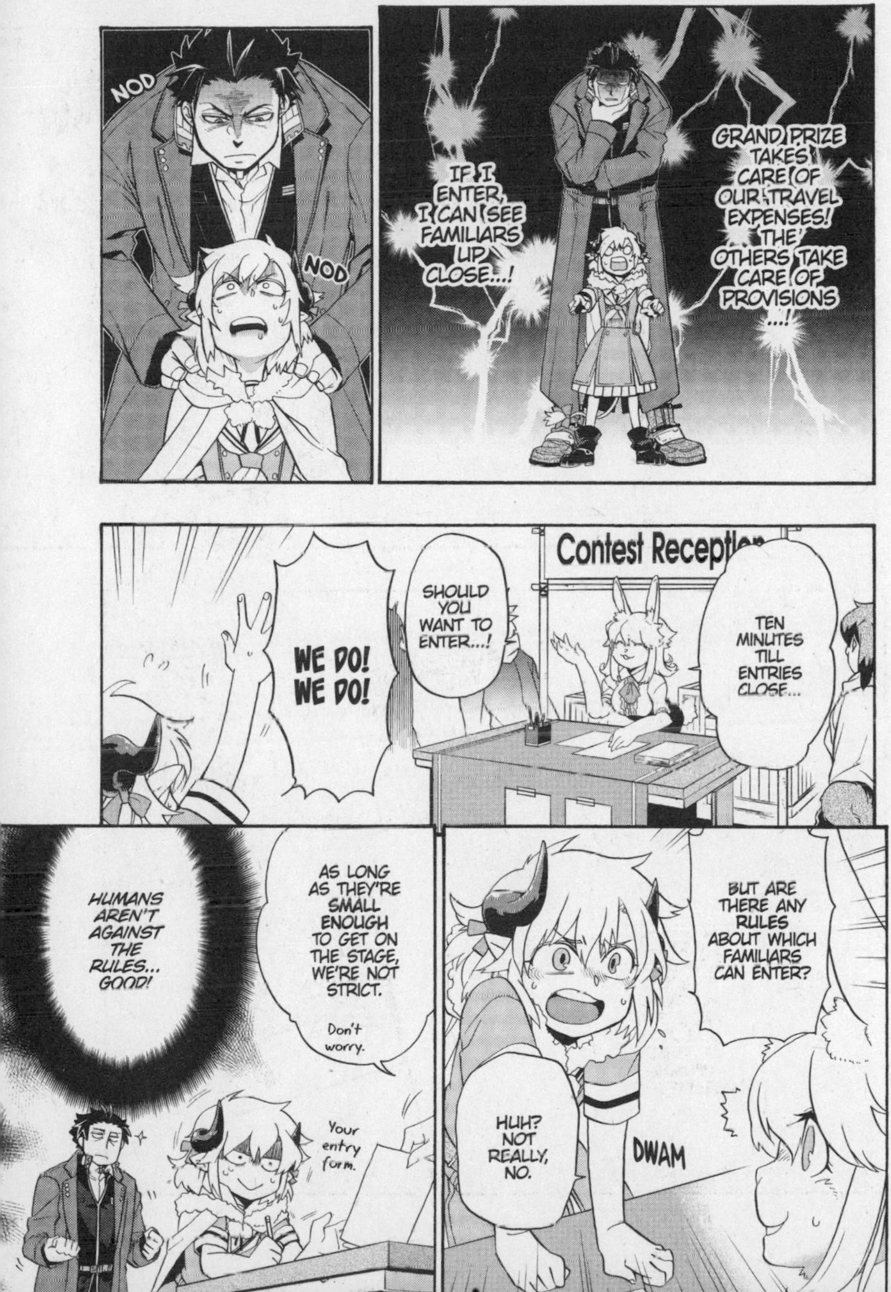
GRAND PRIZE TAKES CARE OF OUR TRAVEL EXPENSES! THE OTHERS TAKE CARE OF PROVISIONS ...!
IF I ENTER, I CAN SEE FAMILIARS UP CLOSE...!
NOD
NOD
TEN MINUTES TILL ENTRIES CLOSE...
Contest Recept
SHOULD YOU WANT TO ENTER...!
WE DO! WE DO!
BUT ARE THERE ANY RULES ABOUT WHICH FAMILIARS CAN ENTER?
HUH? NOT REALLY, NO.
DWAM
AS LONG AS THEY'RE SMALL ENOUGH TO GET ON THE STAGE, WE'RE NOT STRICT.
Don't worry.
HUMANS AREN'T AGAINST THE RULES... GOOD!
Your entry form.

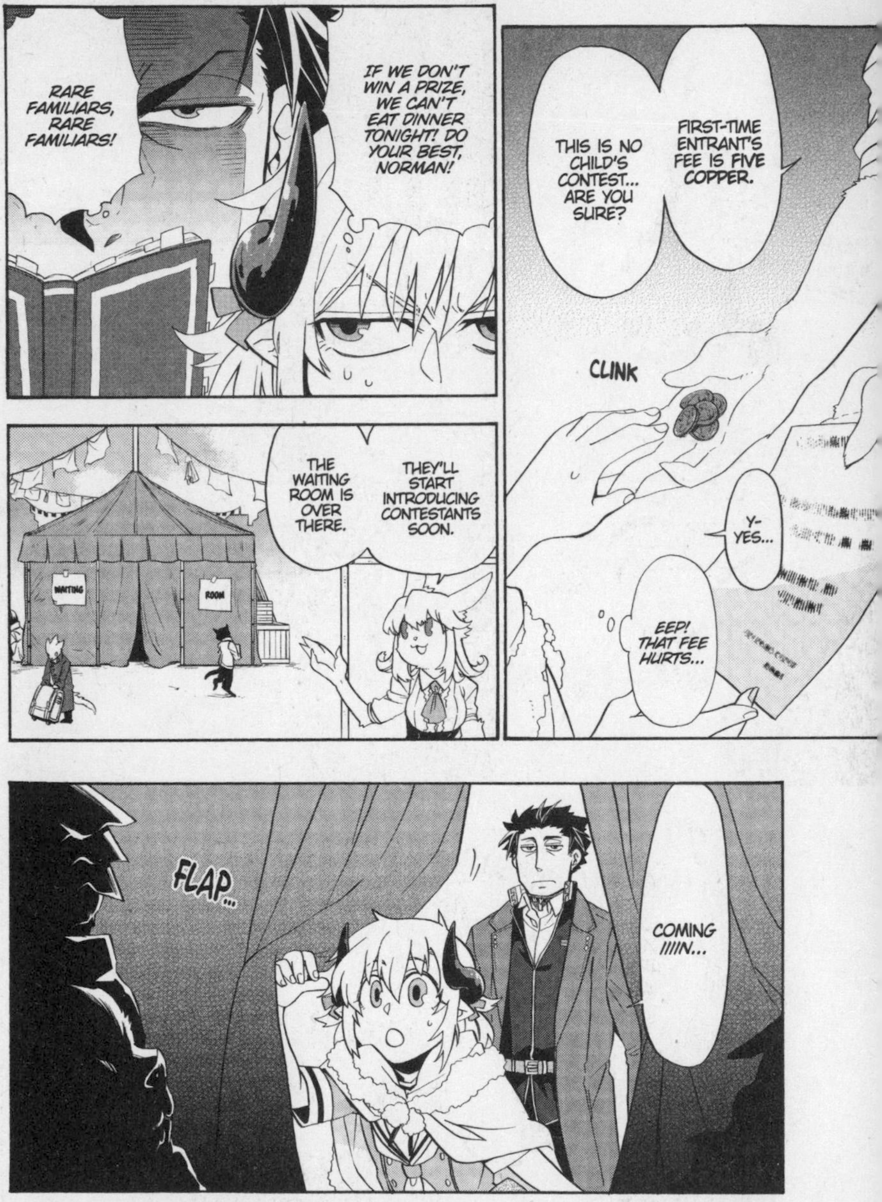
FIRST-TIME ENTRANT'S FEE IS FIVE COPPER.
THIS IS NO CHILD'S CONTEST... ARE YOU SURE?
CLINK
Y-YES...
EEP! THAT FEE HURTS...
IF WE DON'T WIN A PRIZE, WE CAN'T EAT DINNER TONIGHT! DO YOUR BEST, NORMAN!
RARE FAMILIARS, RARE FAMILIARS!
THEY'LL START INTRODUCING CONTESTANTS SOON.
THE WAITING ROOM IS OVER THERE.
WAITING
ROOM
COMING IIIIN...
FLAP...

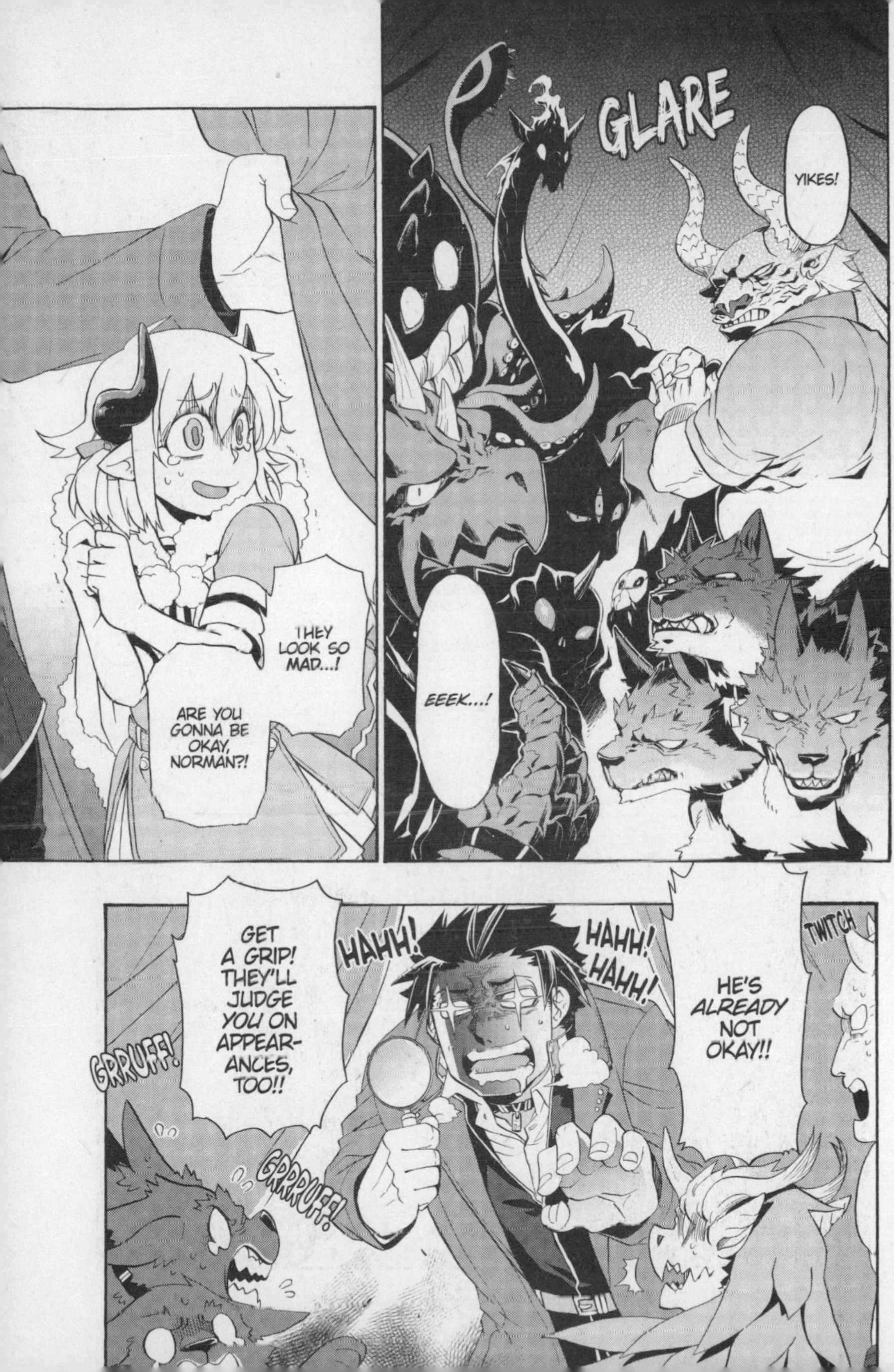
GLARE
YIKES!
EEEK...!
THEY LOOK SO MAD...!
ARE YOU GONNA BE OKAY, NORMAN?!
TWITCH
HE'S ALREADY NOT OKAY!!
HAHH! HAHH!
HAHH!
GET A GRIP! THEY'LL JUDGE YOU ON APPEAR-ANCES, TOO!!
GRRUFF!
GRRRUFF!

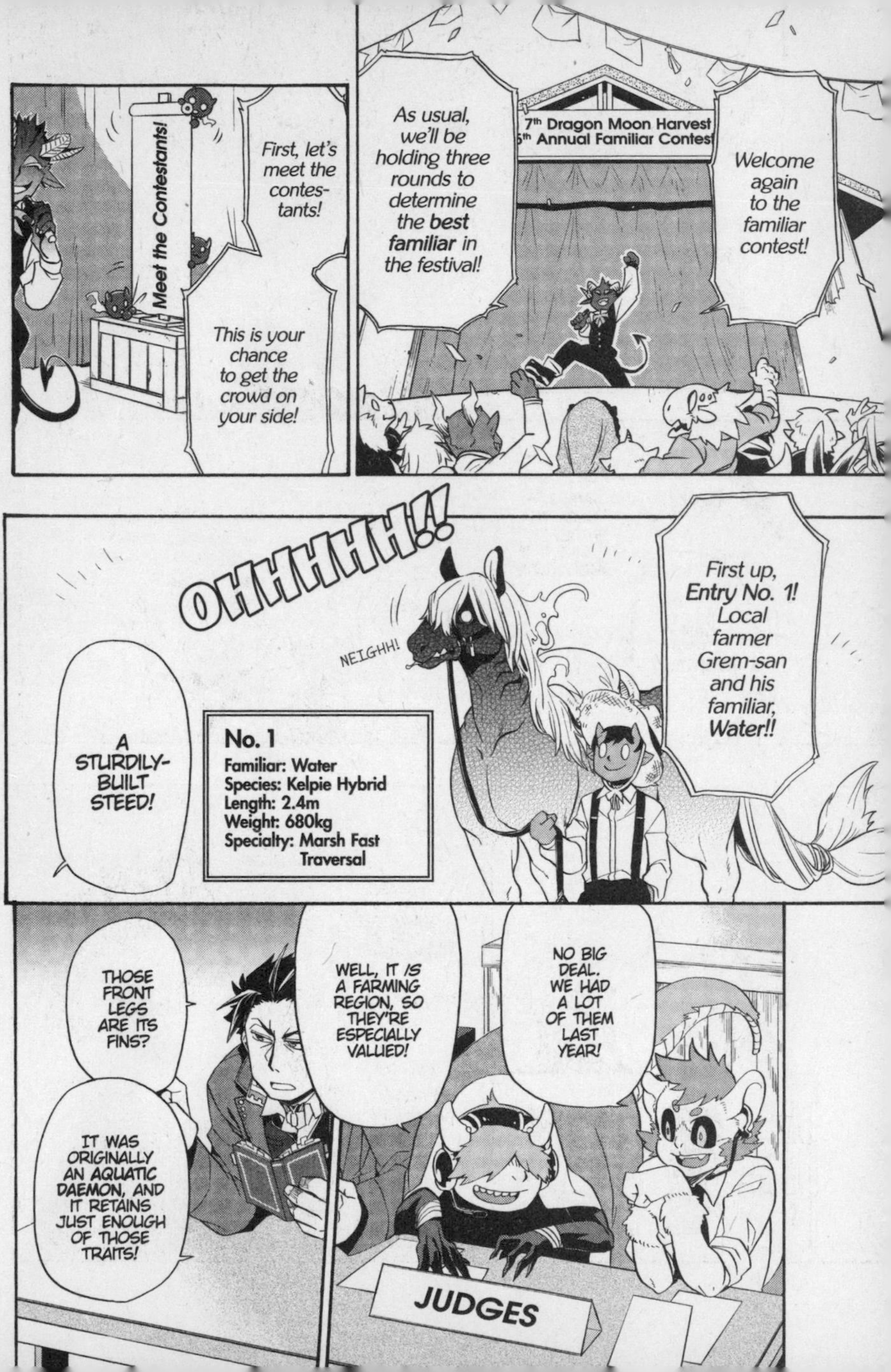

Welcome again to the familiar contest!
7th Dragon Moon Harvest
th Annual Familiar Contes
As usual, we'll be holding three rounds to determine the best familiar in the festival!
First, let's meet the contestants!
Meet the Contestants!
This is your chance to get the crowd on your side!
First up, Entry No. 1! Local farmer Grem-san and his familiar, Water!!
OHHHHHH!!
NEIGHH!
No. 1
Familiar: Water
Species: Kelpie Hybrid
Length: 2.4m
Weight: 680kg
Specialty: Marsh Fast Traversal
A STURDILY-BUILT STEED!
NO BIG DEAL. WE HAD A LOT OF THEM LAST YEAR!
WELL, IT IS A FARMING REGION, SO THEY'RE ESPECIALLY VALUED!
THOSE FRONT LEGS ARE ITS FINS?
IT WAS ORIGINALLY AN AQUATIC DAEMON, AND IT RETAINS JUST ENOUGH OF THOSE TRAITS!
JUDGES

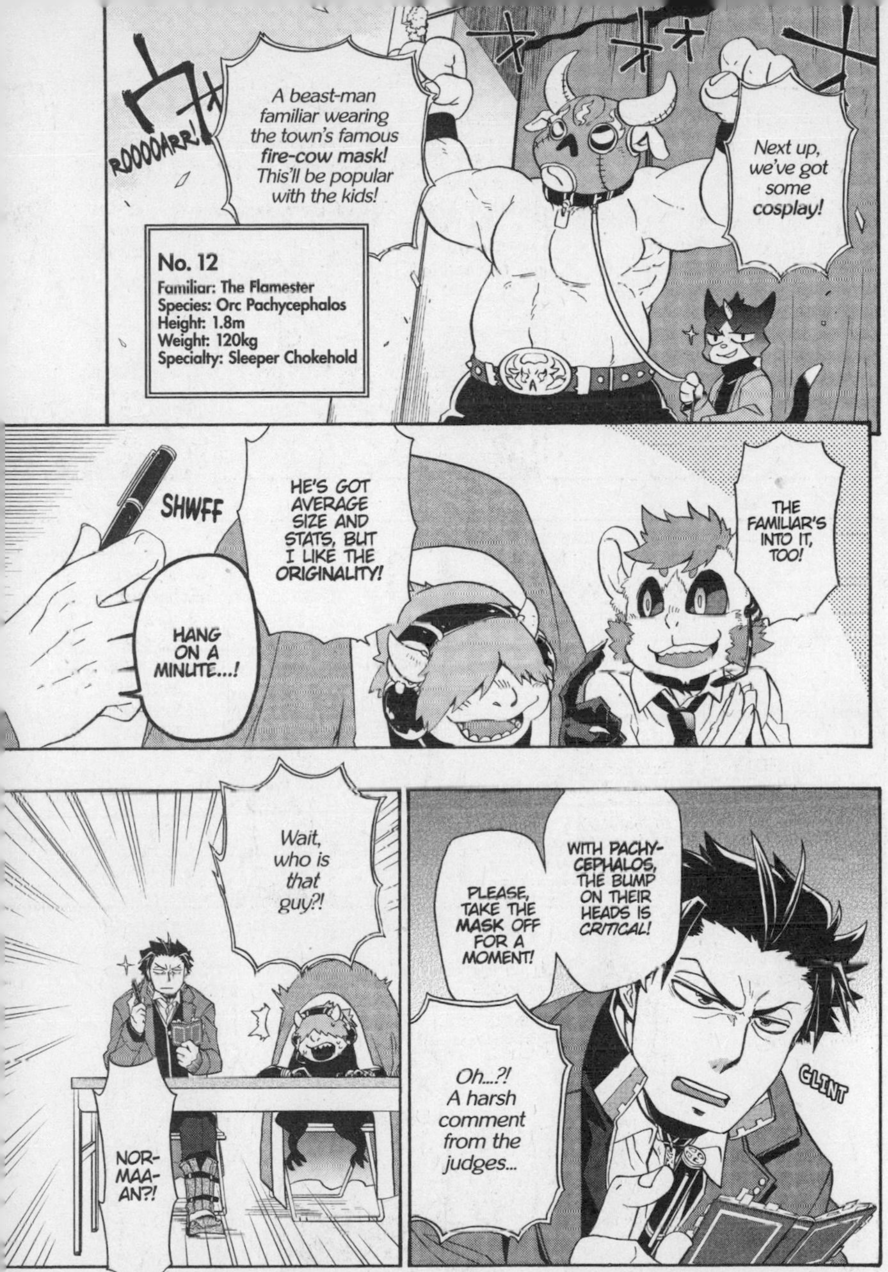
Next up, we've got some cosplay!
A beast-man familiar wearing the town's famous fire-cow mask! This'll be popular with the kids!
ROOOOARR!
No. 12
Familiar: The Flamester
Species: Orc Pachycephalos
Height: 1.8m
Weight: 120kg
Specialty: Sleeper Chokehold
THE FAMILIAR'S INTO IT, TOO!
HE'S GOT AVERAGE SIZE AND STATS, BUT I LIKE THE ORIGINALITY!
SHWFF
HANG ON A MINUTE...!
WITH PACHY-CEPHALOS, THE BUMP ON THEIR HEADS IS CRITICAL!
PLEASE, TAKE THE MASK OFF FOR A MOMENT!
CLINT
Oh...?! A harsh comment from the judges...
Wait, who is that guy?!
NOR-MAA-AN?!

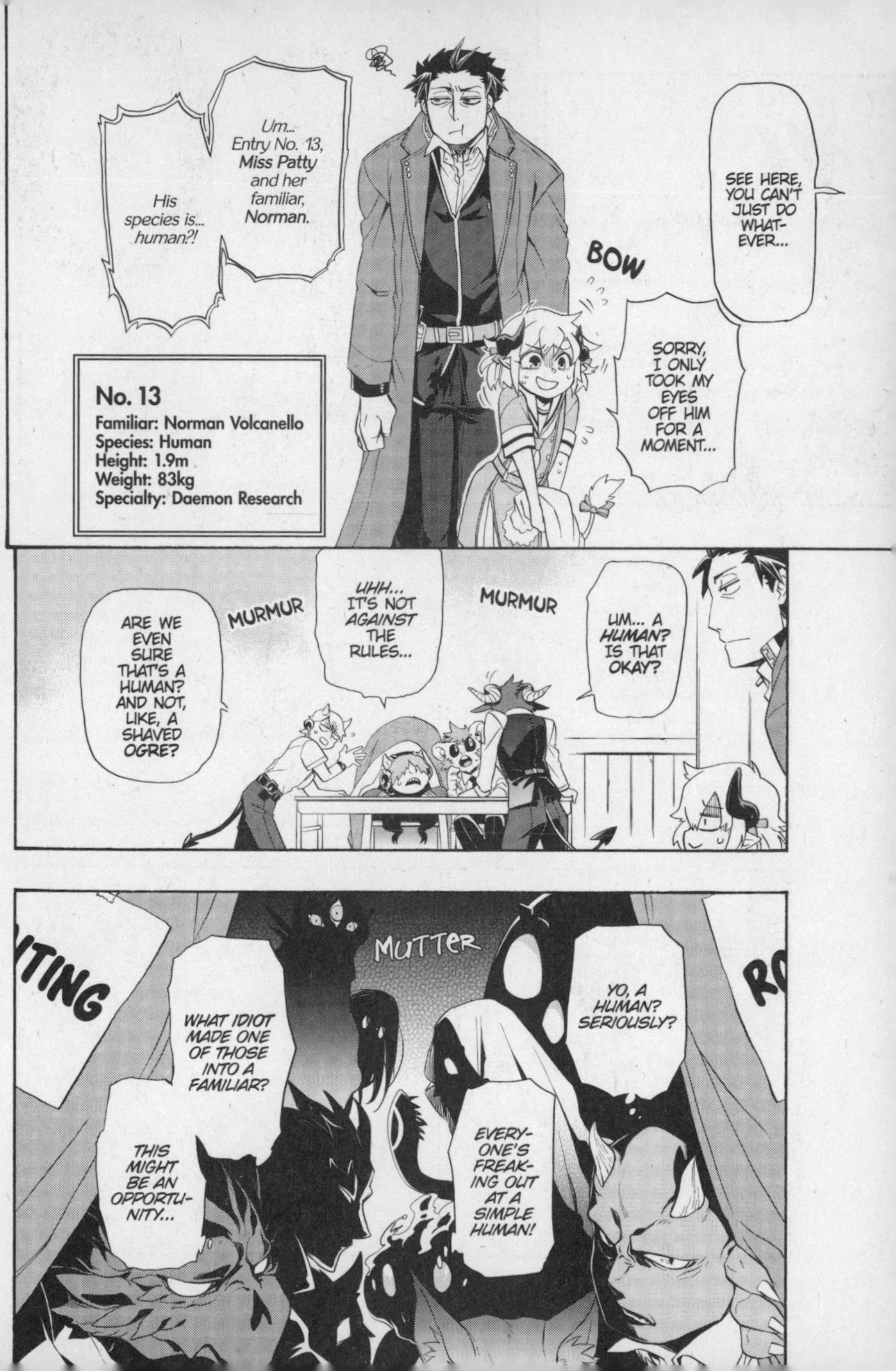
SEE HERE, YOU CAN'T JUST DO WHAT-EVER...
BOW
SORRY, I ONLY TOOK MY EYES OFF HIM FOR A MOMENT...
Um... Entry No. 13, Miss Patty and her familiar, Norman.
His species is... human?!
No. 13
Familiar: Norman Volcanello
Species: Human
Height: 1.9m
Weight: 83kg
Specialty: Daemon Research
UM... A HUMAN? IS THAT OKAY?
MURMUR
UHH... IT'S NOT AGAINST THE RULES...
MURMUR
ARE WE EVEN SURE THAT'S A HUMAN? AND NOT, LIKE, A SHAVED OGRE?
YO, A HUMAN? SERIOUSLY?
MUTTER
WHAT IDIOT MADE ONE OF THOSE INTO A FAMILIAR?
EVERY-ONE'S FREAK-ING OUT AT A SIMPLE HUMAN!
THIS MIGHT BE AN OPPORTU-NITY...

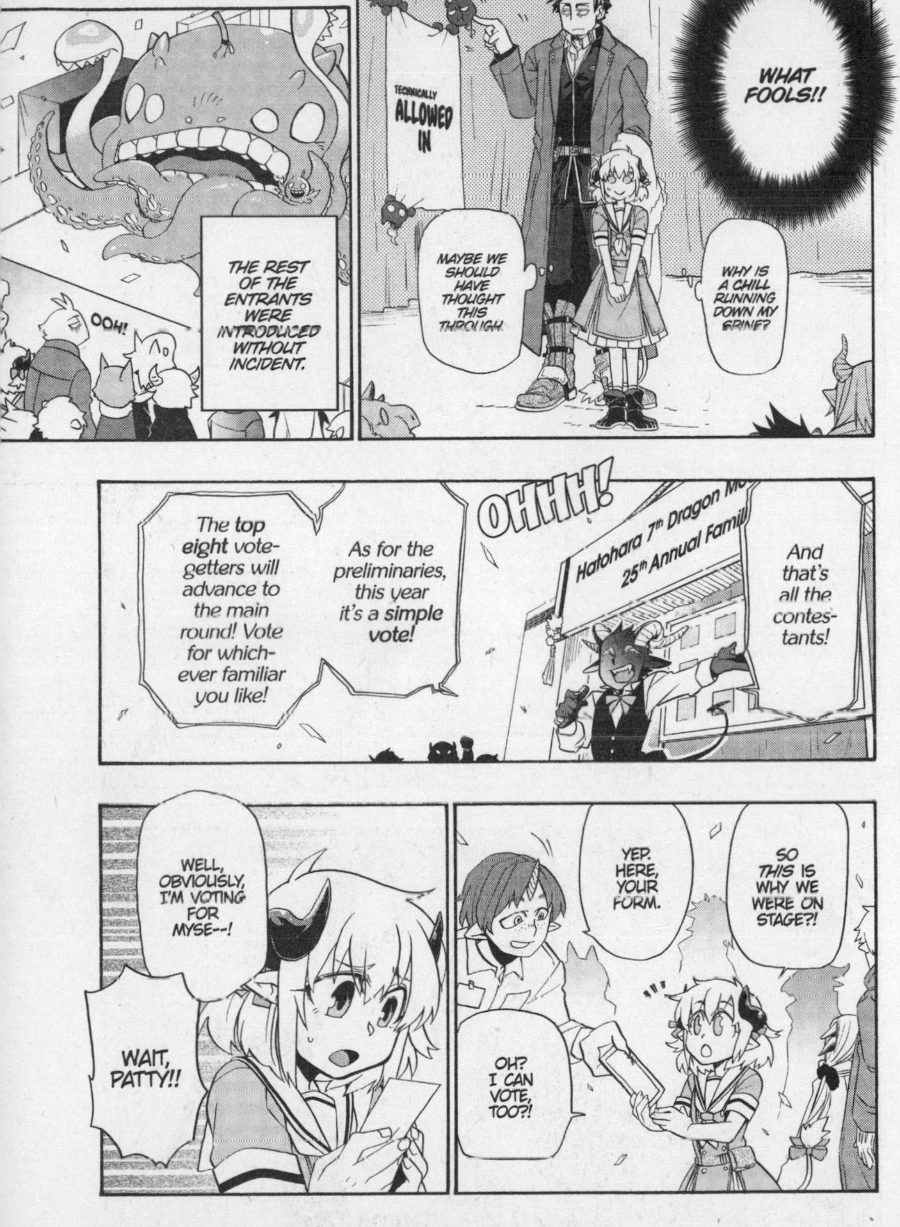
WHAT FOOLS!!
WHY IS A CHILL RUNNING DOWN MY SPINE?
MAYBE WE SHOULD HAVE THOUGHT THIS THROUGH.
TECHNICALLY ALLOWED IN
THE REST OF THE ENTRANTS WERE INTRODUCED WITHOUT INCIDENT.
OOH!
And that's all the contestants!
OHHH!
As for the preliminaries, this year it's a simple vote!
The top eight vote-getters will advance to the main round! Vote for whichever familiar you like!
SO THIS IS WHY WE WERE ON STAGE?!
YEP. HERE, YOUR FORM.
OH? I CAN VOTE, TOO?!
WELL, OBVIOUSLY, I'M VOTING FOR MYSE--!
WAIT, PATTY!!

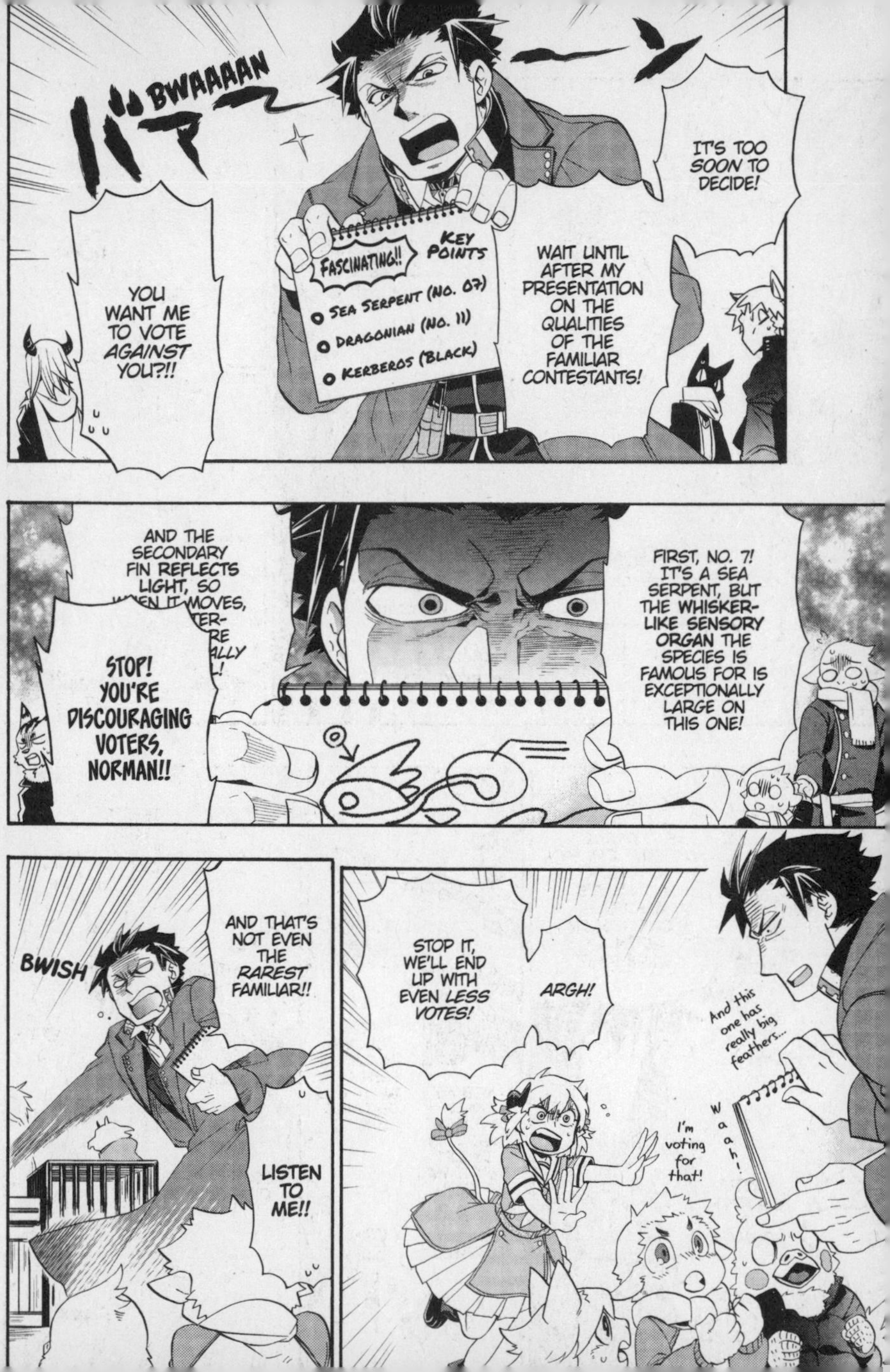
IT'S TOO SOON TO DECIDE!
WAIT UNTIL AFTER MY PRESENTATION ON THE QUALITIES OF THE FAMILIAR CONTESTANTS!
KEY POINTS
FASCINATING!!
Sea Serpent (No. 07)
Dragonian (No. 11)
Kerberos (Black)
BWAAAAN
YOU WANT ME TO VOTE AGAINST YOU?!!
FIRST, NO. 7! IT'S A SEA SERPENT, BUT THE WHISKER-LIKE SENSORY ORGAN THE SPECIES IS FAMOUS FOR IS EXCEPTIONALLY LARGE ON THIS ONE!
AND THE SECONDARY FIN REFLECTS LIGHT, SO
STOP! YOU'RE DISCOURAGING VOTERS, NORMAN!!
And this one has really big feathers...
Waah!
I'm voting for that!
ARGH!
STOP IT, WE'LL END UP WITH EVEN LESS VOTES!
AND THAT'S NOT EVEN THE RAREST FAMILIAR!!
BWISH
LISTEN TO ME!!

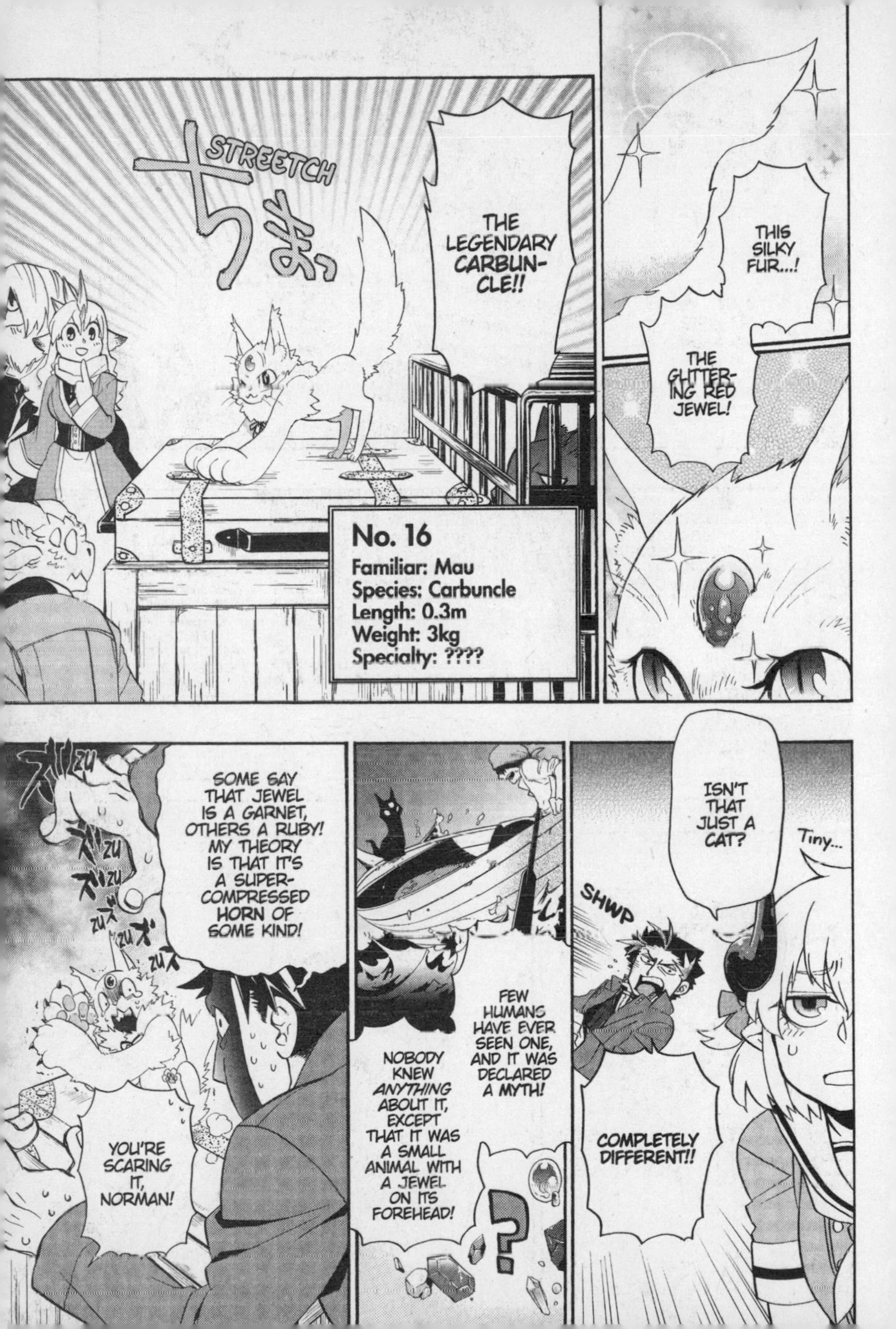
THIS SILKY FUR...!
THE GLITTERING RED JEWEL!
STREETCH
ちまっ
THE LEGENDARY CARBUNCLE!!
No. 16
Familiar: Mau
Species: Carbuncle
Length: 0.3m
Weight: 3kg
Specialty: ????
Tiny...
ISN'T THAT JUST A CAT?
SHWP
COMPLETELY DIFFERENT!!
FEW HUMANS HAVE EVER SEEN ONE, AND IT WAS DECLARED A MYTH!
NOBODY KNEW ANYTHING ABOUT IT, EXCEPT THAT IT WAS A SMALL ANIMAL WITH A JEWEL ON ITS FOREHEAD!
ZU
SOME SAY THAT JEWEL IS A GARNET, OTHERS A RUBY! MY THEORY IS THAT IT'S A SUPER-COMPRESSED HORN OF SOME KIND!
YOU'RE SCARING IT, NORMAN!

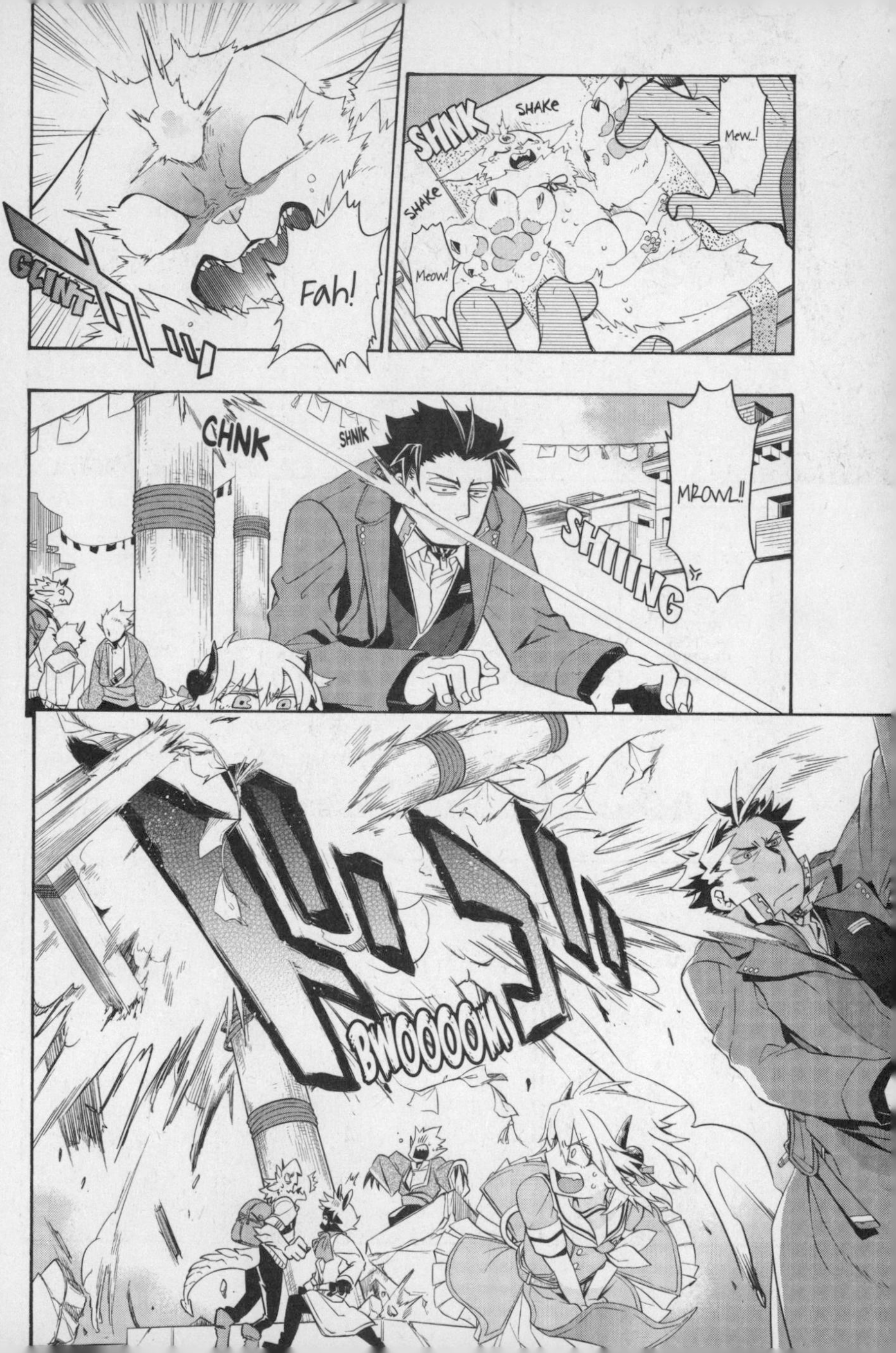
Mew...!
SHAKE
SHNK
SHAKE
Meow!
Fah!
CLINT
MROWL!!
SHIIING
SHNIK
CHNK
BWOOOOM

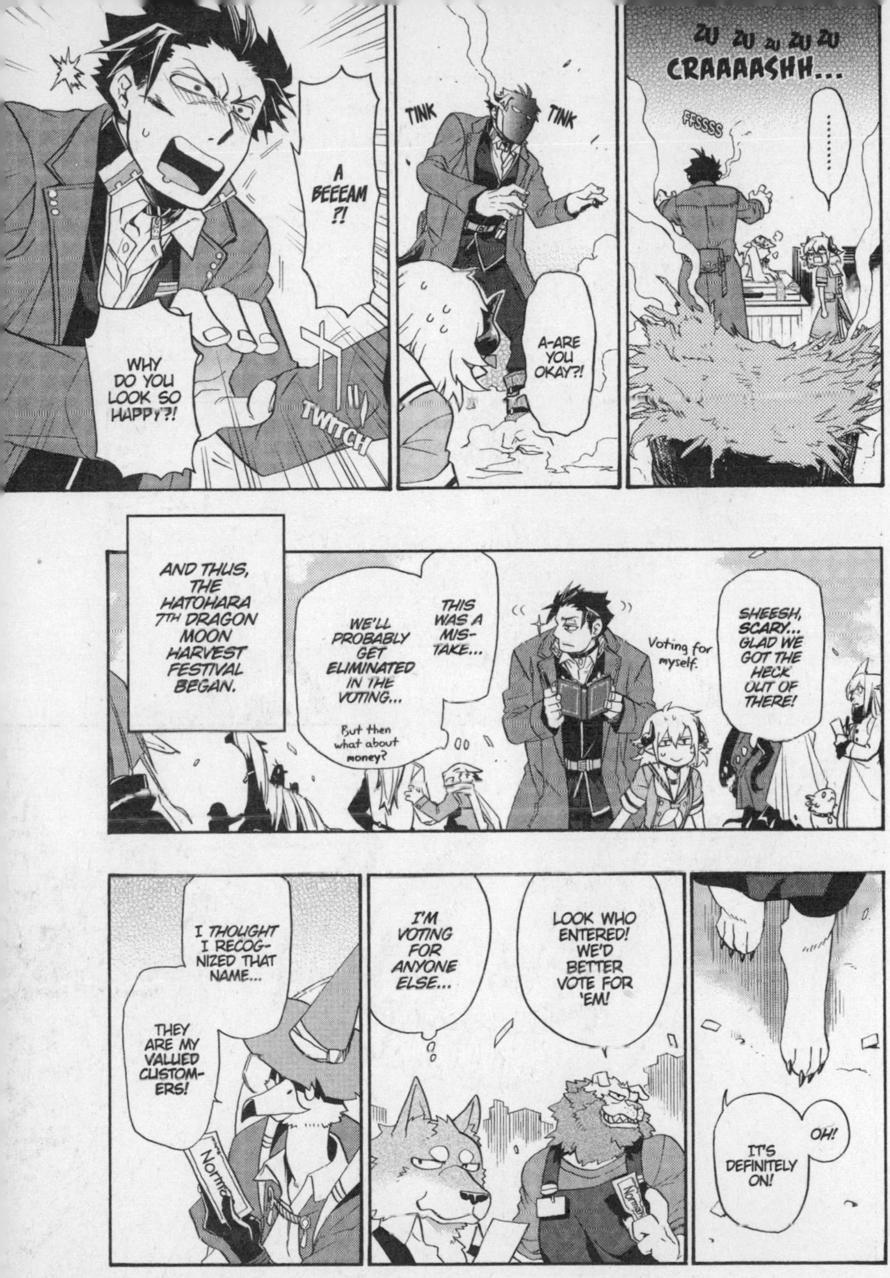
ZU ZU zu ZU ZU
CRAAAASHH...
FFSSSS
......
TINK
TINK
A-ARE YOU OKAY?!
A BEEEAM ?!
WHY DO YOU LOOK SO HAPPY?!
TWITCH
SHEESH, SCARY... GLAD WE GOT THE HECK OUT OF THERE!
Voting for myself.
THIS WAS A MIS-TAKE...
WE'LL PROBABLY GET ELIMINATED IN THE VOTING...
But then what about money?
AND THUS, THE HATOHARA 7TH DRAGON MOON HARVEST FESTIVAL BEGAN.
OH!
IT'S DEFINITELY ON!
LOOK WHO ENTERED! WE'D BETTER VOTE FOR 'EM!
I'M VOTING FOR ANYONE ELSE...
I THOUGHT I RECOG-NIZED THAT NAME...
THEY ARE MY VALUED CUSTOM-ERS!

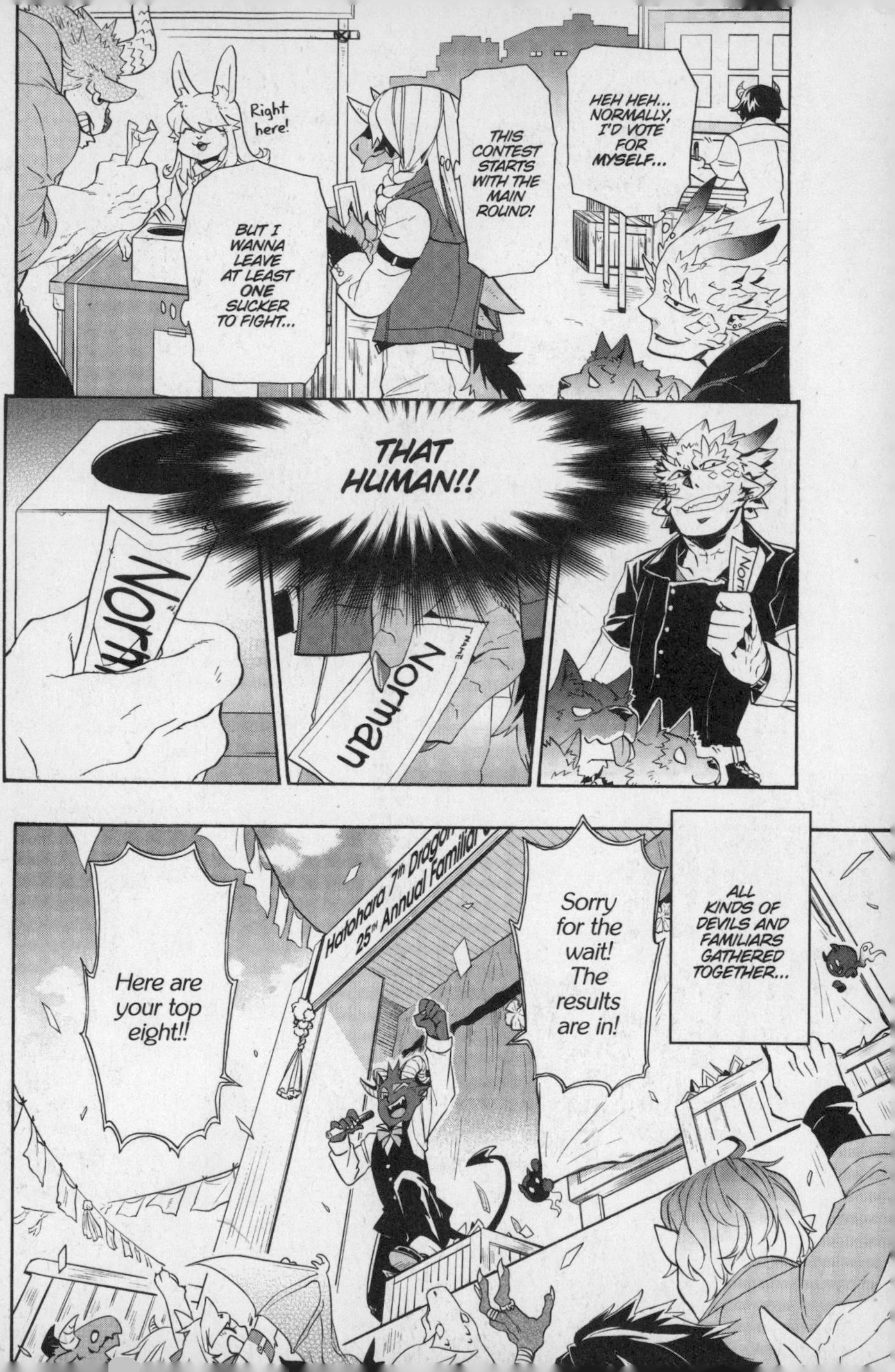
HEH HEH... NORMALLY, I'D VOTE FOR MYSELF...
THIS CONTEST STARTS WITH THE MAIN ROUND!
Right here!
BUT I WANNA LEAVE AT LEAST ONE SUCKER TO FIGHT...
THAT HUMAN!!
Norm
NAME
Norman
Norm
ALL KINDS OF DEVILS AND FAMILIARS GATHERED TOGETHER...
Sorry for the wait! The results are in!
Hatohara 7th Dragon
25th Annual Familiar
Here are your top eight!!

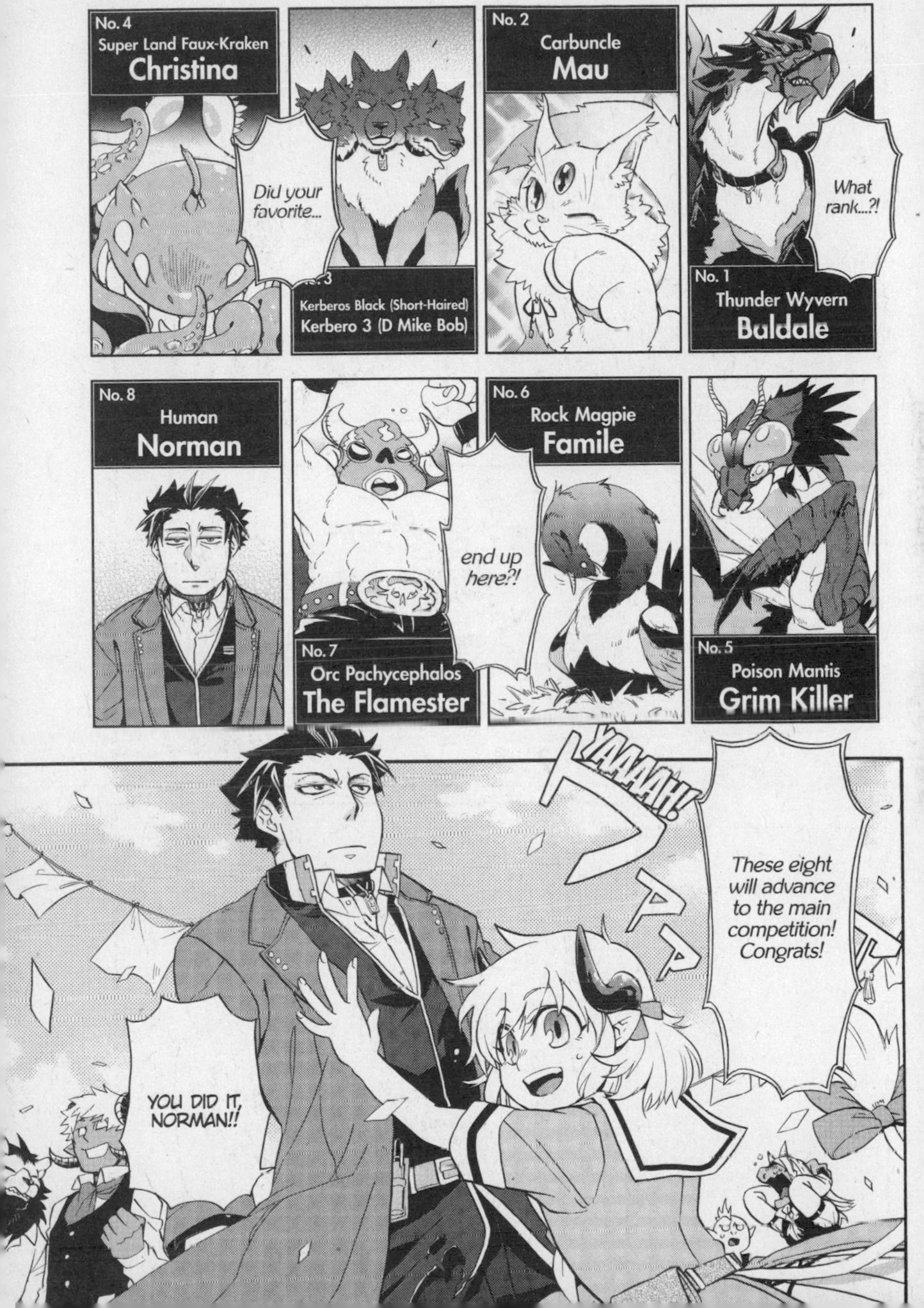
What rank...?!
No. 1
Thunder Wyvern
Baldale
No. 2
Carbuncle
Mau
Did your favorite...
No. 3
Kerberos Black (Short-Haired)
Kerbero 3 (D Mike Bob)
No. 4
Super Land Faux-Kraken
Christina
No. 5
Poison Mantis
Grim Killer
No. 6
Rock Magpie
Famile
end up here?!
No. 7
Orc Pachycephalos
The Flamester
No. 8
Human
Norman
YAAAAAH!
These eight will advance to the main competition! Congrats!
YOU DID IT, NORMAN!!

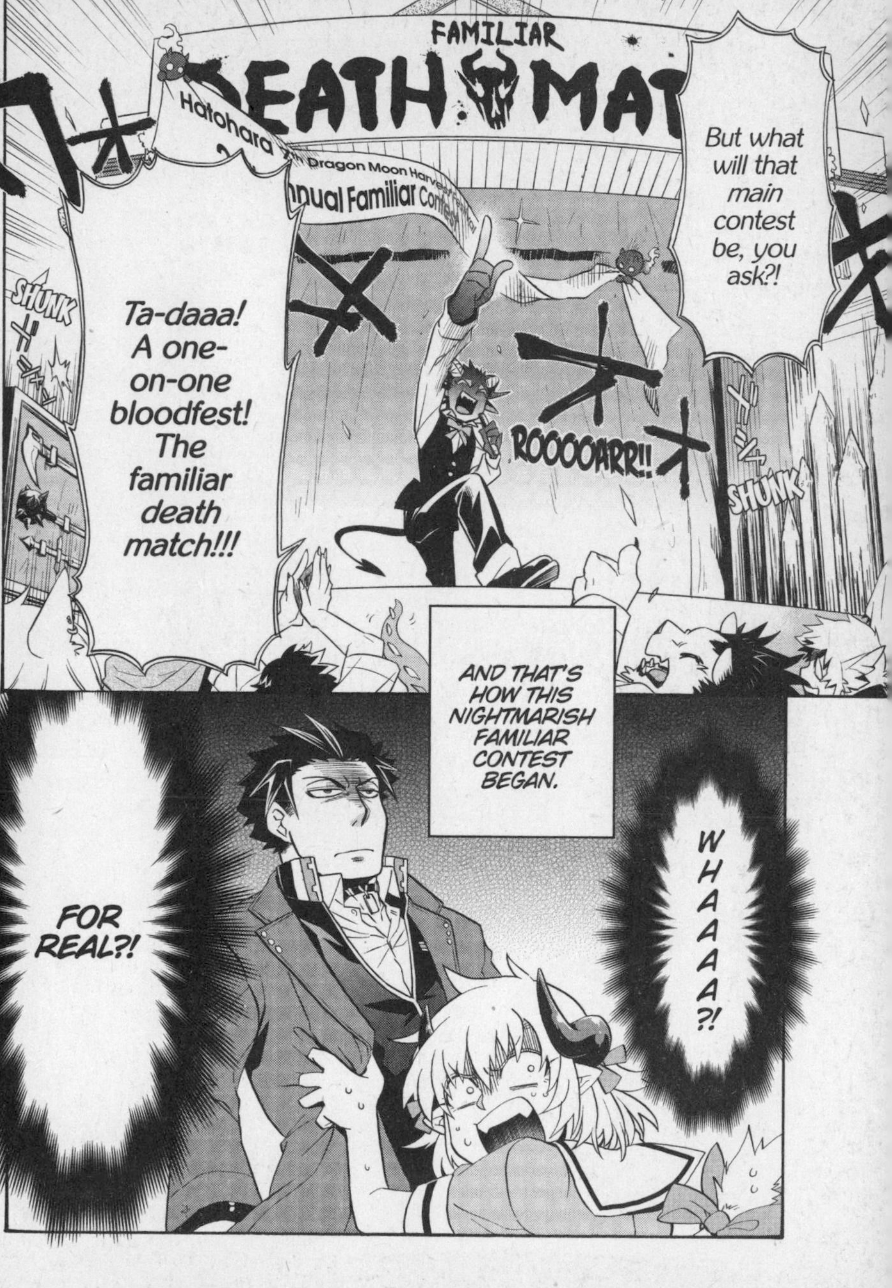

FAMILIAR
Hatohara
Dragon Moon
But what will that main contest be, you ask?!
SHUNK
ROOOOARR!!
Ta-daaa! A one-on-one bloodfest! The familiar death match!!!
SHUNK
AND THAT'S HOW THIS NIGHTMARISH FAMILIAR CONTEST BEGAN.
WHAAAAA?!
FOR REAL?!

Sorry For My Familiar

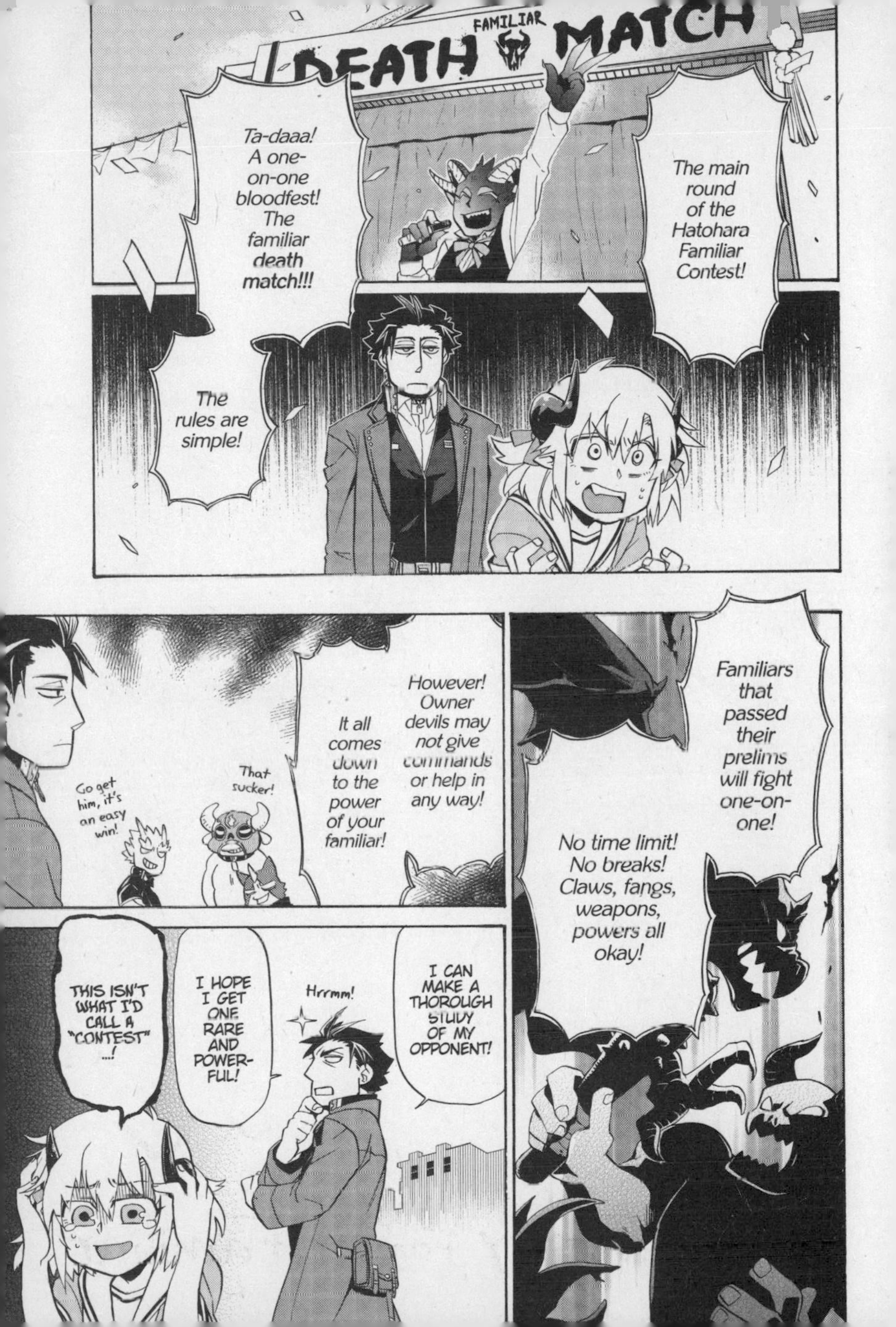
FAMILIAR DEATH MATCH
The main round of the Hatohara Familiar Contest!
Ta-daaa! A one-on-one bloodfest! The familiar death match!!!
The rules are simple!
Familiars that passed their prelims will fight one-on-one!
No time limit! No breaks! Claws, fangs, weapons, powers all okay!
However! Owner devils may not give commands or help in any way!
It all comes down to the power of your familiar!
That sucker!
Go get him, it's an easy win!
I CAN MAKE A THOROUGH STUDY OF MY OPPONENT!
Hrrmm!
I HOPE I GET ONE RARE AND POWERFUL!
THIS ISN'T WHAT I'D CALL A "CONTEST" ...!

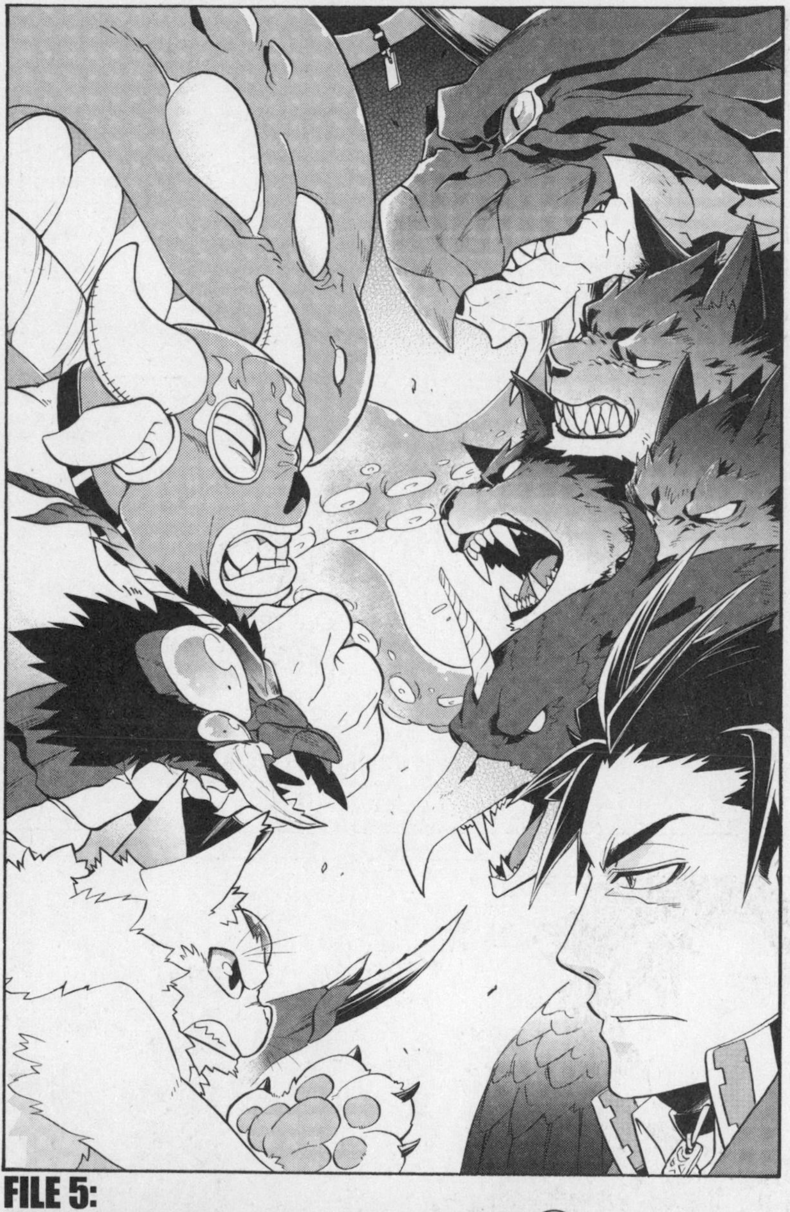

FILE 5:
7th Dragon Moon Harvest Festival ②

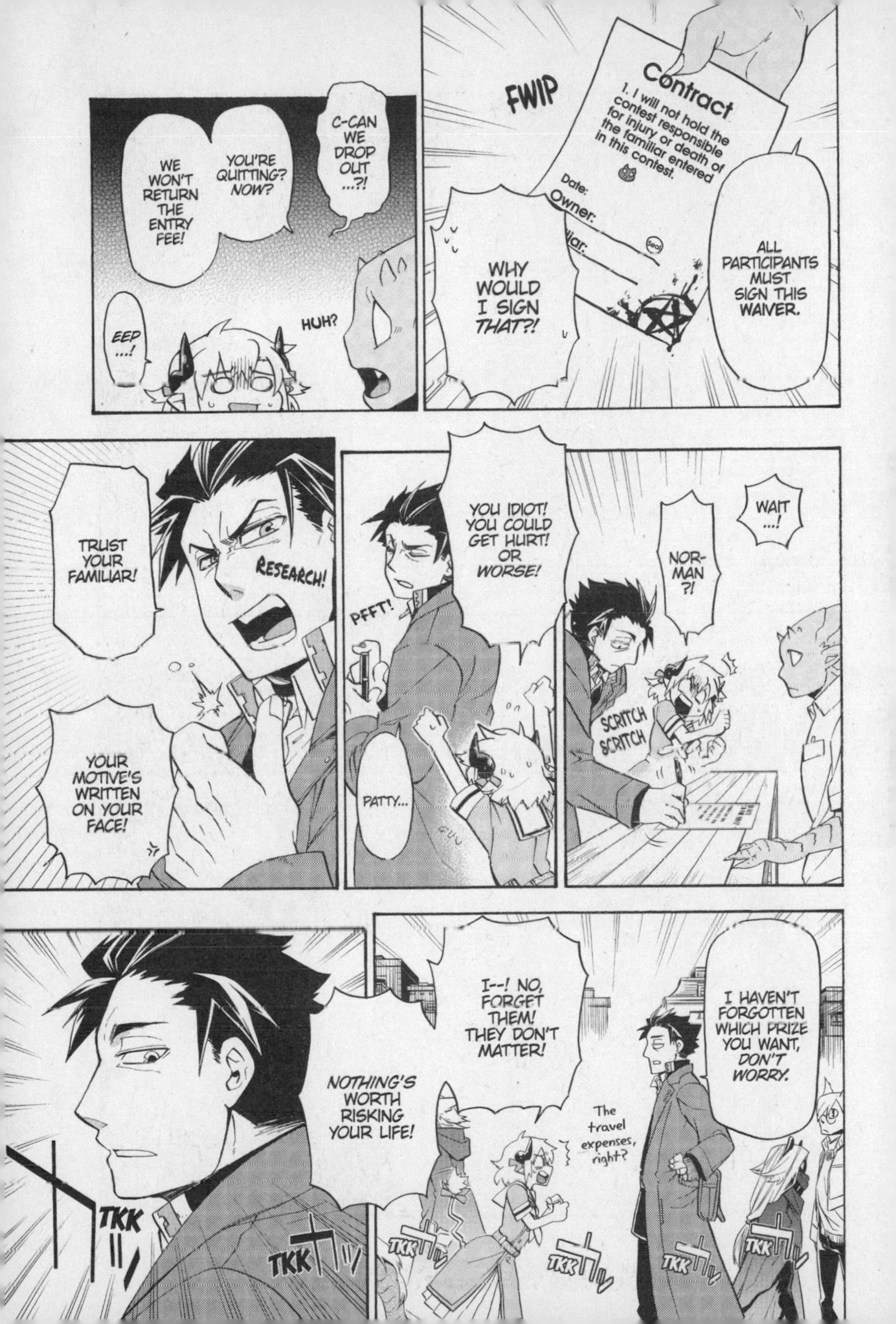
FWIP
Contract
1. I will not hold the contest responsible for injury or death of the familiar entered in this contest.
Date:
Owner:
Seal
ALL PARTICIPANTS MUST SIGN THIS WAIVER.
WHY WOULD I SIGN THAT?!
C-CAN WE DROP OUT ...?!
YOU'RE QUITTING? NOW?
WE WON'T RETURN THE ENTRY FEE!
HUH?
EEP ...!
WAIT ...!
NOR-MAN ?!
SCRITCH SCRITCH
YOU IDIOT! YOU COULD GET HURT! OR WORSE!
PFFT!
PATTY...
TRUST YOUR FAMILIAR!
RESEARCH!
YOUR MOTIVE'S WRITTEN ON YOUR FACE!
I HAVEN'T FORGOTTEN WHICH PRIZE YOU WANT, DON'T WORRY.
The travel expenses, right?
I--! NO, FORGET THEM! THEY DON'T MATTER!
NOTHING'S WORTH RISKING YOUR LIFE!
TKK
TKK
TKK
TKK
TKK
TKK

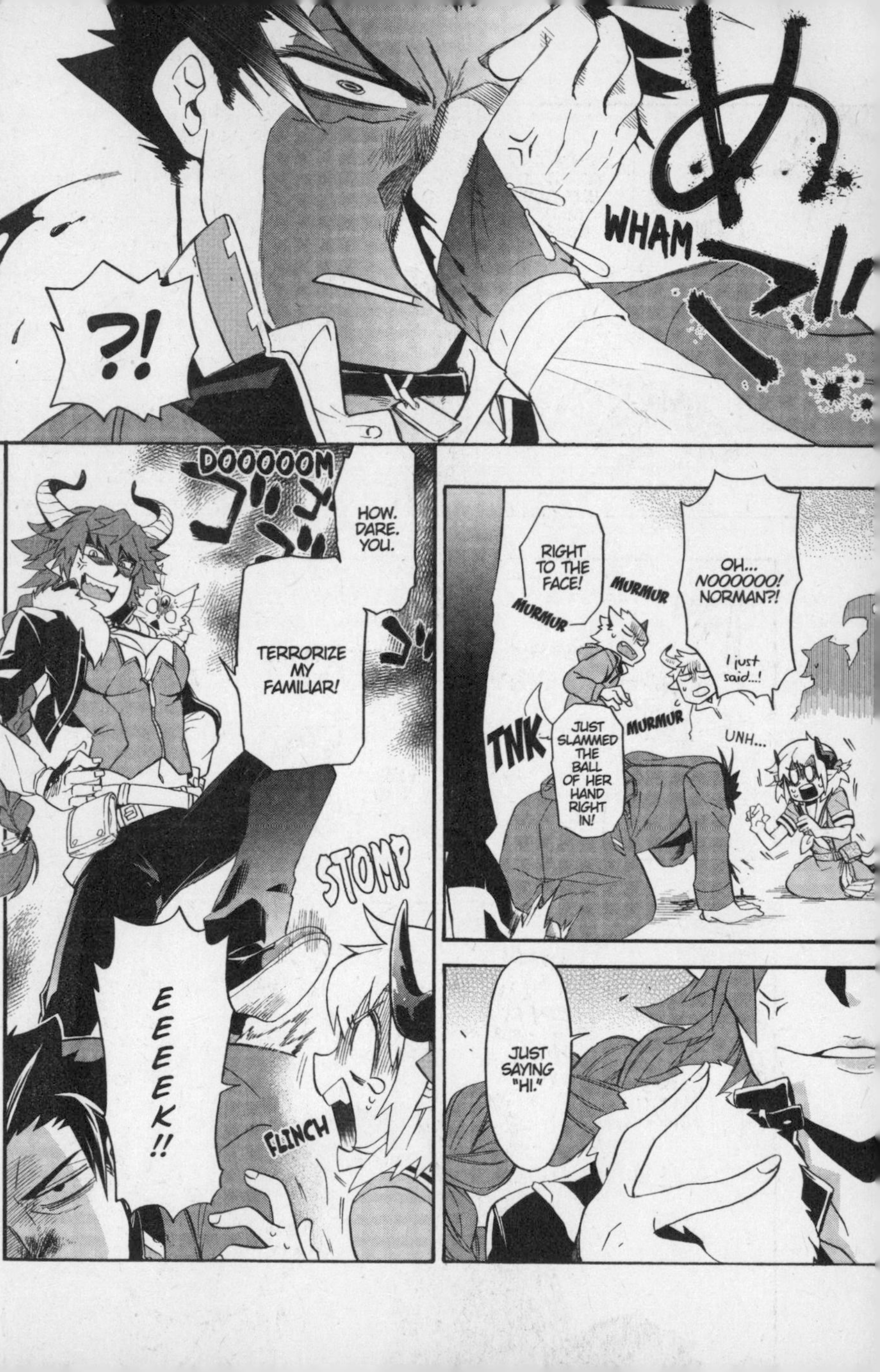
WHAM
?!
OH... NOOOOOO! NORMAN?!
I just said...!
RIGHT TO THE FACE!
MURMUR
MURMUR
UNH...
JUST SLAMMED THE BALL OF HER HAND RIGHT IN!
MURMUR
TNK
JUST SAYING "HI."
DOOOOOM
HOW. DARE. YOU.
TERRORIZE MY FAMILIAR!
STOMP
FLINCH
EEEEEK!!

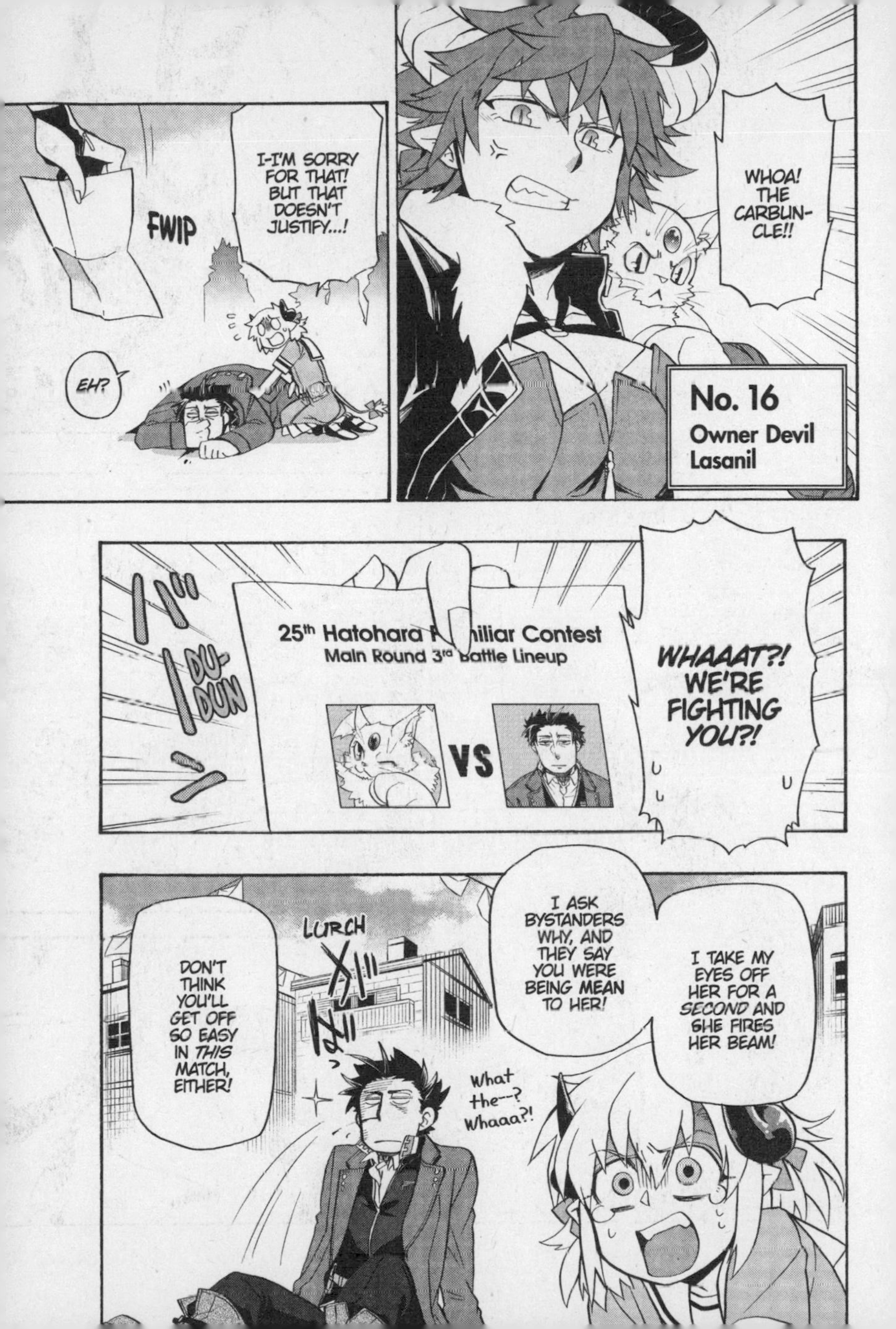
WHOA! THE CARBUNCLE!!
No. 16
Owner Devil
Lasanil
I-I'M SORRY FOR THAT! BUT THAT DOESN'T JUSTIFY...!
FWIP
EH?
WHAAAT?! WE'RE FIGHTING YOU?!
25th Hatohara F miliar Contest
Main Round 3rd Battle Lineup
VS
DU-DUN
I TAKE MY EYES OFF HER FOR A SECOND AND SHE FIRES HER BEAM!
I ASK BYSTANDERS WHY, AND THEY SAY YOU WERE BEING MEAN TO HER!
LURCH
DON'T THINK YOU'LL GET OFF SO EASY IN THIS MATCH, EITHER!
What the--? Whaaa?!

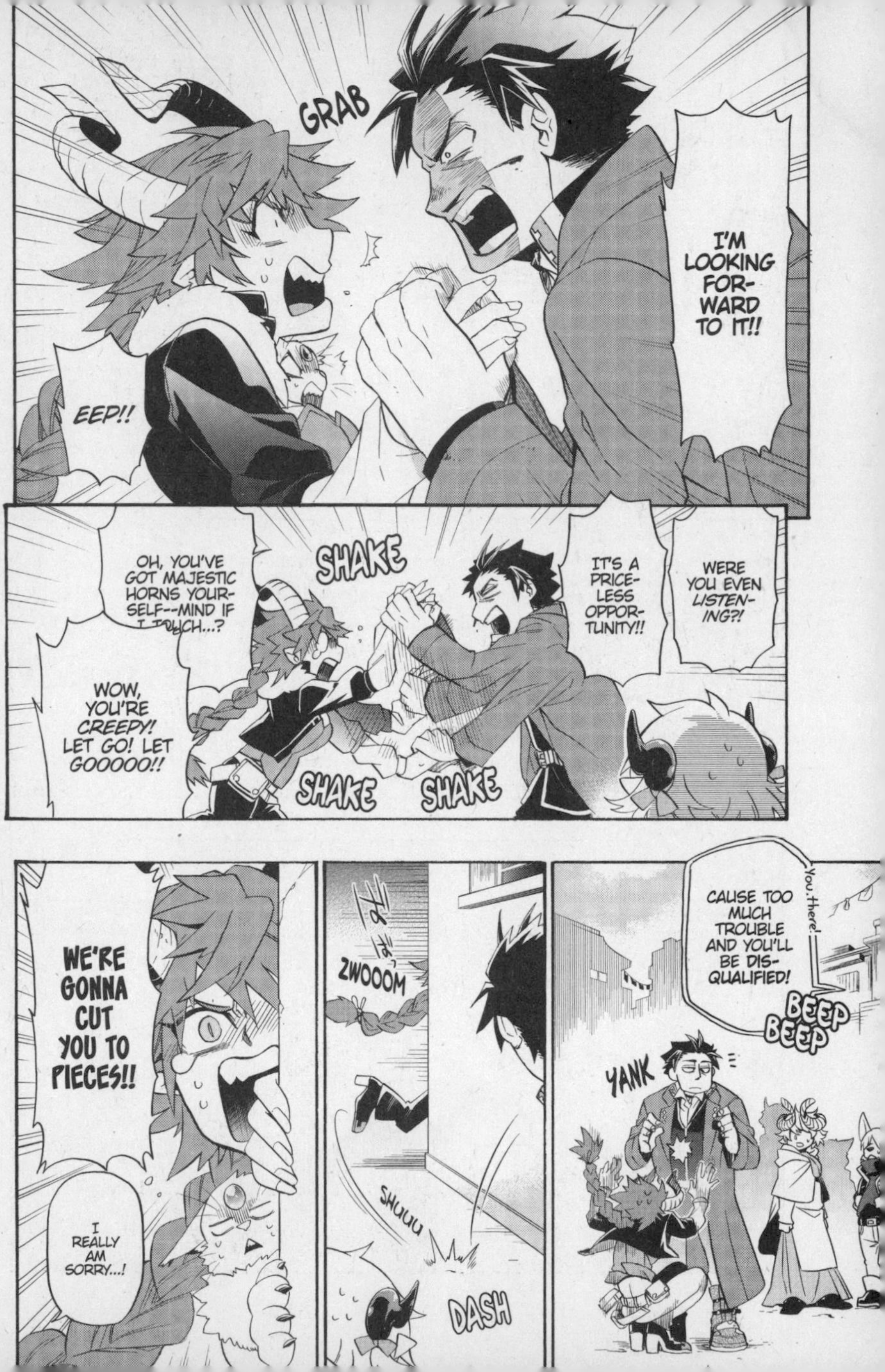
GRAB
I'M LOOKING FOR-WARD TO IT!!
EEP!!
WERE YOU EVEN LISTEN-ING?!
IT'S A PRICE-LESS OPPOR-TUNITY!!
SHAKE
OH, YOU'VE GOT MAJESTIC HORNS YOUR-SELF--MIND IF I TOUCH...?
WOW, YOU'RE CREEPY! LET GO! LET GOOOOO!!
SHAKE
SHAKE
You there!
CAUSE TOO MUCH TROUBLE AND YOU'LL BE DIS-QUALIFIED!
BEEP BEEP
YANK
ZWOOOM
SHUUU
DASH
WE'RE GONNA CUT YOU TO PIECES!!
I REALLY AM SORRY...!

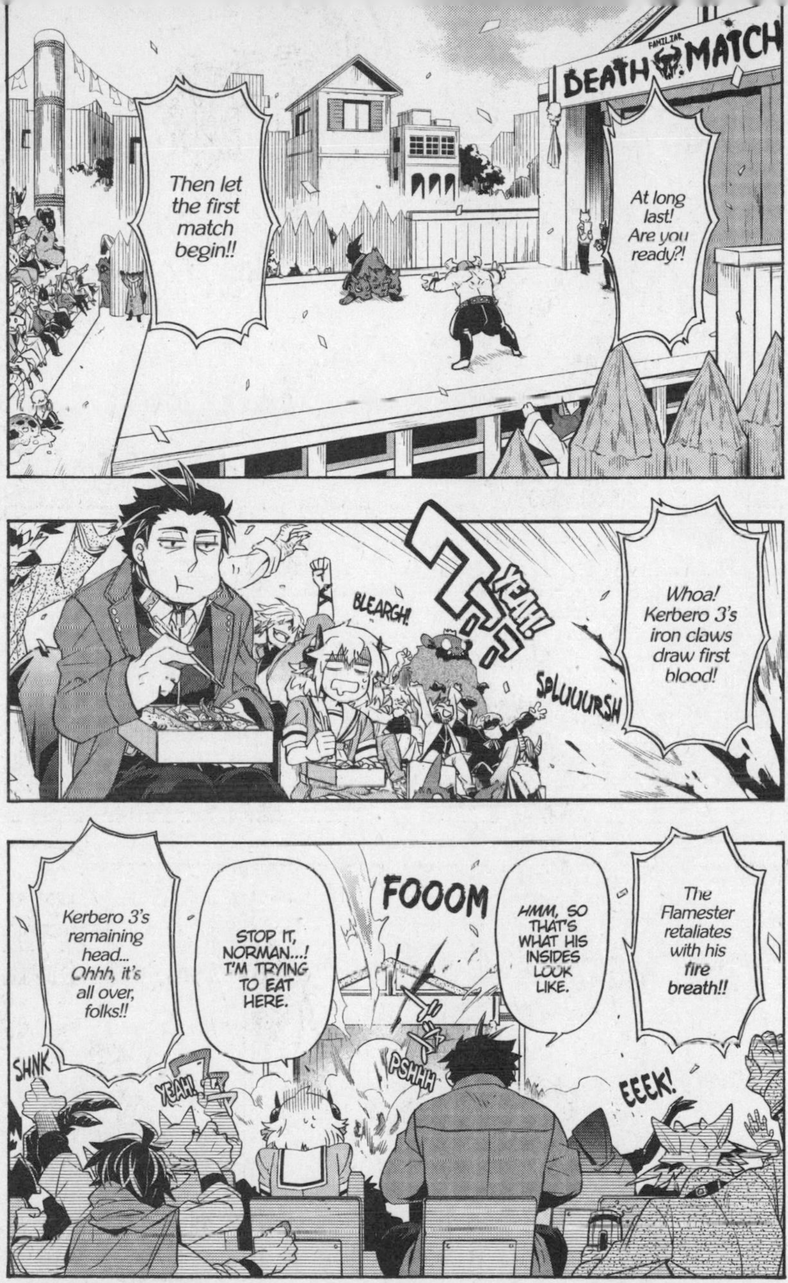
DEATH FAMILIAR MATCH
At long last! Are you ready?!
Then let the first match begin!!
Whoa! Kerbero 3's iron claws draw first blood!
YEAH!
SPLUUURSH
BLEARGH!
The Flamester retaliates with his fire breath!!
HMM, SO THAT'S WHAT HIS INSIDES LOOK LIKE.
FOOOM
STOP IT, NORMAN...! I'M TRYING TO EAT HERE.
Kerbero 3's remaining head... Ohhh, it's all over, folks!!
EEEK!
PSHHH
YEAH!
SHNK

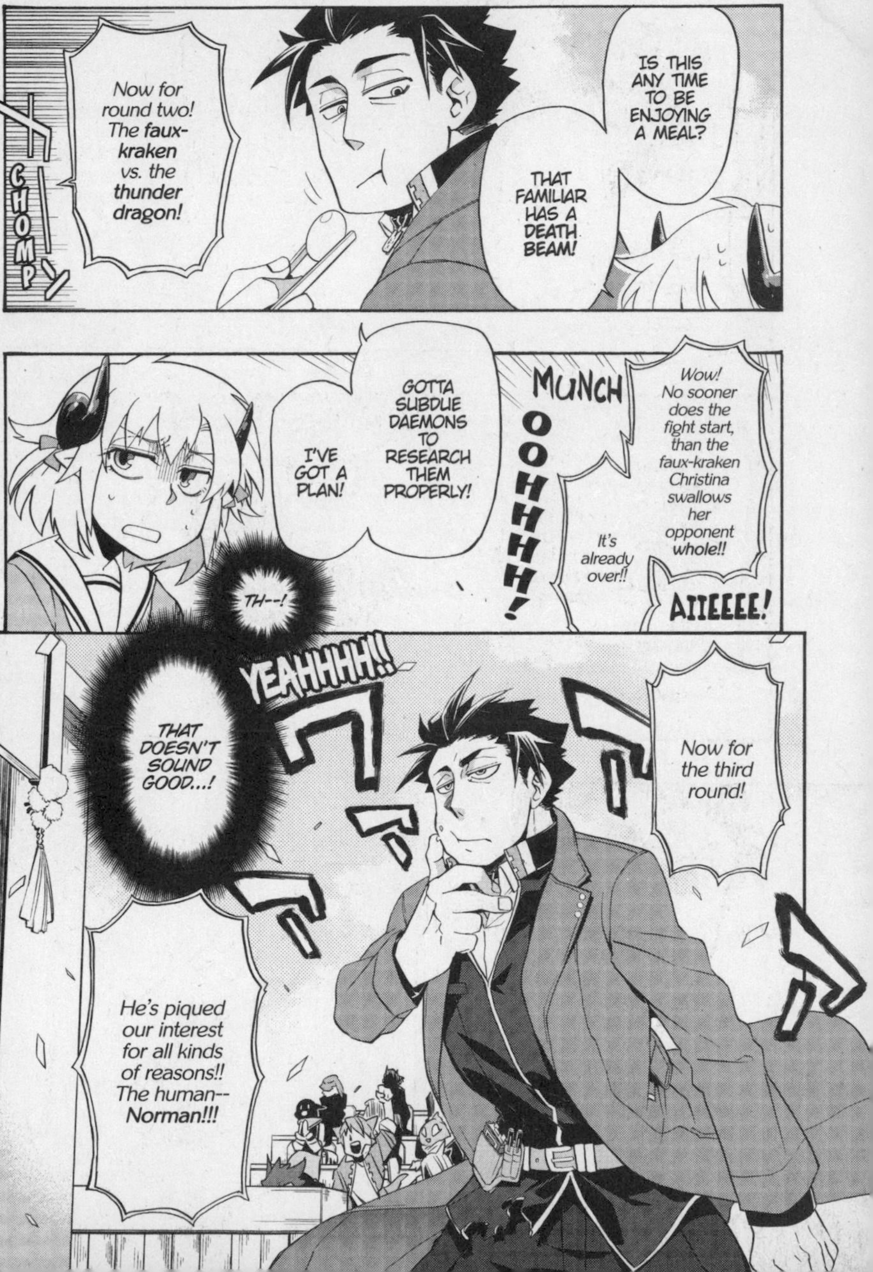
IS THIS ANY TIME TO BE ENJOYING A MEAL?
THAT FAMILIAR HAS A DEATH BEAM!
Now for round two! The faux-kraken vs. the thunder dragon!
CHOMP
Wow! No sooner does the fight start, than the faux-kraken Christina swallows her opponent whole!!
It's already over!!
AIIEEEE!
MUNCH
OOOHHHHH!
GOTTA SUBDUE DAEMONS TO RESEARCH THEM PROPERLY!
I'VE GOT A PLAN!
TH--!
Now for the third round!
YEAHHHH!!
THAT DOESN'T SOUND GOOD...!
He's piqued our interest for all kinds of reasons!! The human-- Norman!!!

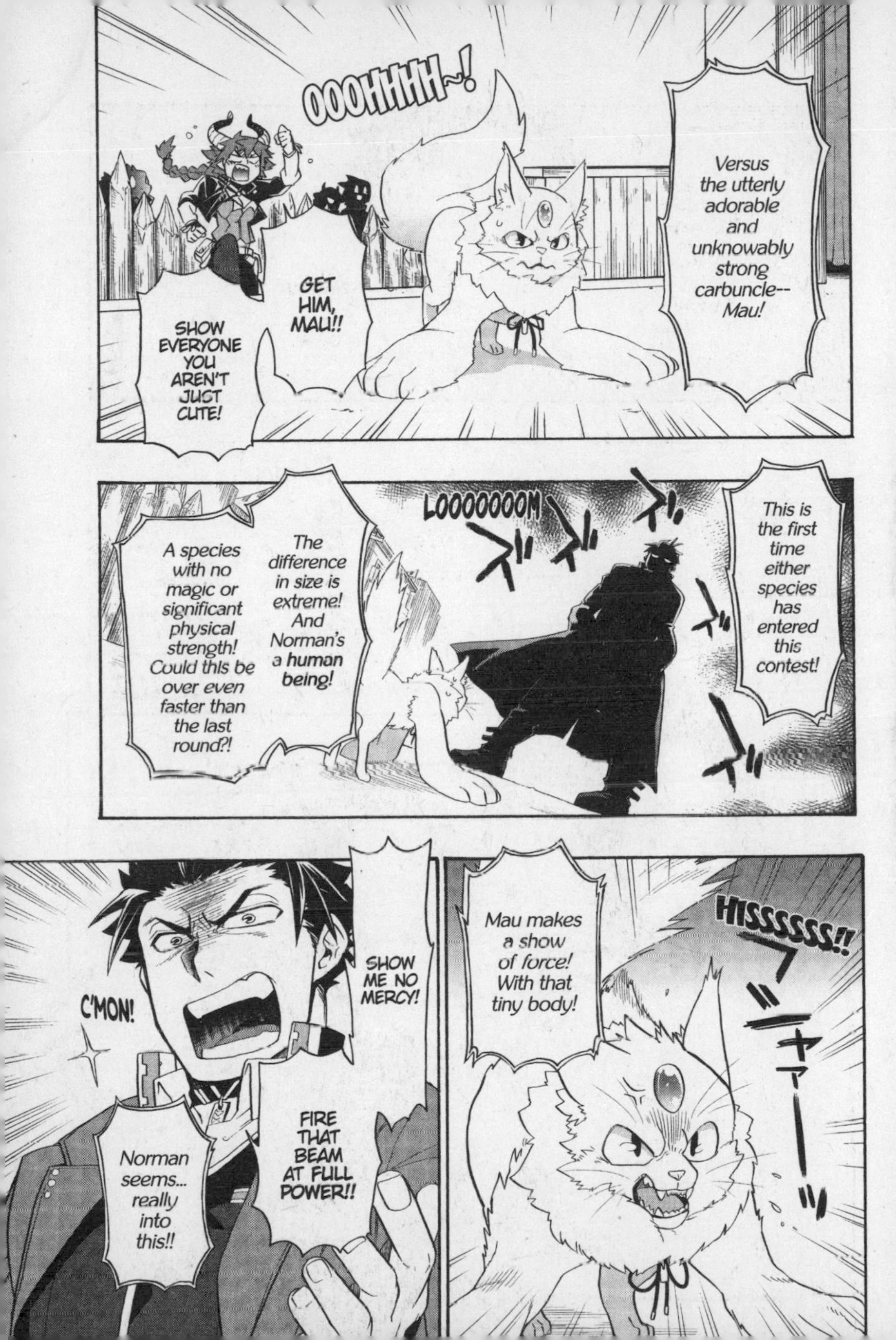
Versus the utterly adorable and unknowably strong carbuncle-- Mau!
OOOHHHH~!
GET HIM, MAU!!
SHOW EVERYONE YOU AREN'T JUST CUTE!
This is the first time either species has entered this contest!
LOOOOOOOM
The difference in size is extreme! And Norman's a human being!
A species with no magic or significant physical strength! Could this be over even faster than the last round?!
HISSSSSSS?!
Mau makes a show of force! With that tiny body!
SHOW ME NO MERCY!
C'MON!
FIRE THAT BEAM AT FULL POWER!!
Norman seems... really into this!!

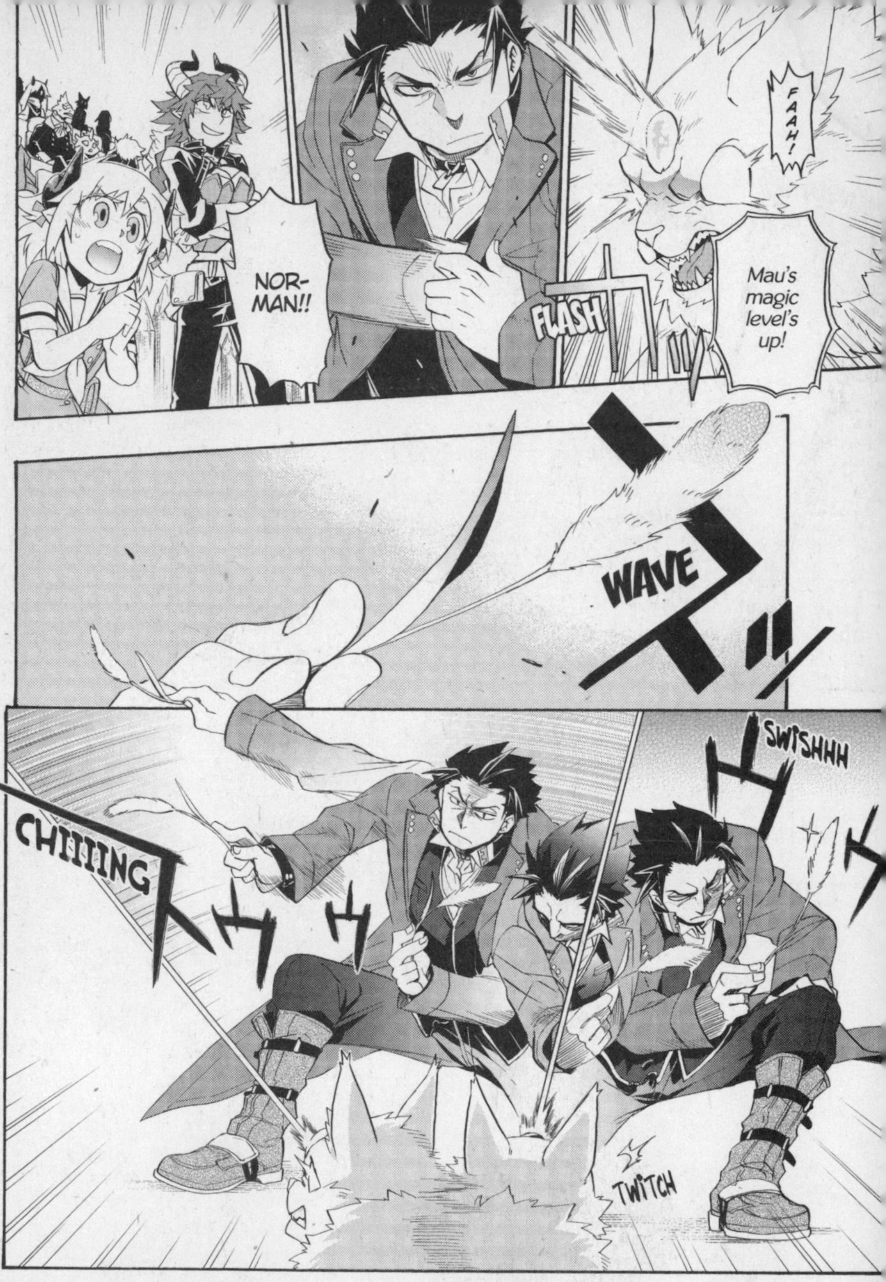
FAAH!
Mau's magic level's up!
FLASH
NOR-MAN!!
WAVE
SWISHHH
CHIIING
TWITCH

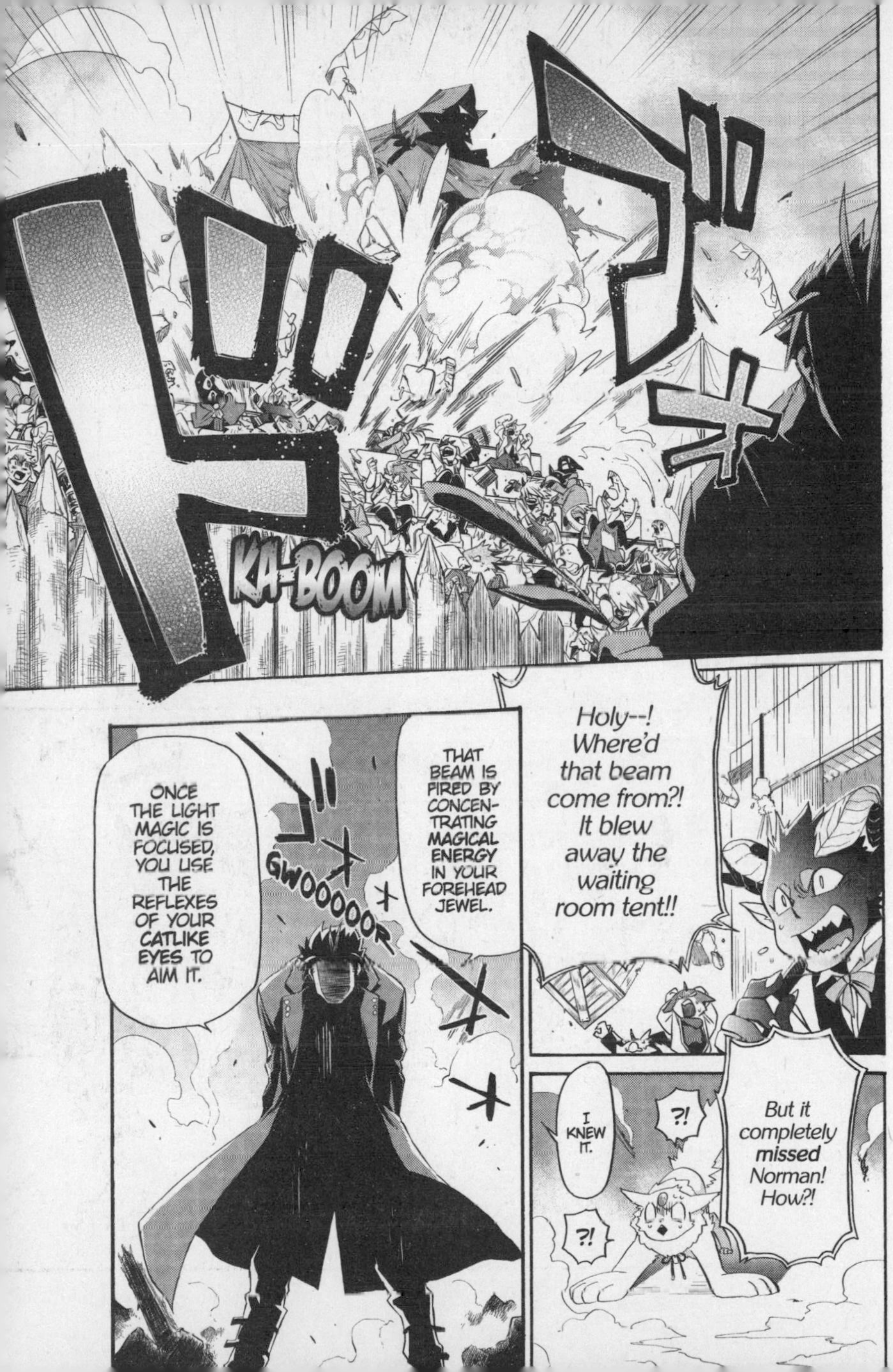
KA-BOOM
Holy--! Where'd that beam come from?! It blew away the waiting room tent!!
But it completely missed Norman! How?!
?!
I KNEW IT.
?!
THAT BEAM IS FIRED BY CONCEN-TRATING MAGICAL ENERGY IN YOUR FOREHEAD JEWEL.
ONCE THE LIGHT MAGIC IS FOCUSED, YOU USE THE REFLEXES OF YOUR CATLIKE EYES TO AIM IT.
GWOOOOOOR

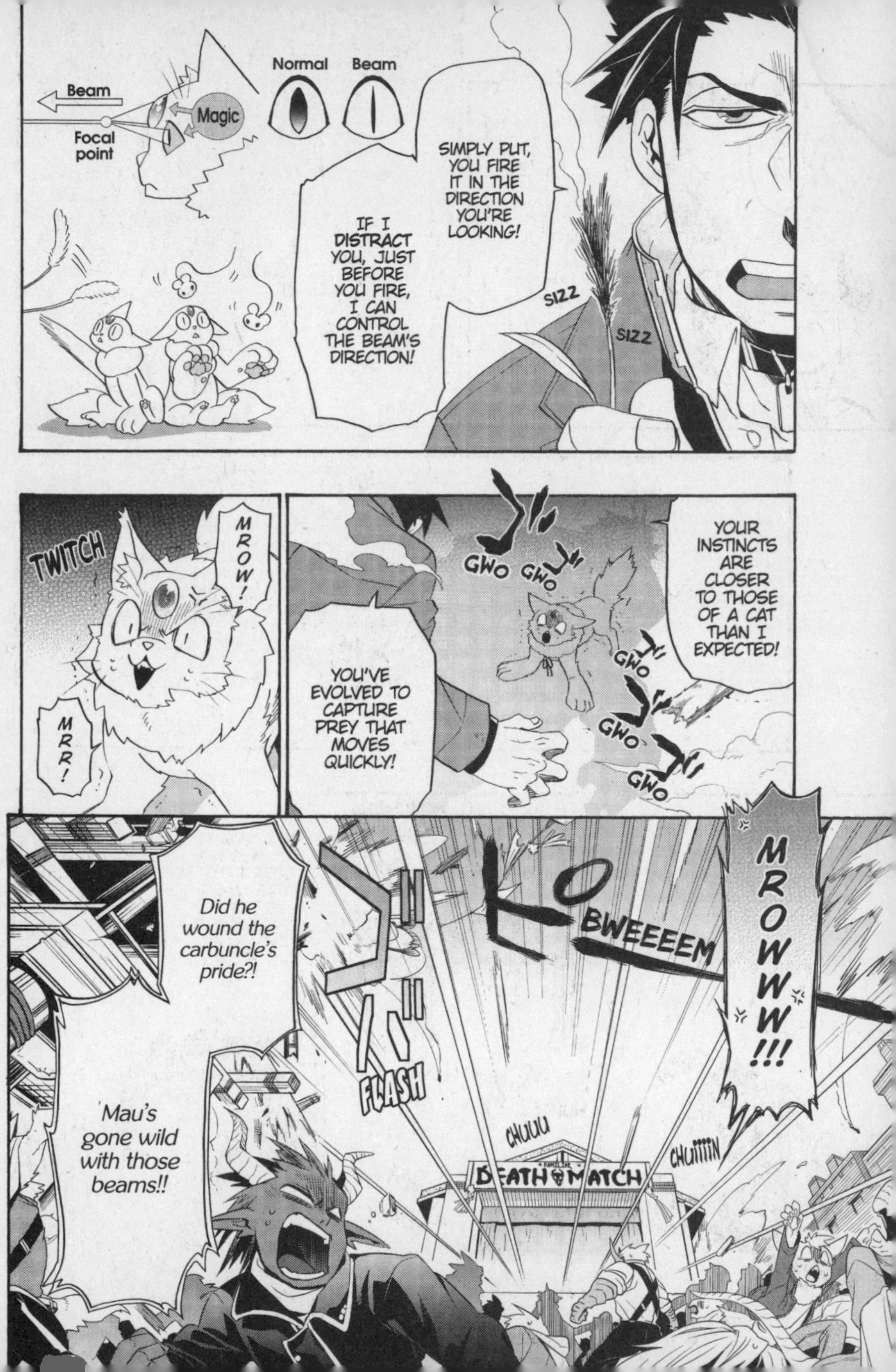
SIMPLY PUT, YOU FIRE IT IN THE DIRECTION YOU'RE LOOKING!
Normal
Beam
Beam
Magic
Focal point
SIZZ
SIZZ
IF I DISTRACT YOU, JUST BEFORE YOU FIRE, I CAN CONTROL THE BEAM'S DIRECTION!
YOUR INSTINCTS ARE CLOSER TO THOSE OF A CAT THAN I EXPECTED!
GWO GWO
GWO
GWO
GWO
YOU'VE EVOLVED TO CAPTURE PREY THAT MOVES QUICKLY!
MROW!
TWITCH
MRR!
MROWWW!!!
BWEEEEM
FLASH
Did he wound the carbuncle's pride?!
Mau's gone wild with those beams!!
CHUUU
CHUIIIIN
DEATH MATCH

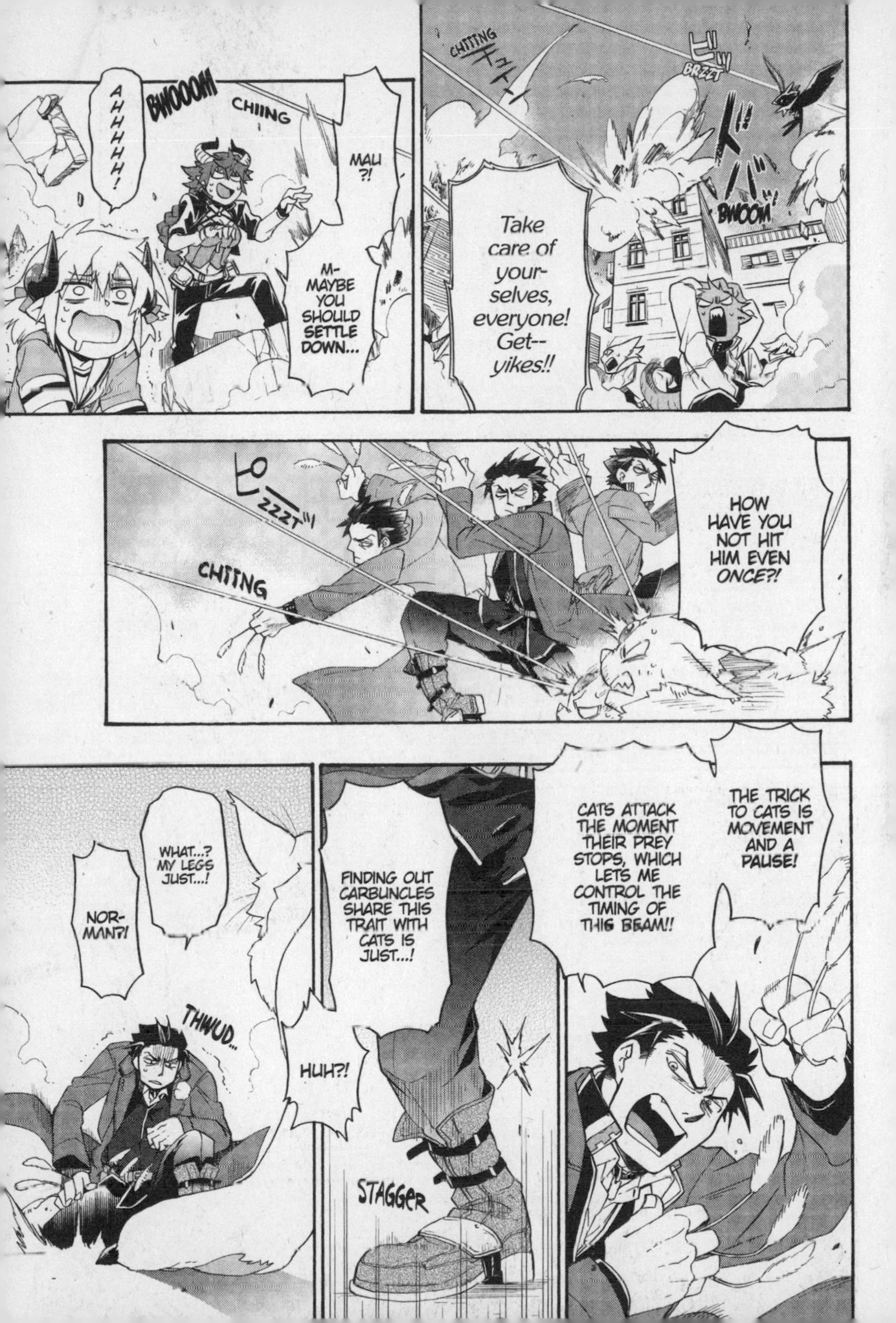
CHITING
BRZZT
BWOOM
Take care of your-selves, everyone! Get-- yikes!!
BWOOOM!
CHIING
AHHHHHH!
MAU ?!
M-MAYBE YOU SHOULD SETTLE DOWN...
HOW HAVE YOU NOT HIT HIM EVEN ONCE?!
ZZZZT
CHIING
THE TRICK TO CATS IS MOVEMENT AND A PAUSE!
CATS ATTACK THE MOMENT THEIR PREY STOPS, WHICH LETS ME CONTROL THE TIMING OF THIS BEAM!!
FINDING OUT CARBUNCLES SHARE THIS TRAIT WITH CATS IS JUST...!
HUH?!
STAGGER
WHAT...? MY LEGS JUST...!
NOR-MAN?!
THWUD...

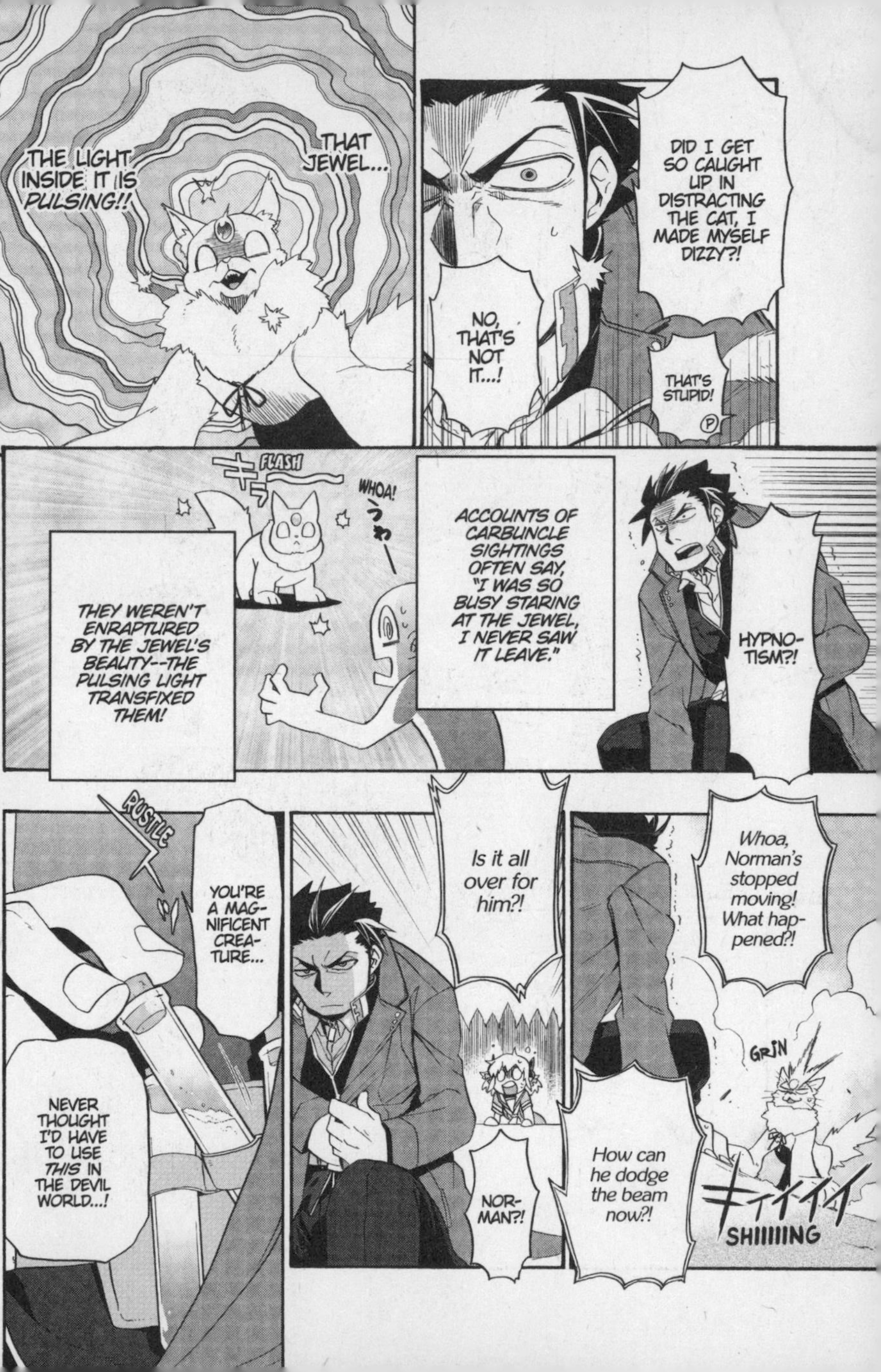

DID I GET SO CAUGHT UP IN DISTRACTING THE CAT, I MADE MYSELF DIZZY?!
NO, THAT'S NOT IT...!
THAT'S STUPID!
P
THAT JEWEL...
THE LIGHT INSIDE IT IS *PULSING!!*
HYPNOTISM?!
ACCOUNTS OF CARBUNCLE SIGHTINGS OFTEN SAY, "I WAS SO BUSY STARING AT THE JEWEL, I NEVER SAW IT LEAVE."
FLASH
WHOA!
THEY WEREN'T ENRAPTURED BY THE JEWEL'S BEAUTY--THE PULSING LIGHT TRANSFIXED THEM!
Whoa, Norman's stopped moving! What happened?!
GRIN
SHIIIIING
How can he dodge the beam now?!
Is it all over for him?!
NORMAN?!
RUSTLE
YOU'RE A MAGNIFICENT CREATURE...
NEVER THOUGHT I'D HAVE TO USE *THIS* IN THE DEVIL WORLD...!

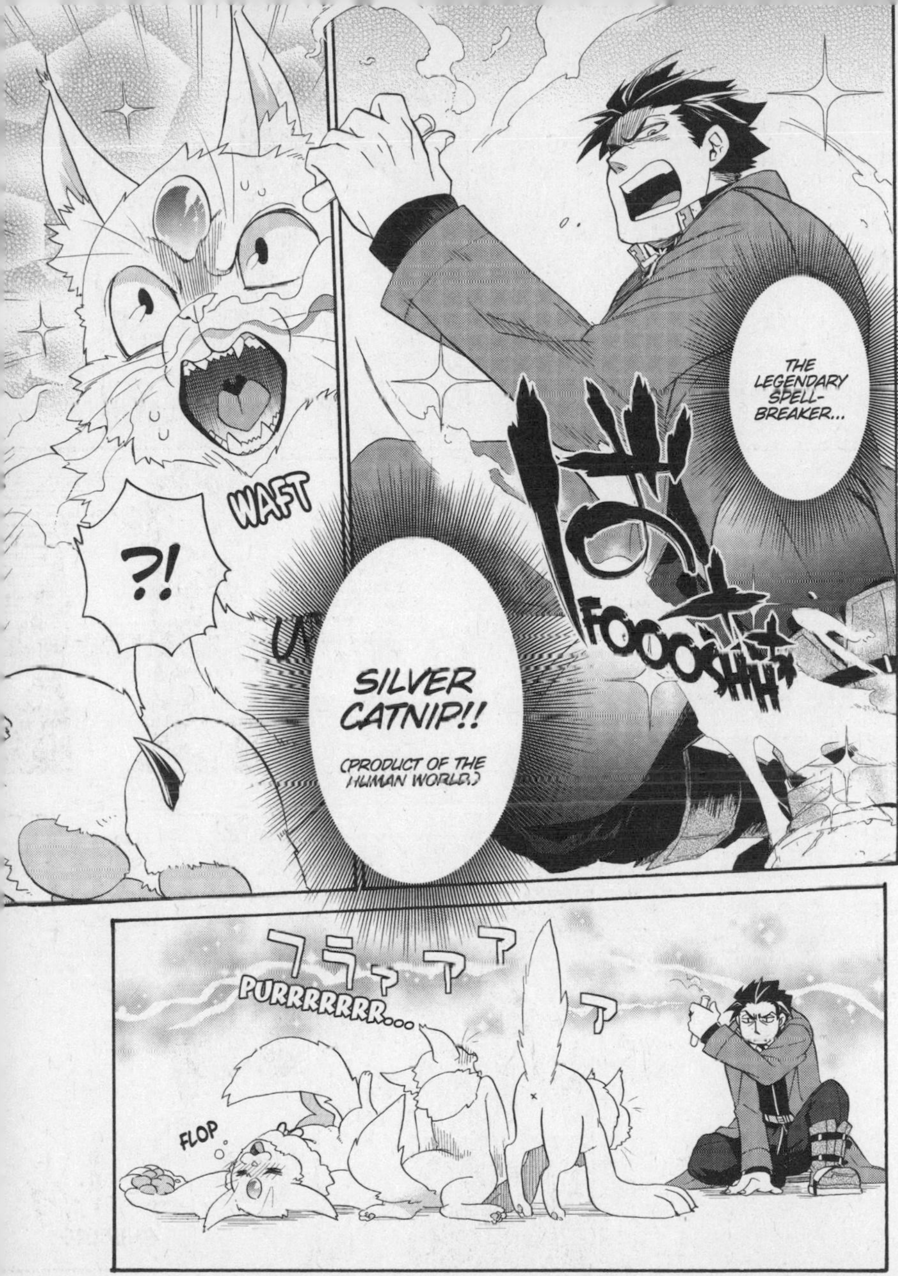
THE LEGENDARY SPELL-BREAKER...
FOOOOSHH
SILVER CATNIP!!
(PRODUCT OF THE HUMAN WORLD.)
WAFT
?!
PURRRRRRRR...
FLOP

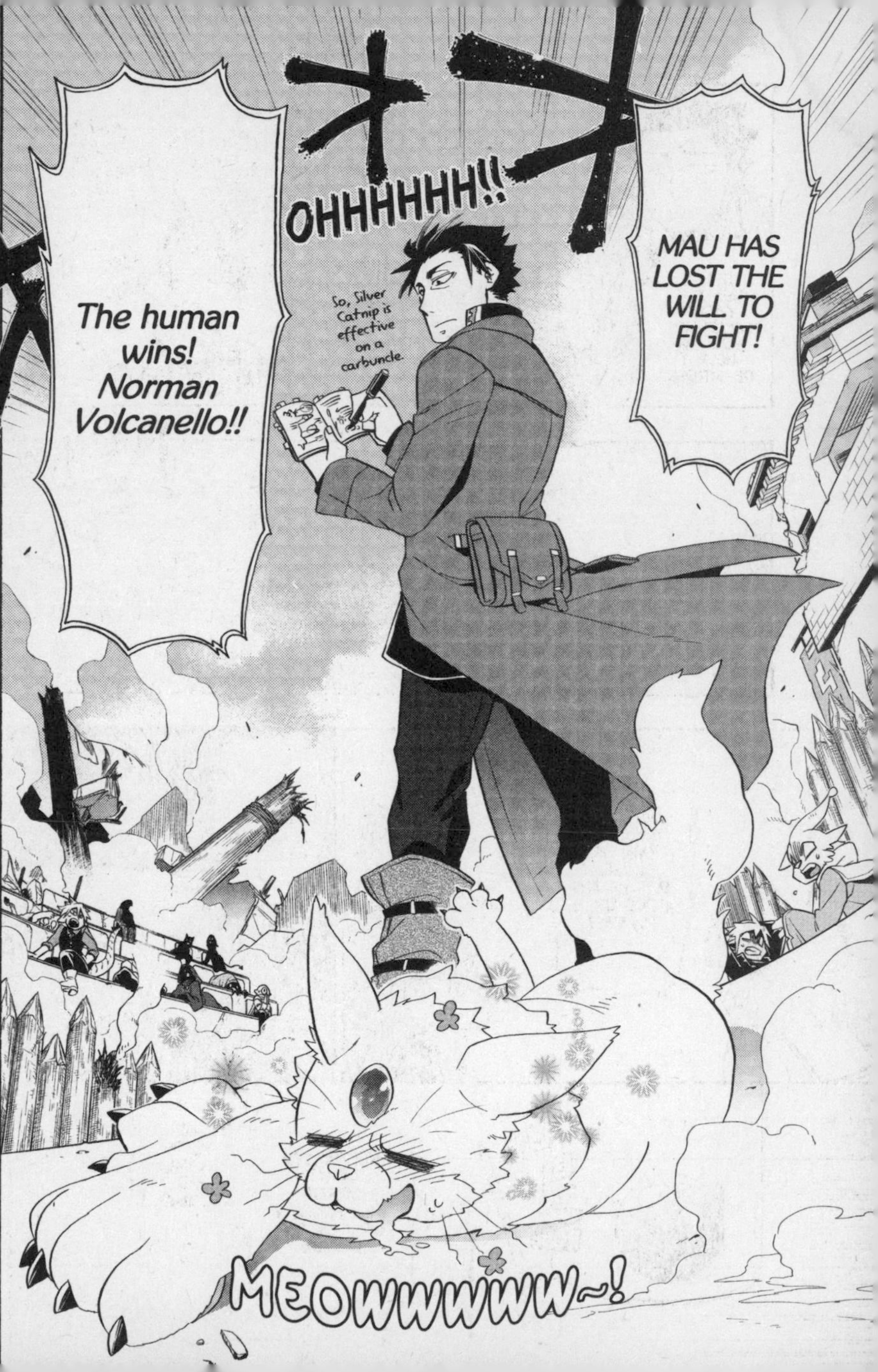
MAU HAS LOST THE WILL TO FIGHT!
OHHHHHH!!
So, Silver Catnip is effective on a carbuncle.
The human wins! Norman Volcanello!!
MEOWWWWWW~!

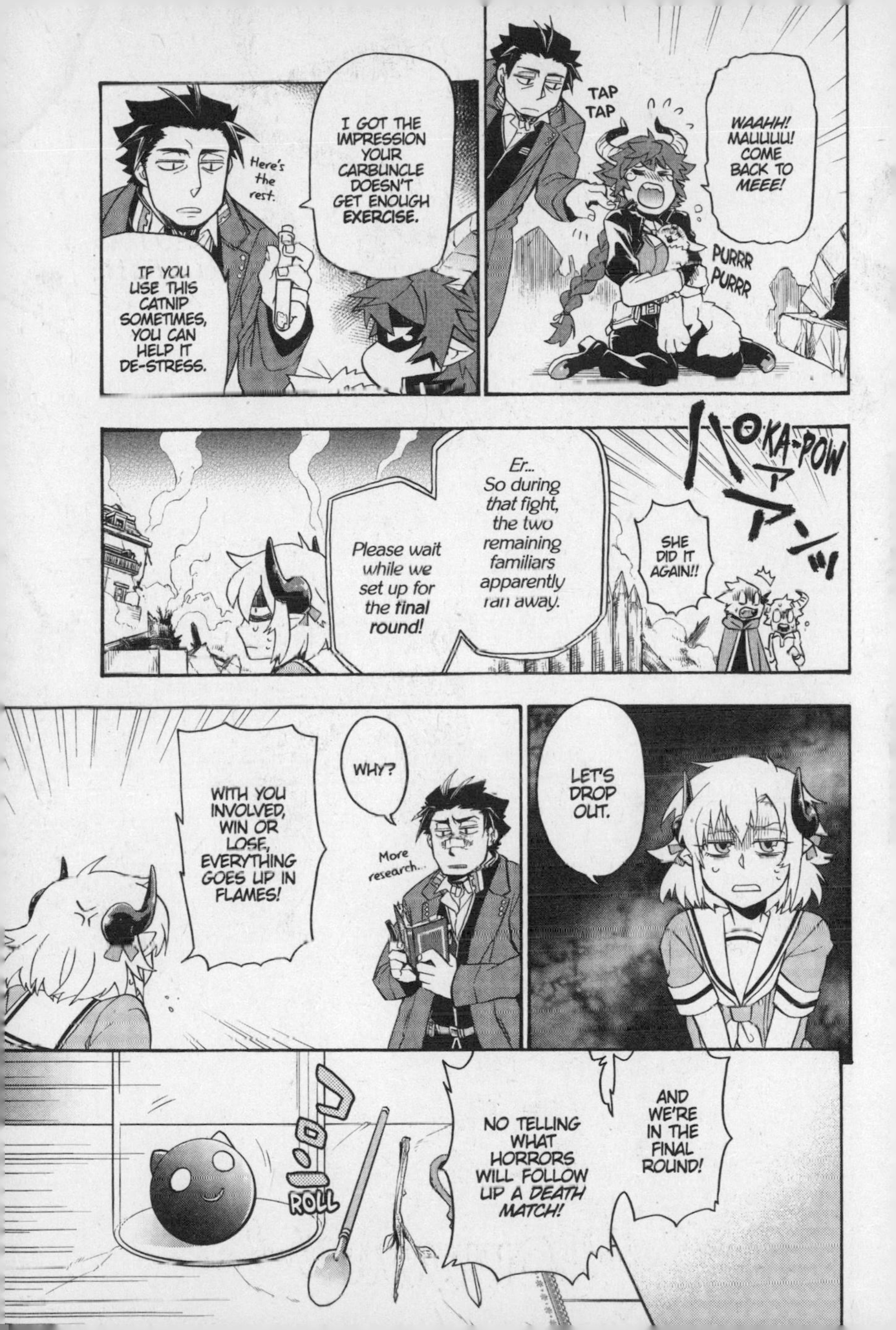

TAP TAP
WAAHH! MAUUUU! COME BACK TO MEEE!
PURRR PURRR
I GOT THE IMPRESSION YOUR CARBUNCLE DOESN'T GET ENOUGH EXERCISE.
Here's the rest.
IF YOU USE THIS CATNIP SOMETIMES, YOU CAN HELP IT DE-STRESS.
KA-POW
SHE DID IT AGAIN!!
Er... So during that fight, the two remaining familiars apparently ran away.
Please wait while we set up for the final round!
LET'S DROP OUT.
WHY?
More research...
WITH YOU INVOLVED, WIN OR LOSE, EVERYTHING GOES UP IN FLAMES!
AND WE'RE IN THE FINAL ROUND!
NO TELLING WHAT HORRORS WILL FOLLOW UP A DEATH MATCH!
ROLL

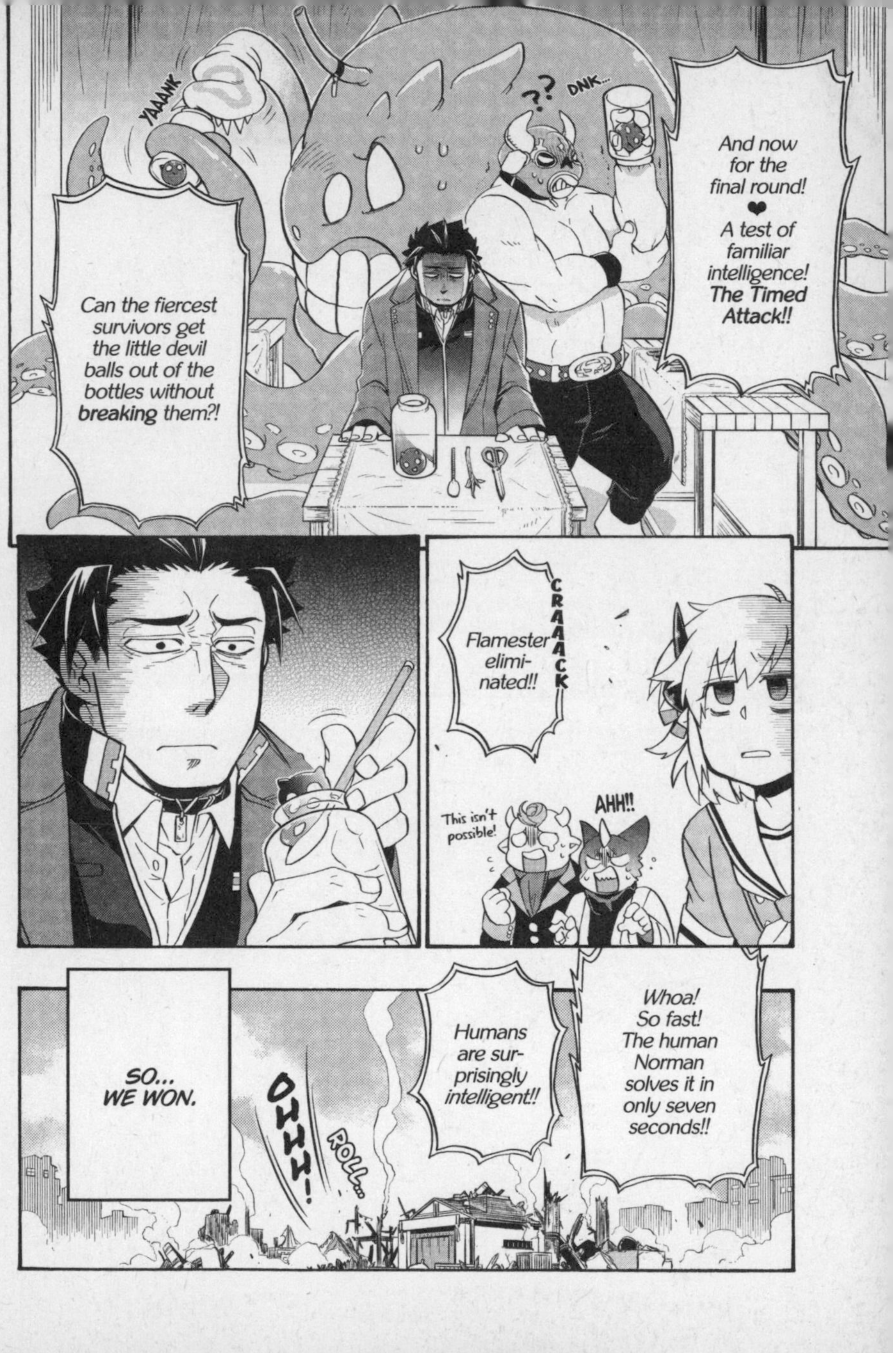
And now for the final round! ❤ A test of familiar intelligence! The Timed Attack!!
DNK...
??
YAAANK
Can the fiercest survivors get the little devil balls out of the bottles without **breaking** them?!
Flamester elimi-nated!!
CRAAACK
AHH!!
This isn't possible!
Whoa! So fast! The human Norman solves it in only seven seconds!!
Humans are sur-prisingly intelligent!!
ROLL...
OHHH!
SO... WE WON.

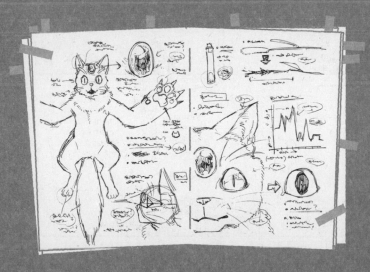

Sorry For My Familiar

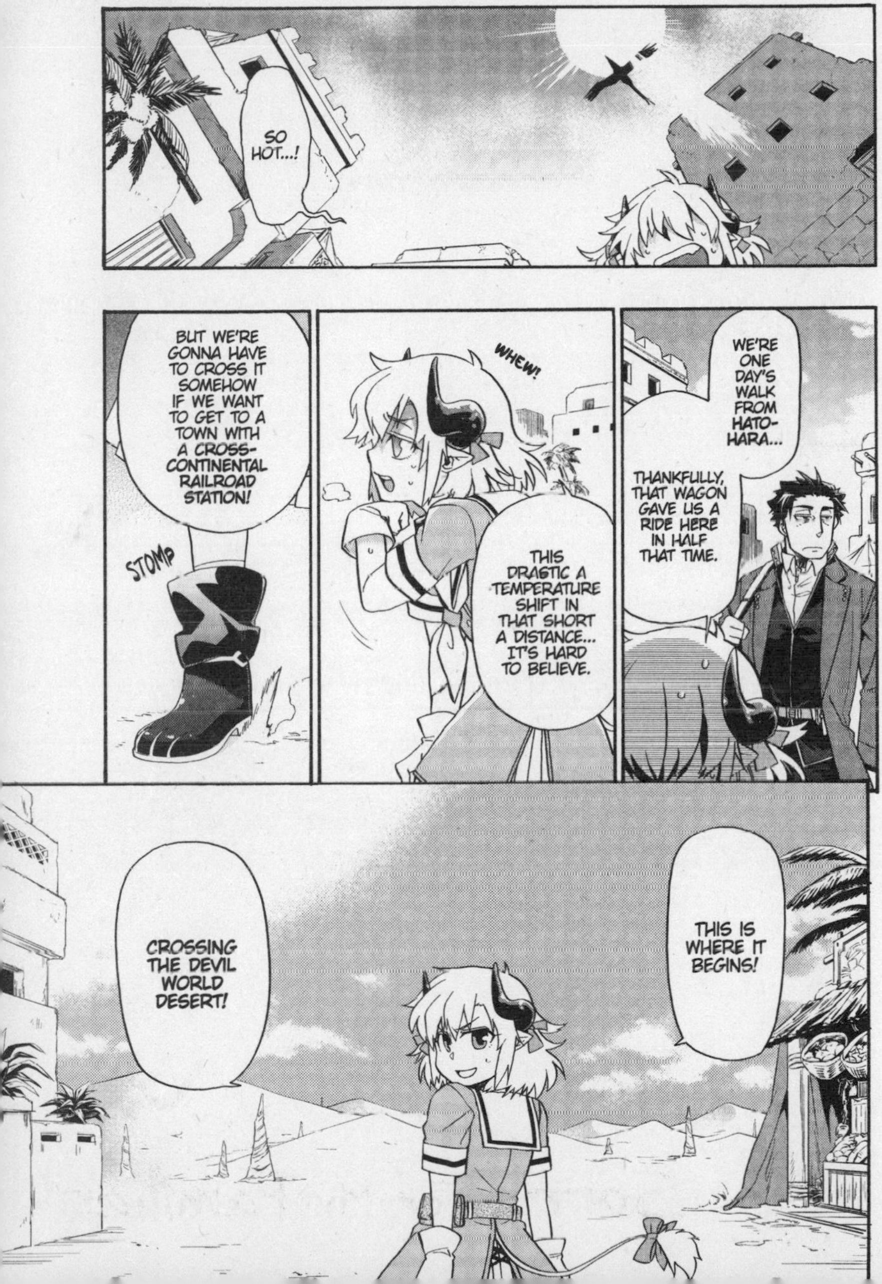
SO HOT...!
WE'RE ONE DAY'S WALK FROM HATO-HARA...
THANKFULLY, THAT WAGON GAVE US A RIDE HERE IN HALF THAT TIME.
WHEW!
THIS DRASTIC A TEMPERATURE SHIFT IN THAT SHORT A DISTANCE... IT'S HARD TO BELIEVE.
BUT WE'RE GONNA HAVE TO CROSS IT SOMEHOW IF WE WANT TO GET TO A TOWN WITH A CROSS-CONTINENTAL RAILROAD STATION!
STOMP
THIS IS WHERE IT BEGINS!
CROSSING THE DEVIL WORLD DESERT!

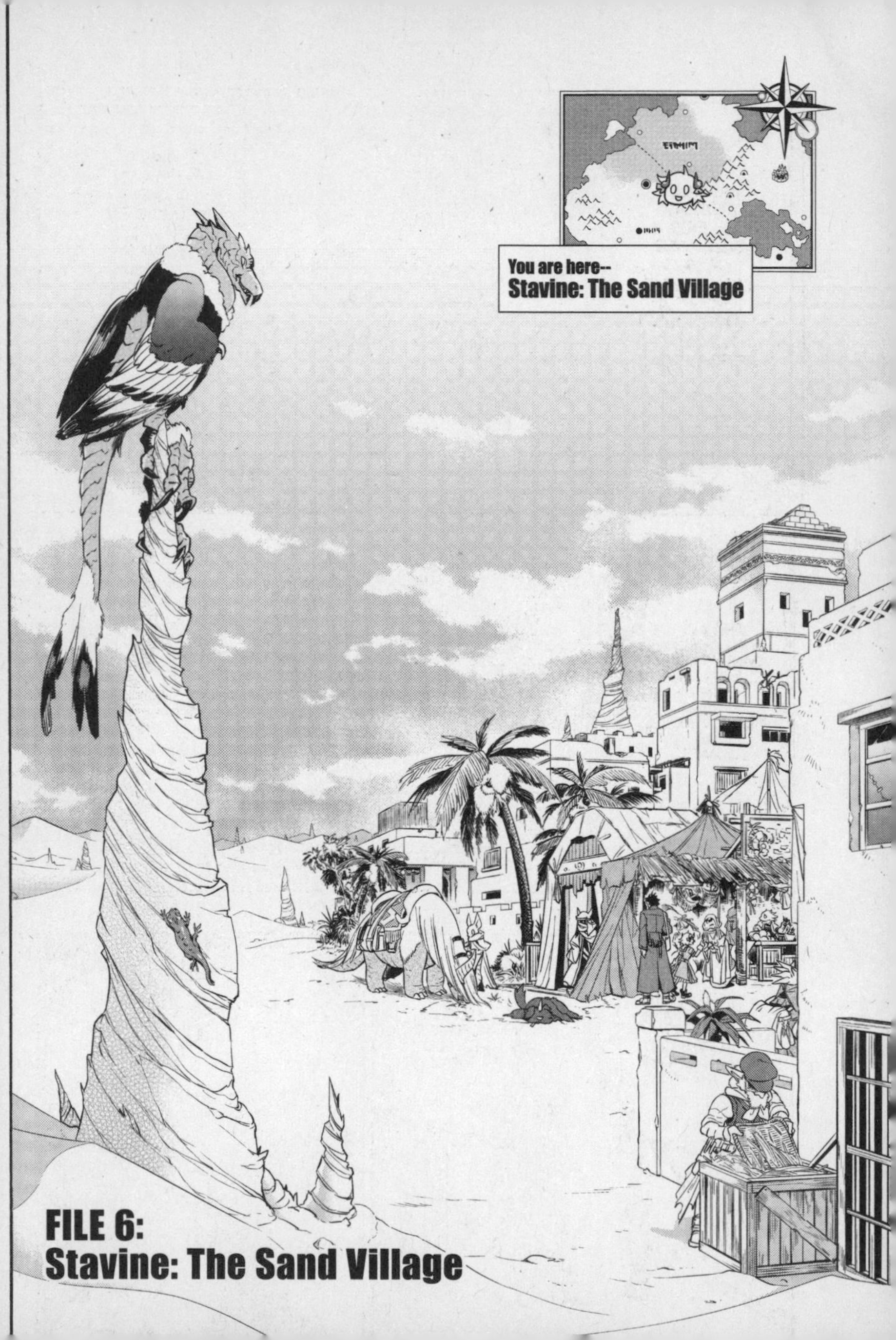
You are here--
Stavine: The Sand Village

FILE 6: Stavine: The Sand Village

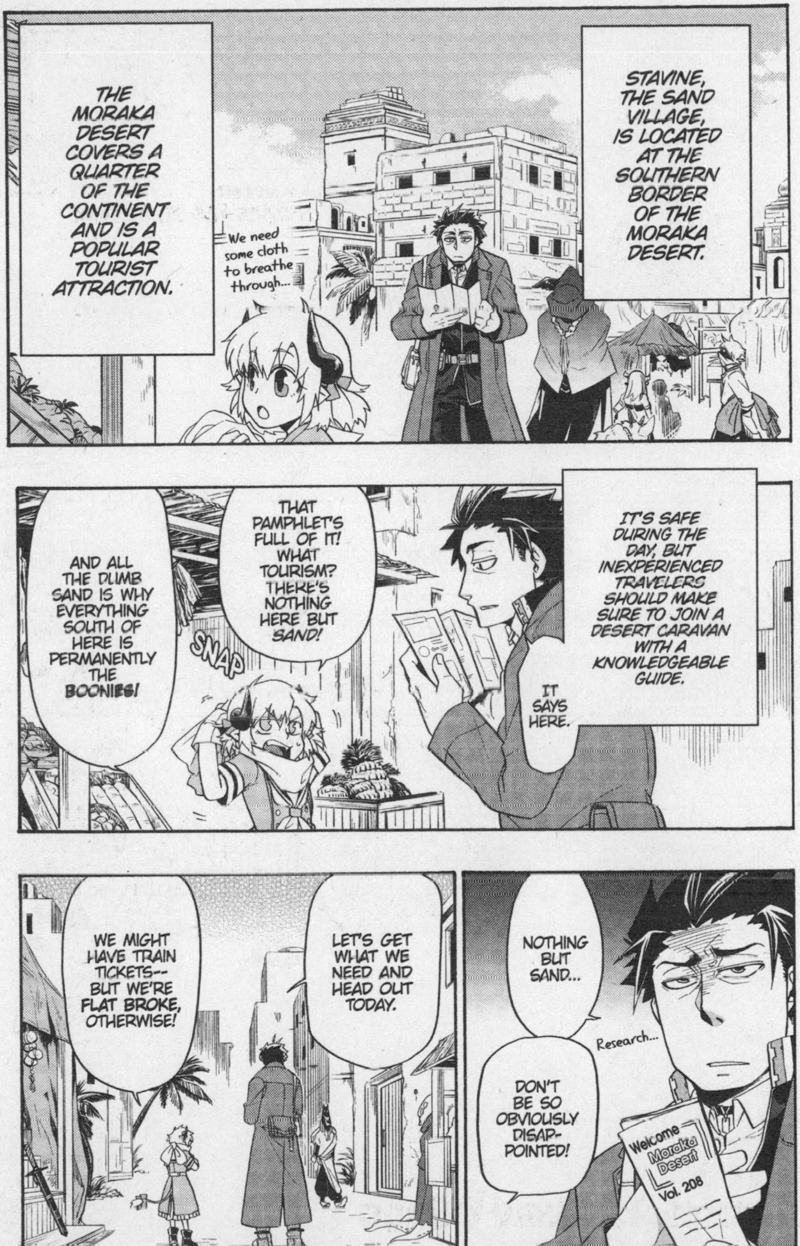
STAVINE, THE SAND VILLAGE, IS LOCATED AT THE SOUTHERN BORDER OF THE MORAKA DESERT.
THE MORAKA DESERT COVERS A QUARTER OF THE CONTINENT AND IS A POPULAR TOURIST ATTRACTION.
We need some cloth to breathe through...
IT'S SAFE DURING THE DAY, BUT INEXPERIENCED TRAVELERS SHOULD MAKE SURE TO JOIN A DESERT CARAVAN WITH A KNOWLEDGEABLE GUIDE.
IT SAYS HERE.
THAT PAMPHLET'S FULL OF IT! WHAT TOURISM? THERE'S NOTHING HERE BUT SAND!
SNAP
AND ALL THE DUMB SAND IS WHY EVERYTHING SOUTH OF HERE IS PERMANENTLY THE BOONIES!
NOTHING BUT SAND...
Research...
DON'T BE SO OBVIOUSLY DISAP-POINTED!
Welcome Moraka Desert Vol. 208
LET'S GET WHAT WE NEED AND HEAD OUT TODAY.
WE MIGHT HAVE TRAIN TICKETS-- BUT WE'RE FLAT BROKE, OTHERWISE!

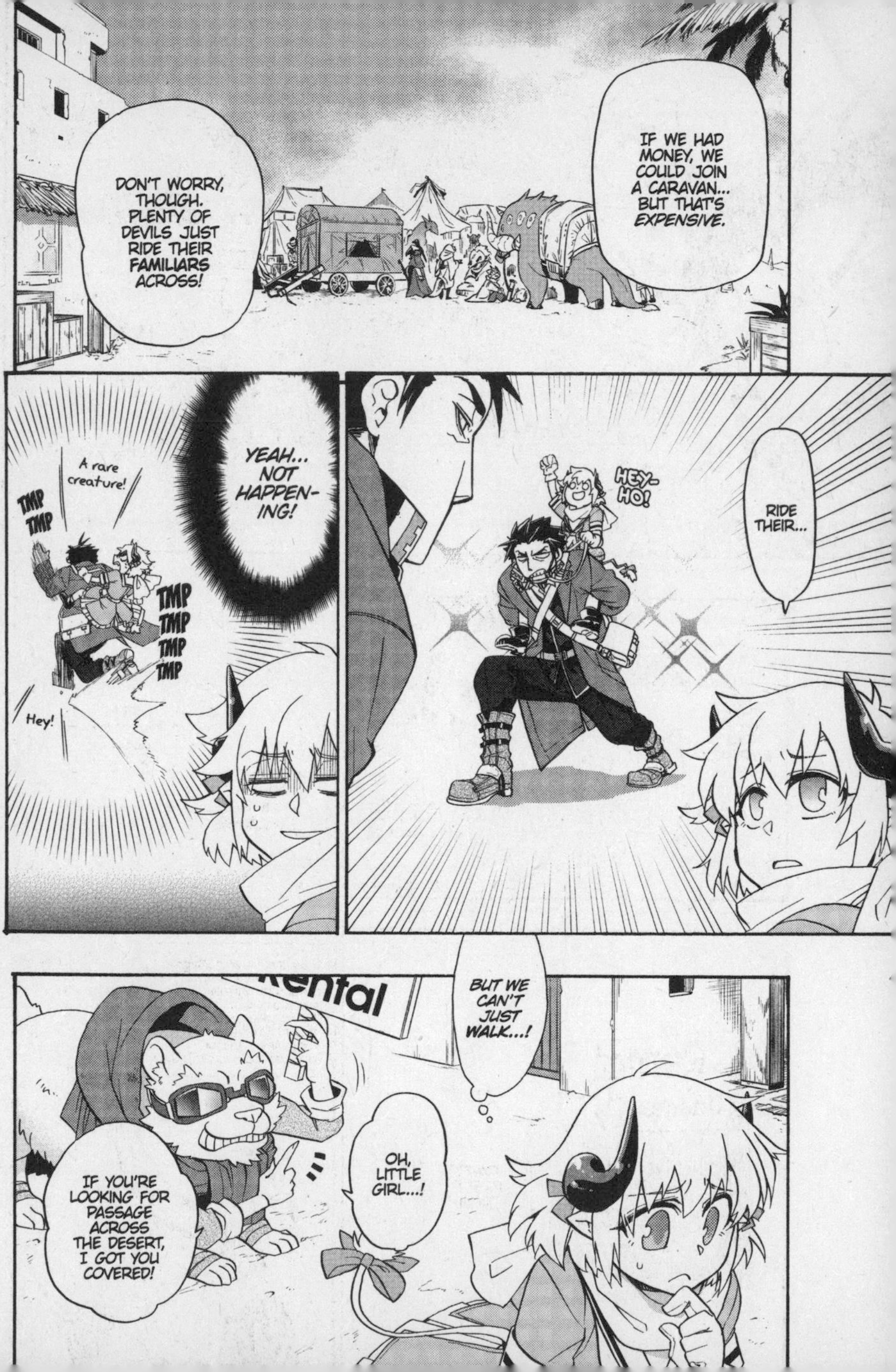
IF WE HAD MONEY, WE COULD JOIN A CARAVAN... BUT THAT'S *EXPENSIVE.*
DON'T WORRY, THOUGH. PLENTY OF DEVILS JUST RIDE THEIR FAMILIARS ACROSS!
RIDE THEIR...
HEY-HO!
YEAH... NOT HAPPEN-ING!
A rare creature!
TMP TMP
TMP TMP TMP TMP
Hey!
BUT WE CAN'T JUST WALK...!
Rental
OH, LITTLE GIRL...!
IF YOU'RE LOOKING FOR PASSAGE ACROSS THE DESERT, I GOT YOU COVERED!

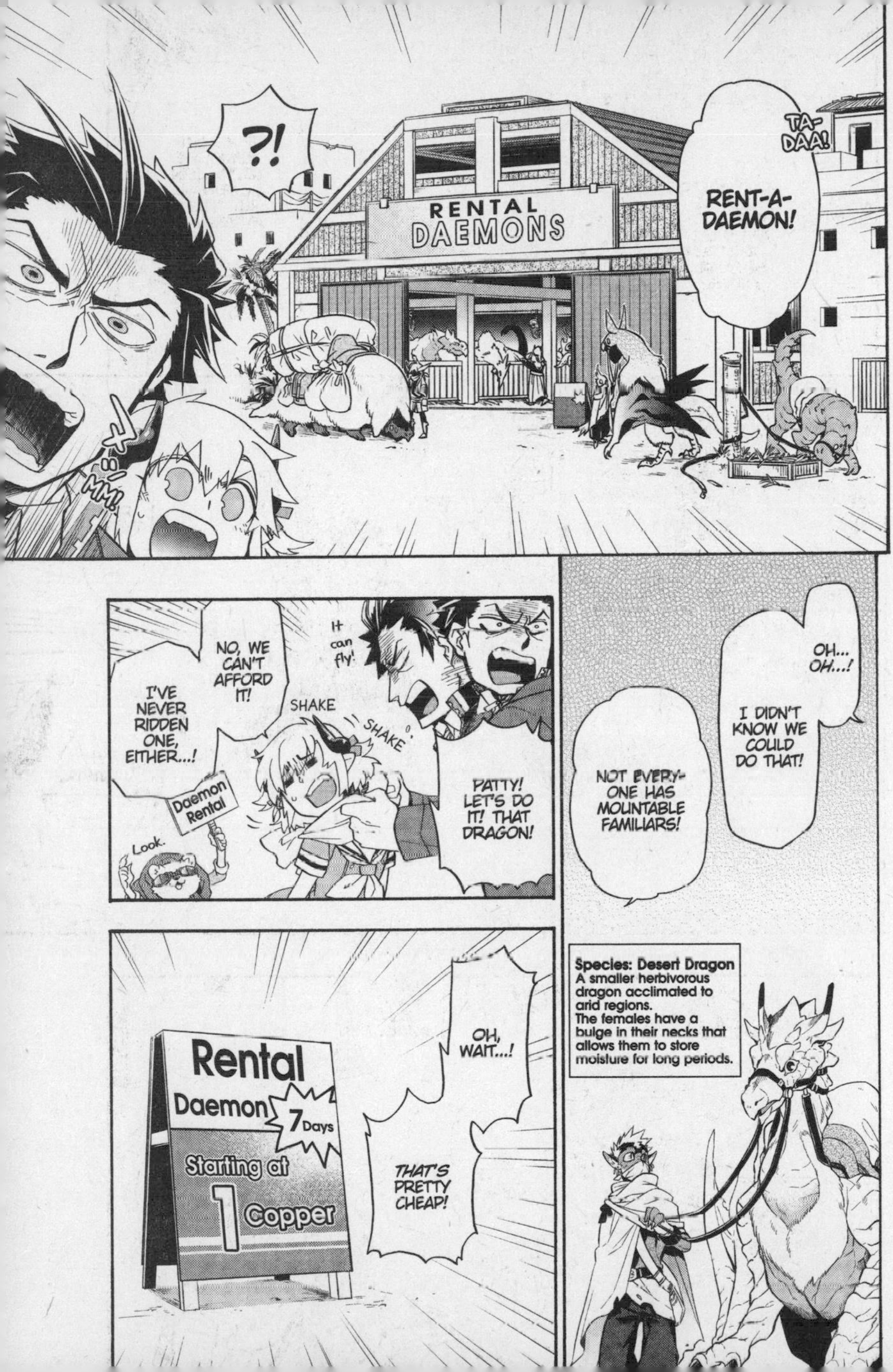
TA-DAA!
RENT-A-DAEMON!
RENTAL DAEMONS
?!
MM!
OH... OH...!
I DIDN'T KNOW WE COULD DO THAT!
NOT EVERYONE HAS MOUNTABLE FAMILIARS!
PATTY! LET'S DO IT! THAT DRAGON!
SHAKE
SHAKE
It can fly!
NO, WE CAN'T AFFORD IT!
I'VE NEVER RIDDEN ONE, EITHER...!
Daemon Rental
Look.
Species: Desert Dragon
A smaller herbivorous dragon acclimated to arid regions.
The females have a bulge in their necks that allows them to store moisture for long periods.
OH, WAIT...!
THAT'S PRETTY CHEAP!
Rental Daemon
7 Days
Starting at 1 Copper

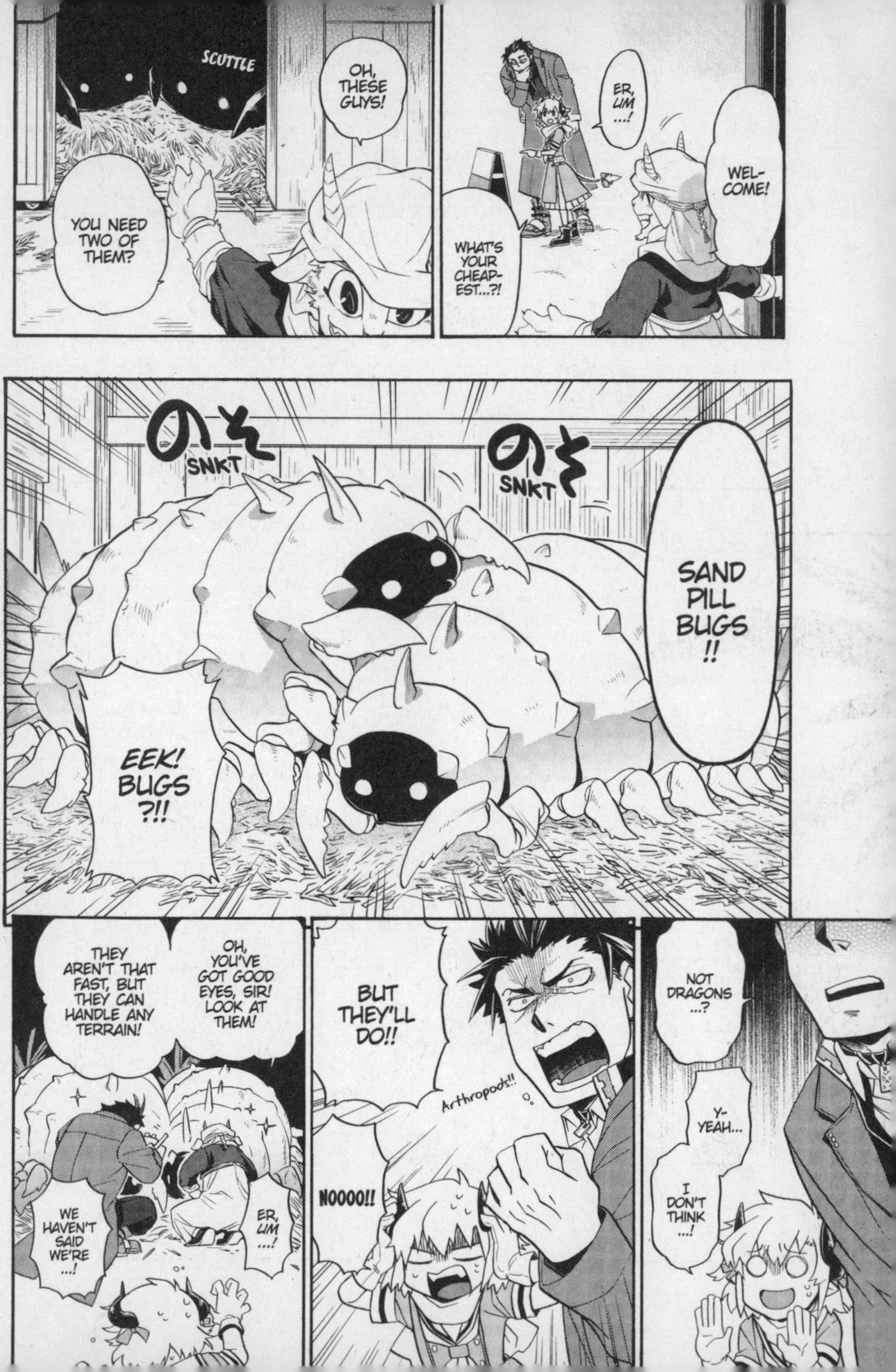
WEL-COME!
ER, UM ...!
WHAT'S YOUR CHEAP-EST...?!
SCUTTLE
OH, THESE GUYS!
YOU NEED TWO OF THEM?
のそ SNKT
のそ SNKT
SAND PILL BUGS!!
EEK! BUGS?!!
NOT DRAGONS ...?
Y-YEAH...
I DON'T THINK ...!
BUT THEY'LL DO!!
Arthropods!!
NOOOO!!
OH, YOU'VE GOT GOOD EYES, SIR! LOOK AT THEM!
THEY AREN'T THAT FAST, BUT THEY CAN HANDLE ANY TERRAIN!
ER, UM ...!
WE HAVEN'T SAID WE'RE ...!

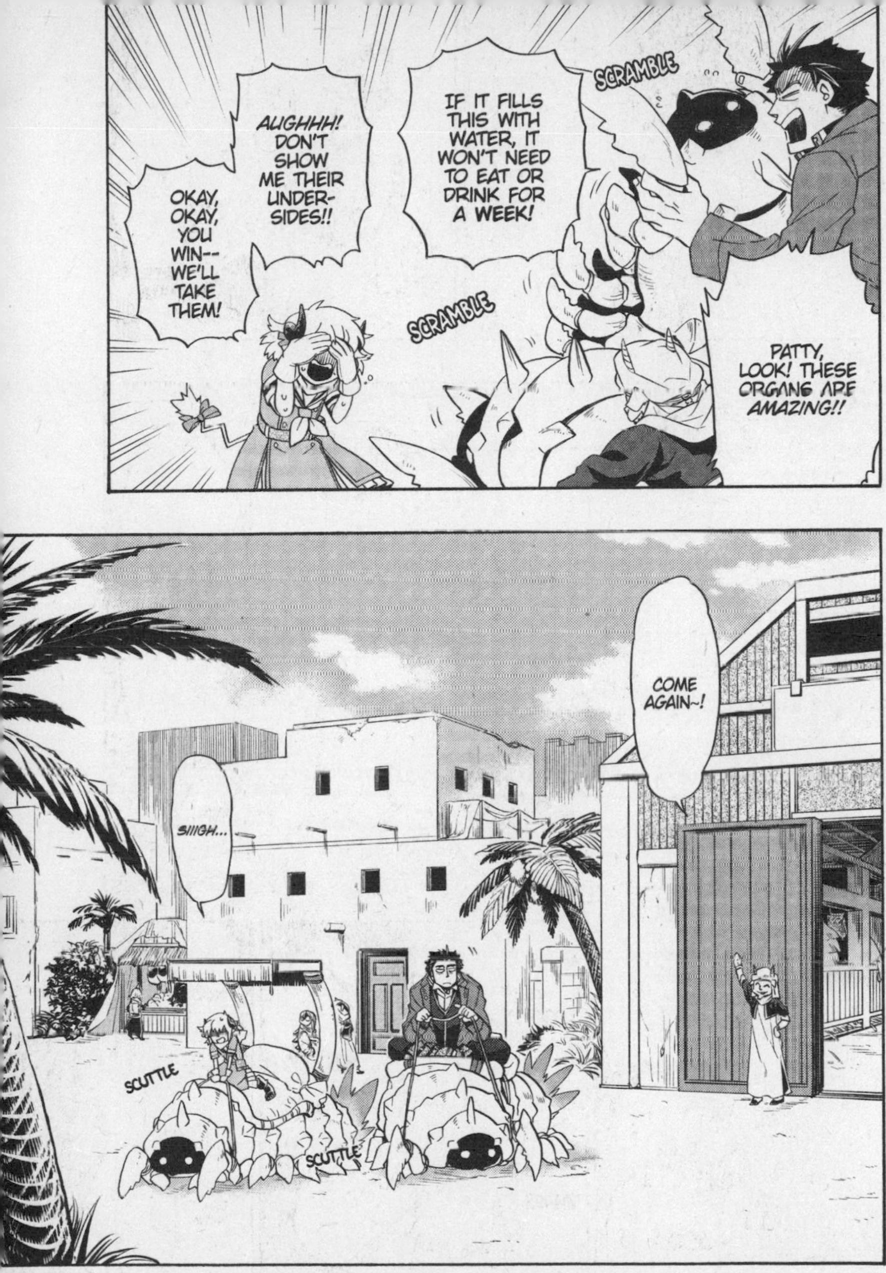

SCRAMBLE
PATTY, LOOK! THESE ORGANS ARE AMAZING!!
IF IT FILLS THIS WITH WATER, IT WON'T NEED TO EAT OR DRINK FOR A WEEK!
SCRAMBLE
AUGHHH! DON'T SHOW ME THEIR UNDER-SIDES!!
OKAY, OKAY, YOU WIN-- WE'LL TAKE THEM!
COME AGAIN~!
SIIIGH...
SCUTTLE
SCUTTLE

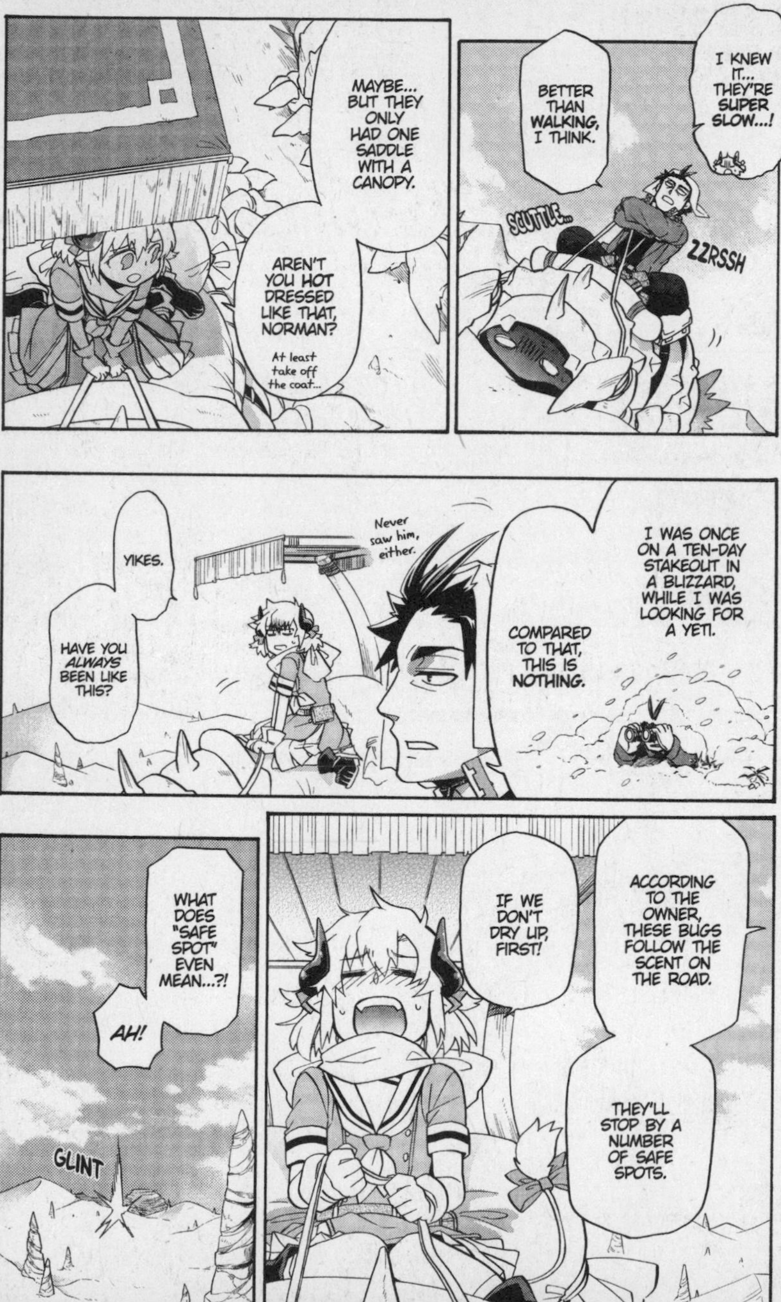
I KNEW IT... THEY'RE SUPER SLOW...!
BETTER THAN WALKING, I THINK.
SCUTTLE...
ZZRSSH
MAYBE... BUT THEY ONLY HAD ONE SADDLE WITH A CANOPY.
AREN'T YOU HOT DRESSED LIKE THAT, NORMAN?
At least take off the coat...
I WAS ONCE ON A TEN-DAY STAKEOUT IN A BLIZZARD, WHILE I WAS LOOKING FOR A YETI.
COMPARED TO THAT, THIS IS NOTHING.
Never saw him, either.
YIKES.
HAVE YOU ALWAYS BEEN LIKE THIS?
ACCORDING TO THE OWNER, THESE BUGS FOLLOW THE SCENT ON THE ROAD.
THEY'LL STOP BY A NUMBER OF SAFE SPOTS.
IF WE DON'T DRY UP, FIRST!
WHAT DOES "SAFE SPOT" EVEN MEAN...?!
AH!
GLINT

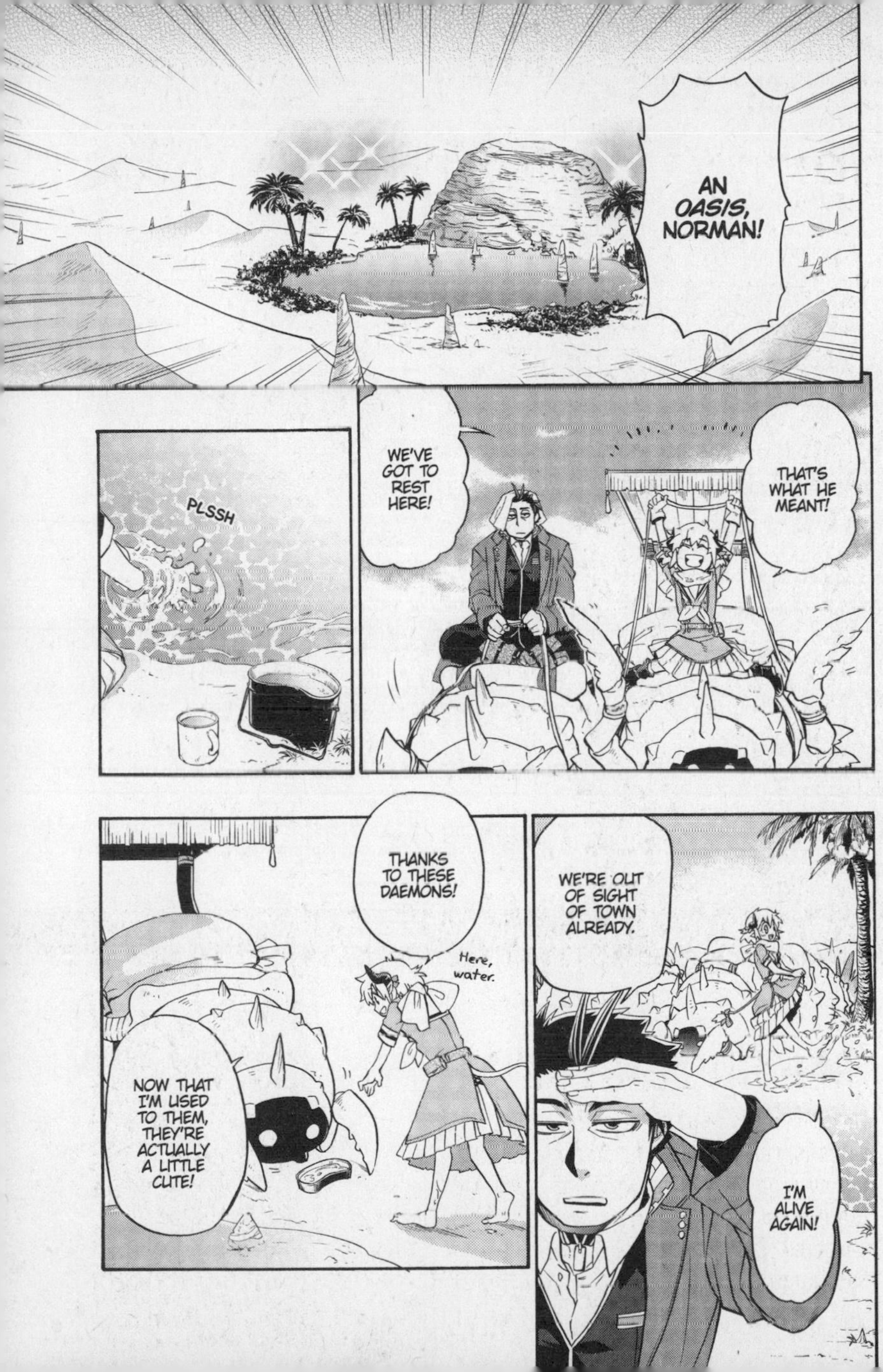
AN OASIS, NORMAN!
THAT'S WHAT HE MEANT!
WE'VE GOT TO REST HERE!
PLSSH
WE'RE OUT OF SIGHT OF TOWN ALREADY.
I'M ALIVE AGAIN!
THANKS TO THESE DAEMONS!
Here, water.
NOW THAT I'M USED TO THEM, THEY'RE ACTUALLY A LITTLE CUTE!

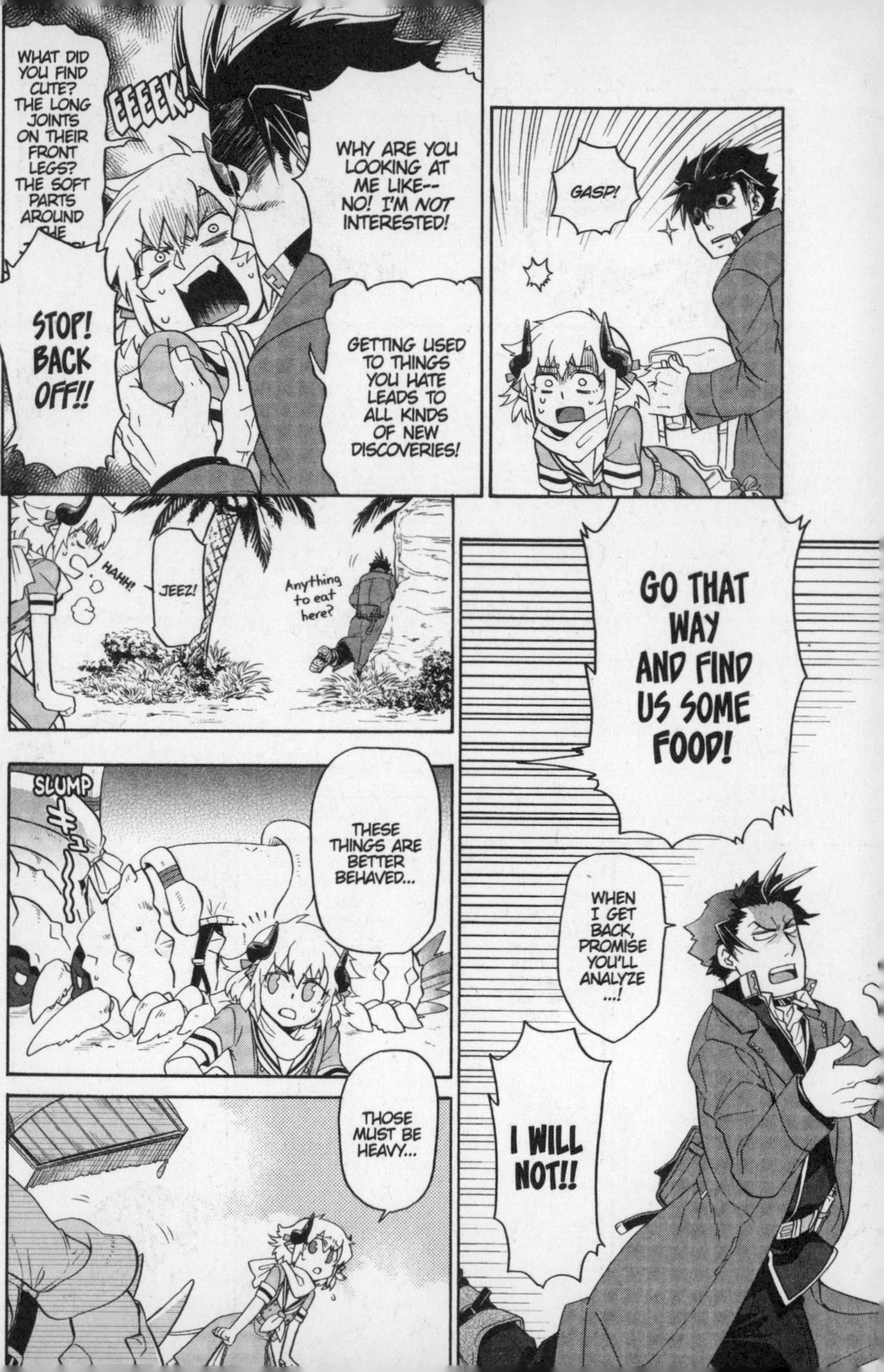
GASP!
WHY ARE YOU LOOKING AT ME LIKE-- NO! I'M NOT INTERESTED!
EEEEK!
WHAT DID YOU FIND CUTE? THE LONG JOINTS ON THEIR FRONT LEGS? THE SOFT PARTS AROUND THE
GETTING USED TO THINGS YOU HATE LEADS TO ALL KINDS OF NEW DISCOVERIES!
STOP! BACK OFF!!
GO THAT WAY AND FIND US SOME FOOD!
WHEN I GET BACK, PROMISE YOU'LL ANALYZE ...!
I WILL NOT!!
Anything to eat here?
HAHH!
JEEZ!
SLUMP
THESE THINGS ARE BETTER BEHAVED...
THOSE MUST BE HEAVY...

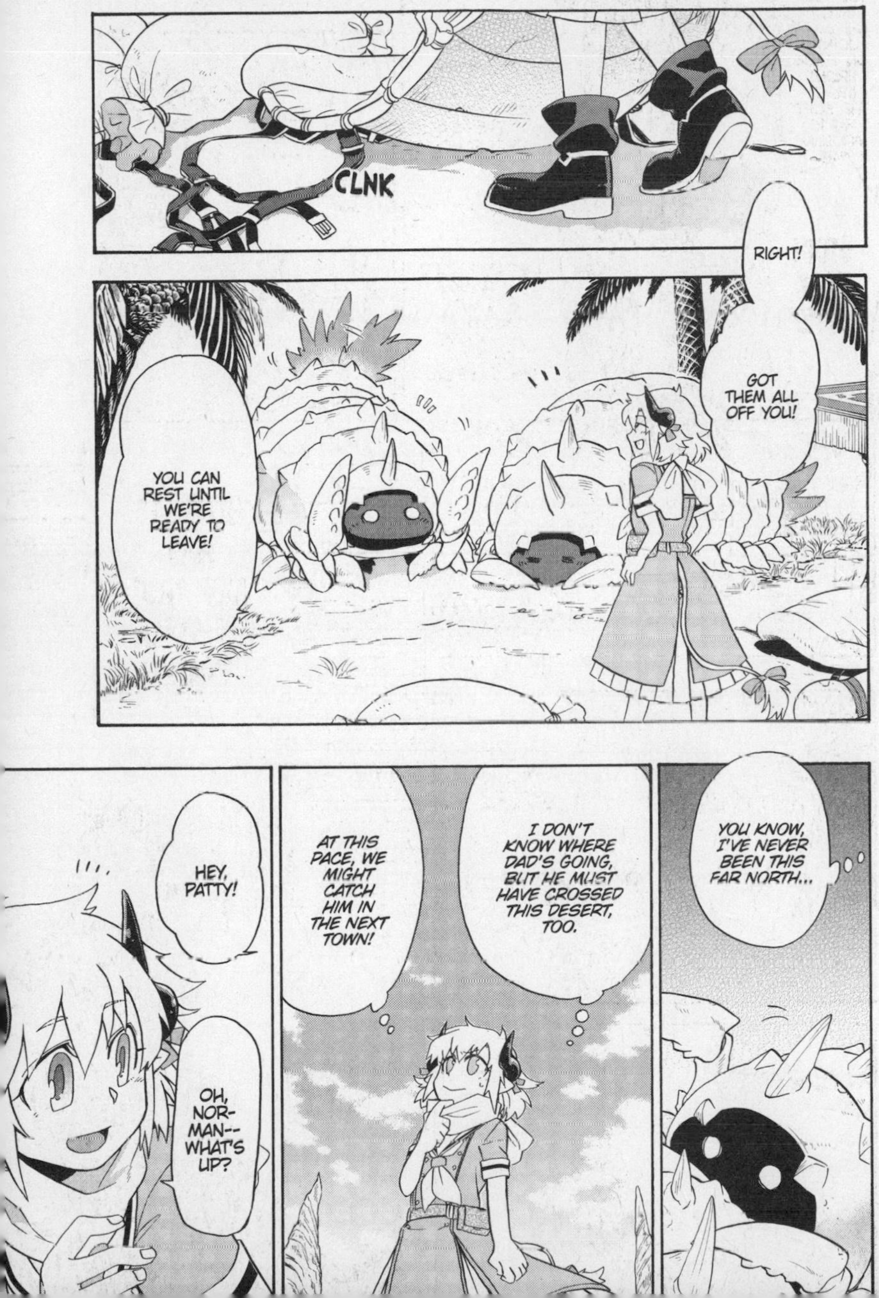
CLNK
RIGHT!
GOT THEM ALL OFF YOU!
YOU CAN REST UNTIL WE'RE READY TO LEAVE!
YOU KNOW, I'VE NEVER BEEN THIS FAR NORTH...
I DON'T KNOW WHERE DAD'S GOING, BUT HE MUST HAVE CROSSED THIS DESERT, TOO.
AT THIS PACE, WE MIGHT CATCH HIM IN THE NEXT TOWN!
HEY, PATTY!
OH, NOR-MAN-- WHAT'S UP?

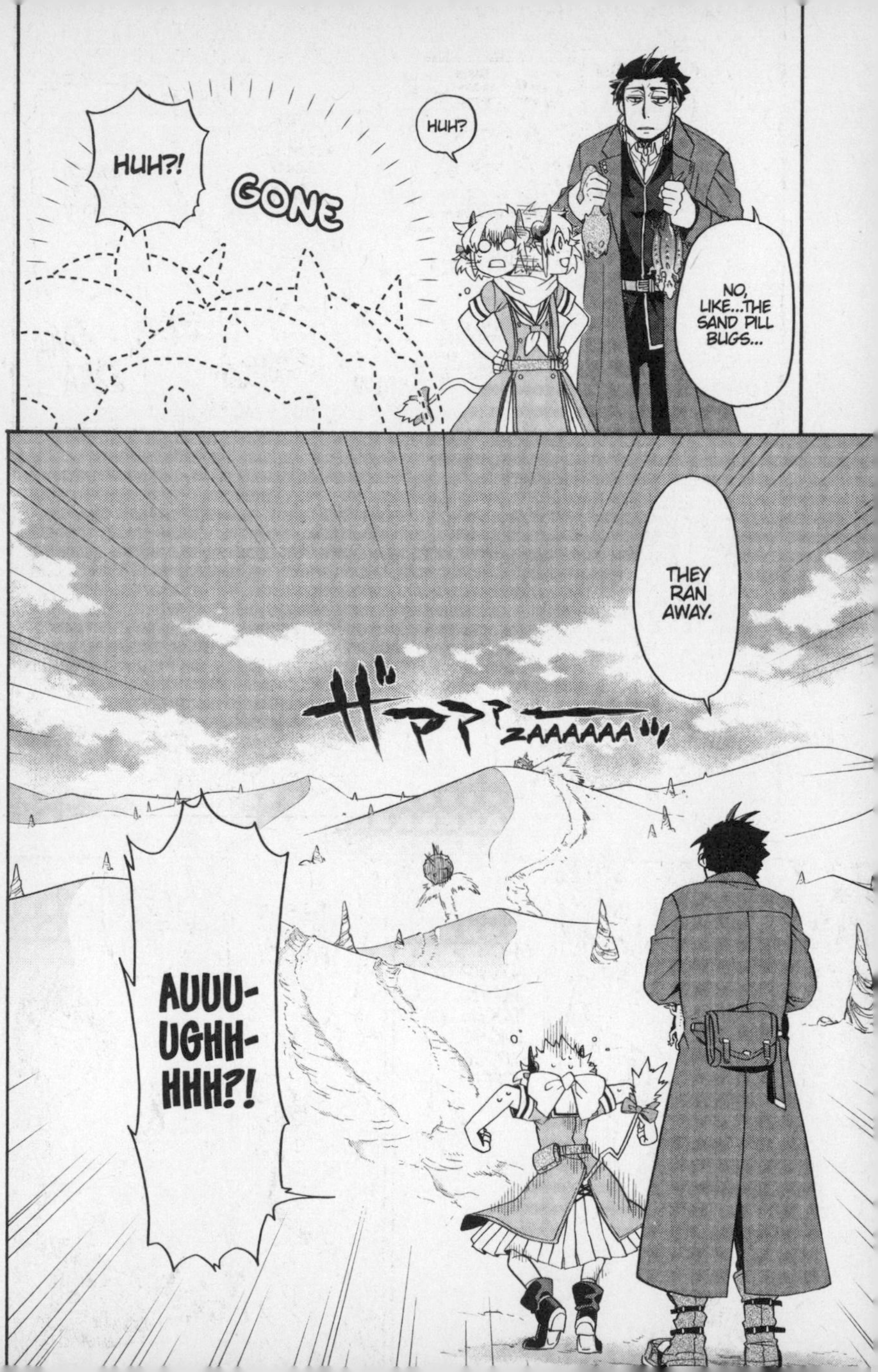
NO, LIKE...THE SAND PILL BUGS...
HUH?
GONE
HUH?!
THEY RAN AWAY.
ZAAAAAA
AUUU-UGHH-HHH?!

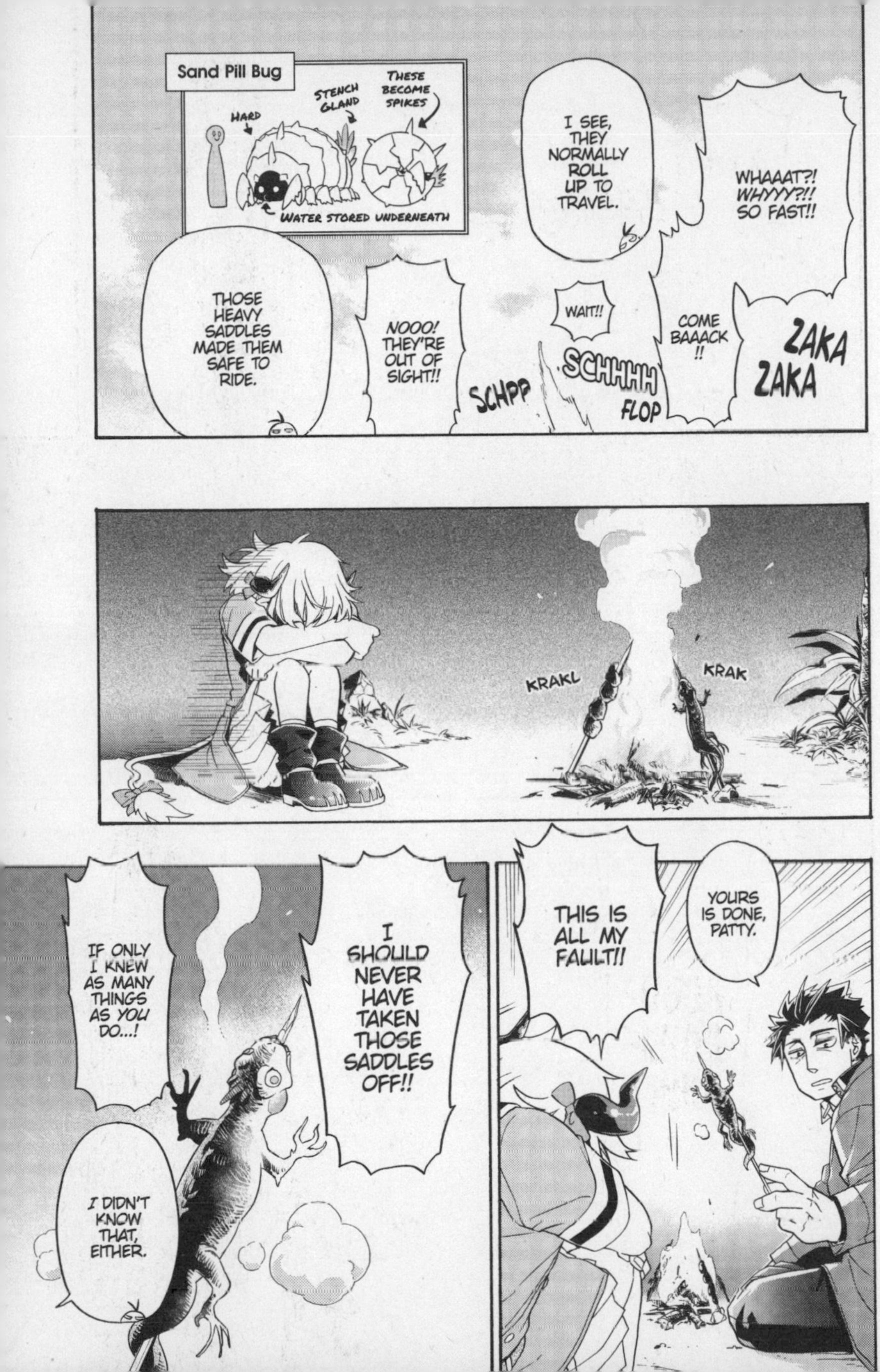
WHAAAT?! *WHYYY?!!* SO FAST!!
I SEE, THEY NORMALLY ROLL UP TO TRAVEL.
Sand Pill Bug
THESE BECOME SPIKES
STENCH GLAND
HARD
WATER STORED UNDERNEATH
ZAKA ZAKA
COME BAAACK!!
WAIT!!
SCHHHH
FLOP
SCHPP
NOOO! THEY'RE OUT OF SIGHT!!
THOSE HEAVY SADDLES MADE THEM SAFE TO RIDE.
KRAK
KRAKL
YOURS IS DONE, PATTY.
THIS IS ALL MY FAULT!!
I SHOULD NEVER HAVE TAKEN THOSE SADDLES OFF!!
IF ONLY I KNEW AS MANY THINGS AS *YOU* DO...!
I DIDN'T KNOW THAT, EITHER.

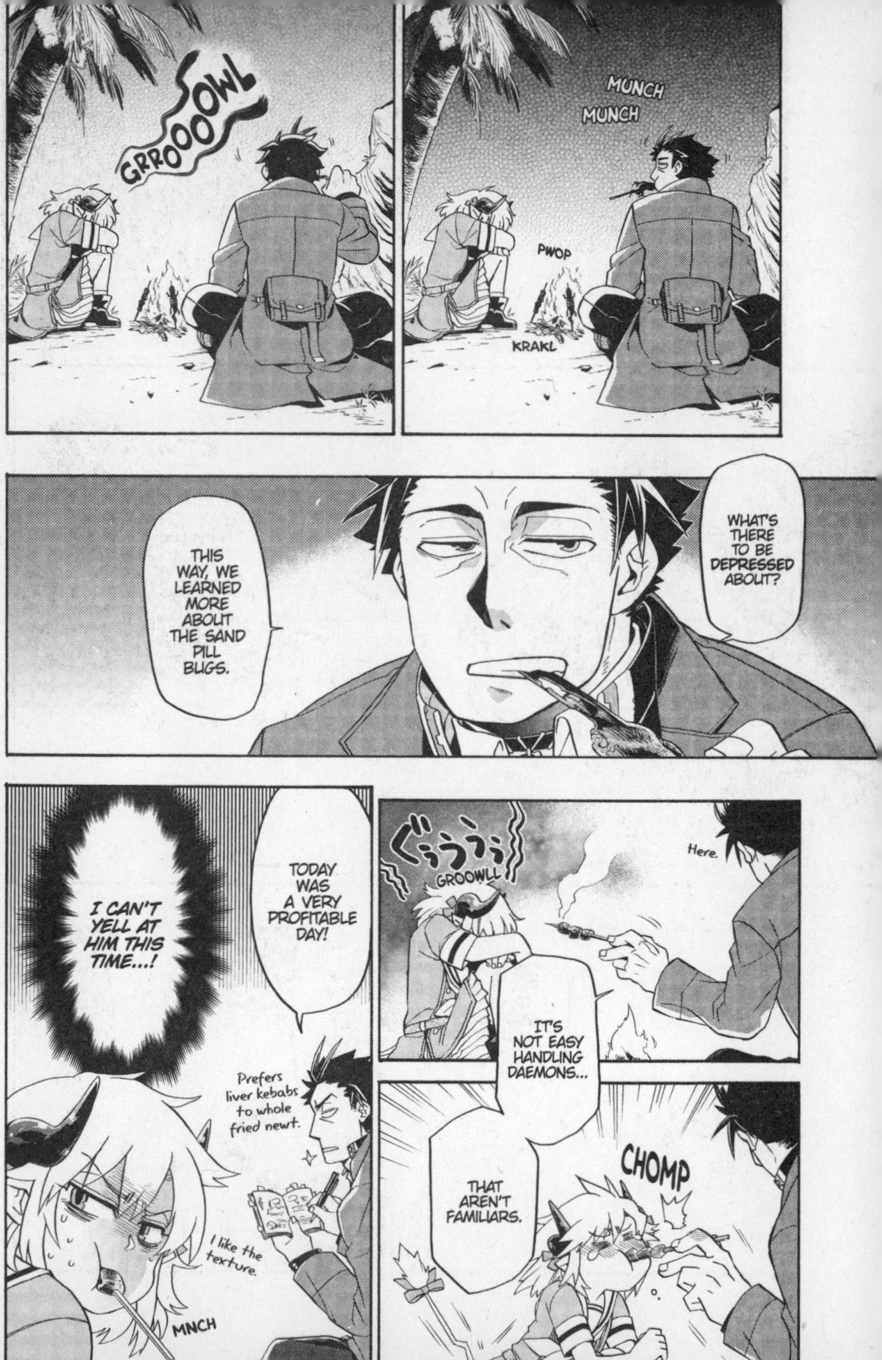
MUNCH
MUNCH
PWOP
KRAKL
GRROOOOWL
WHAT'S THERE TO BE DEPRESSED ABOUT?
THIS WAY, WE LEARNED MORE ABOUT THE SAND PILL BUGS.
Here.
ぐぅぅぅ
GROWLL
IT'S NOT EASY HANDLING DAEMONS...
THAT AREN'T FAMILIARS.
CHOMP
TODAY WAS A VERY PROFITABLE DAY!
I CAN'T YELL AT HIM THIS TIME...!
Prefers liver kebabs to whole fried newt.
I like the texture.
MNCH

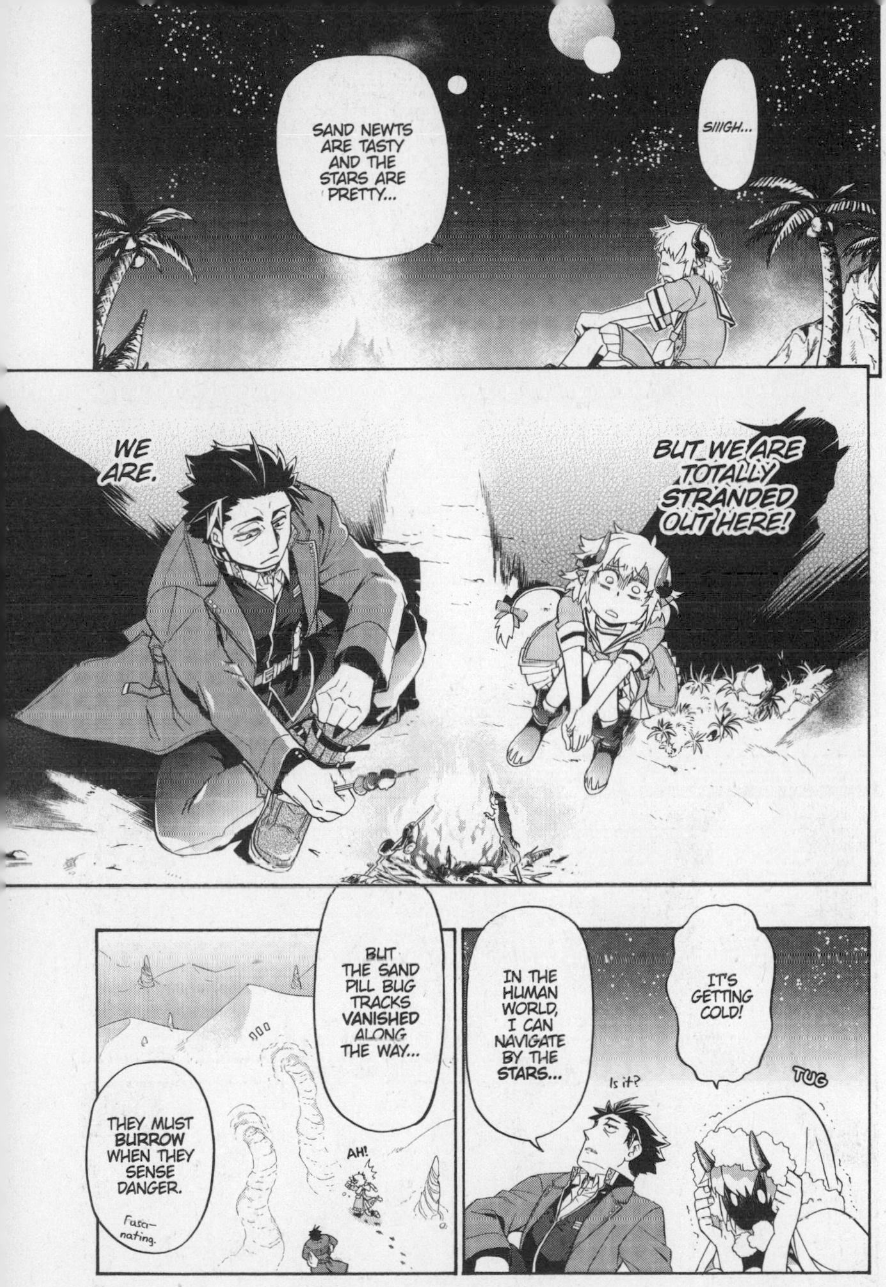
SIIGH...
SAND NEWTS ARE TASTY AND THE STARS ARE PRETTY...
BUT WE ARE TOTALLY STRANDED OUT HERE!
WE ARE.
IT'S GETTING COLD!
IN THE HUMAN WORLD, I CAN NAVIGATE BY THE STARS...
TUG
Is it?
BUT THE SAND PILL BUG TRACKS VANISHED ALONG THE WAY...
AH!
THEY MUST BURROW WHEN THEY SENSE DANGER.
Fasci-nating.

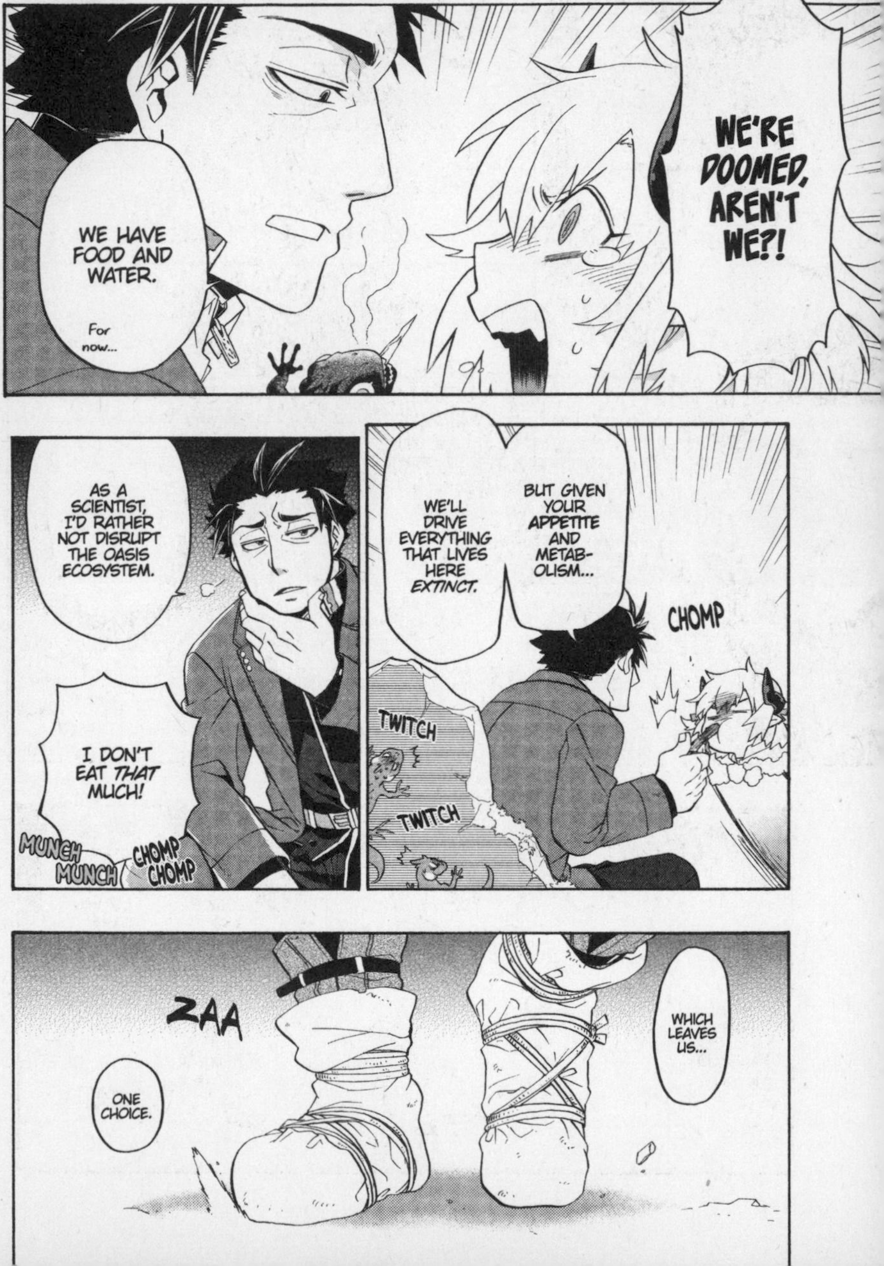
WE'RE DOOMED, AREN'T WE?!
WE HAVE FOOD AND WATER.
For now...
BUT GIVEN YOUR APPETITE AND METAB-OLISM...
WE'LL DRIVE EVERYTHING THAT LIVES HERE *EXTINCT*.
CHOMP
TWITCH
TWITCH
AS A SCIENTIST, I'D RATHER NOT DISRUPT THE OASIS ECOSYSTEM.
I DON'T EAT *THAT* MUCH!
CHOMP CHOMP
MUNCH MUNCH
WHICH LEAVES US...
ZAA
ONE CHOICE.

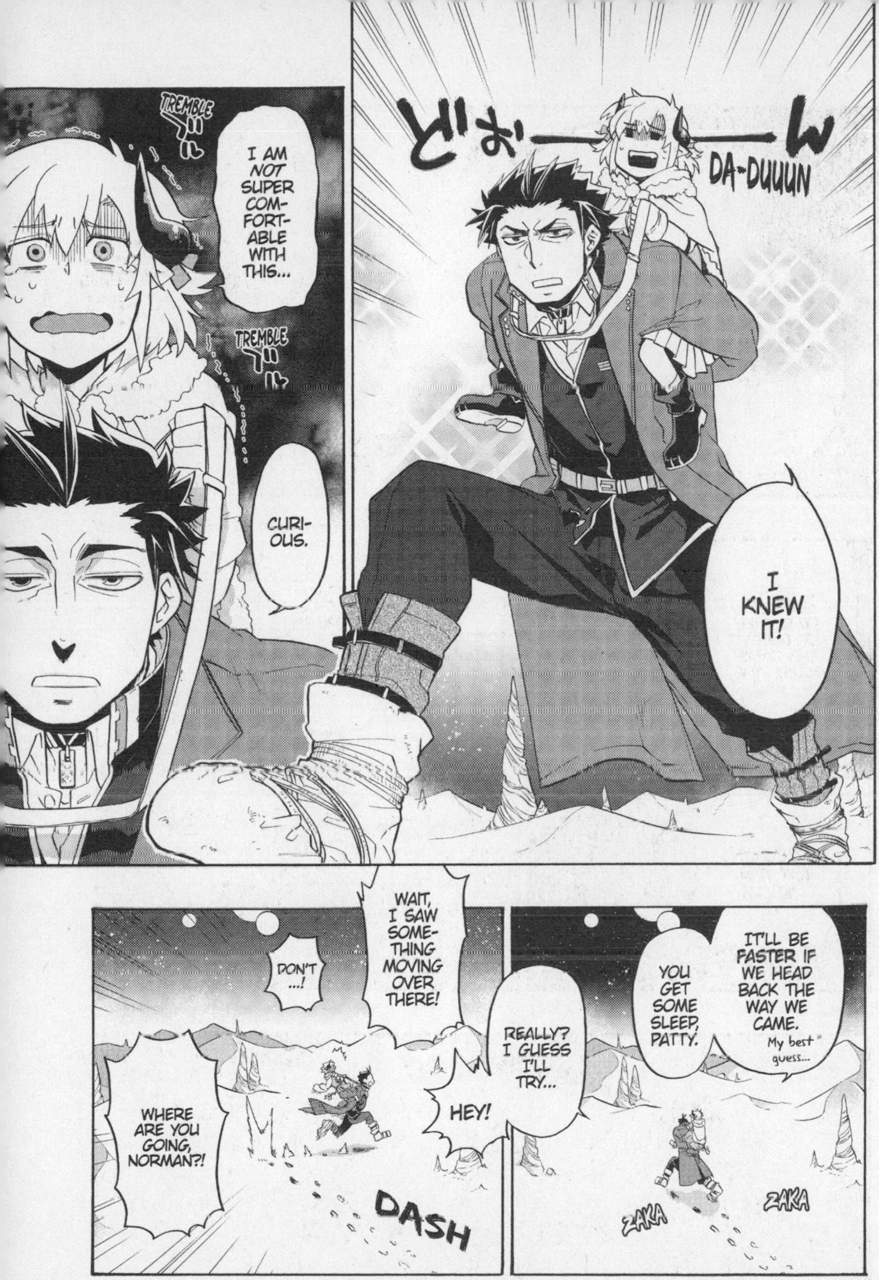
どぉーーーん
DA-DUUUN
I KNEW IT!
TREMBLE ブル
I AM NOT SUPER COMFORTABLE WITH THIS...
TREMBLE ブル
CURIOUS.
IT'LL BE FASTER IF WE HEAD BACK THE WAY WE CAME.
My best guess...
YOU GET SOME SLEEP, PATTY.
REALLY? I GUESS I'LL TRY...
ZAKA
ZAKA
WAIT, I SAW SOMETHING MOVING OVER THERE!
DON'T ...!
HEY!
WHERE ARE YOU GOING, NORMAN?!
DASH

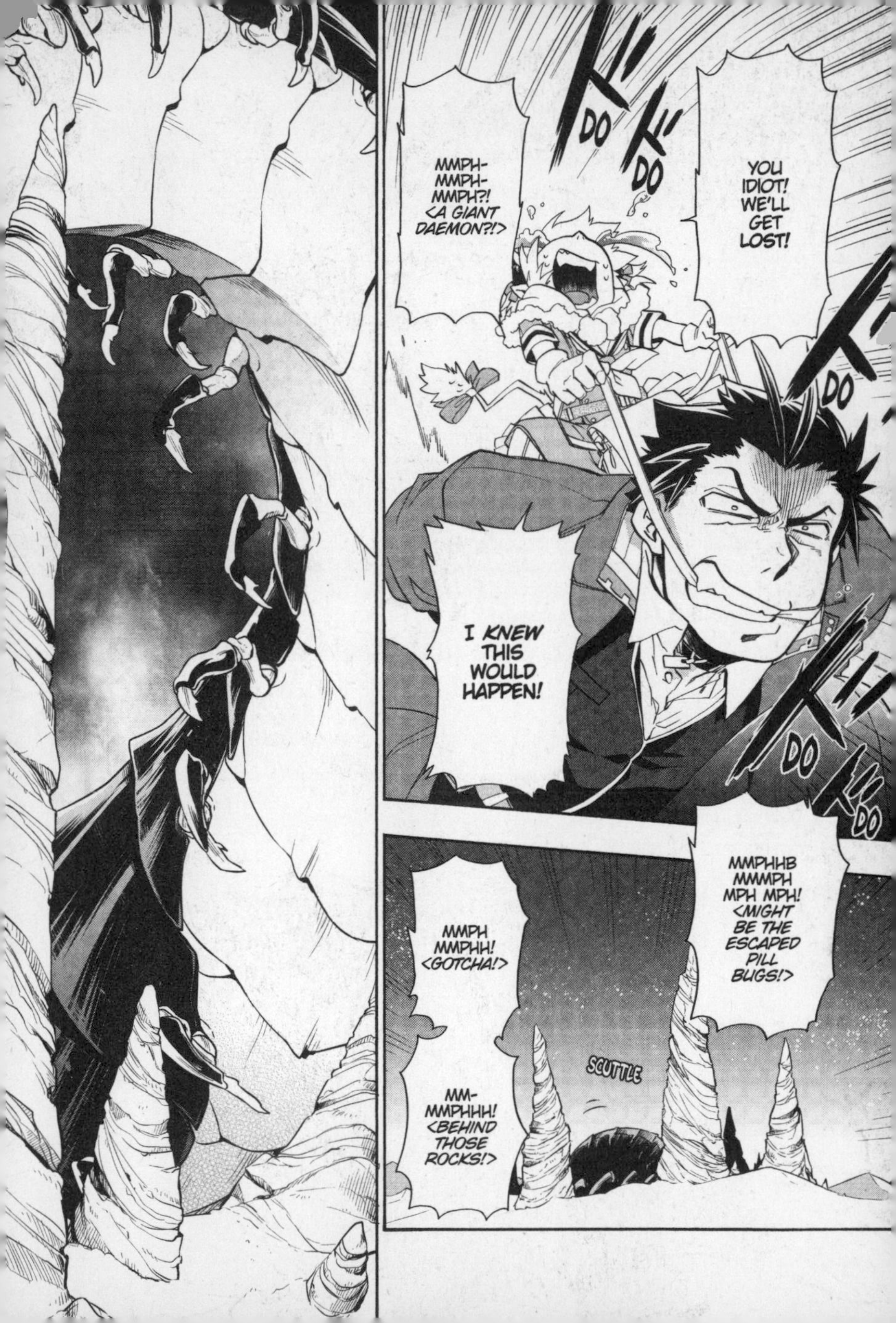
YOU IDIOT! WE'LL GET LOST!
DO DO
MMPH- MMPH- MMPH?! <A GIANT DAEMON?!>
DO DO DO
I KNEW THIS WOULD HAPPEN!
MMPHHB MMMPH MPH MPH! <MIGHT BE THE ESCAPED PILL BUGS!>
MMPH MMPHH! <GOTCHA!>
SCUTTLE
MM-MMPHHH! <BEHIND THOSE ROCKS!>

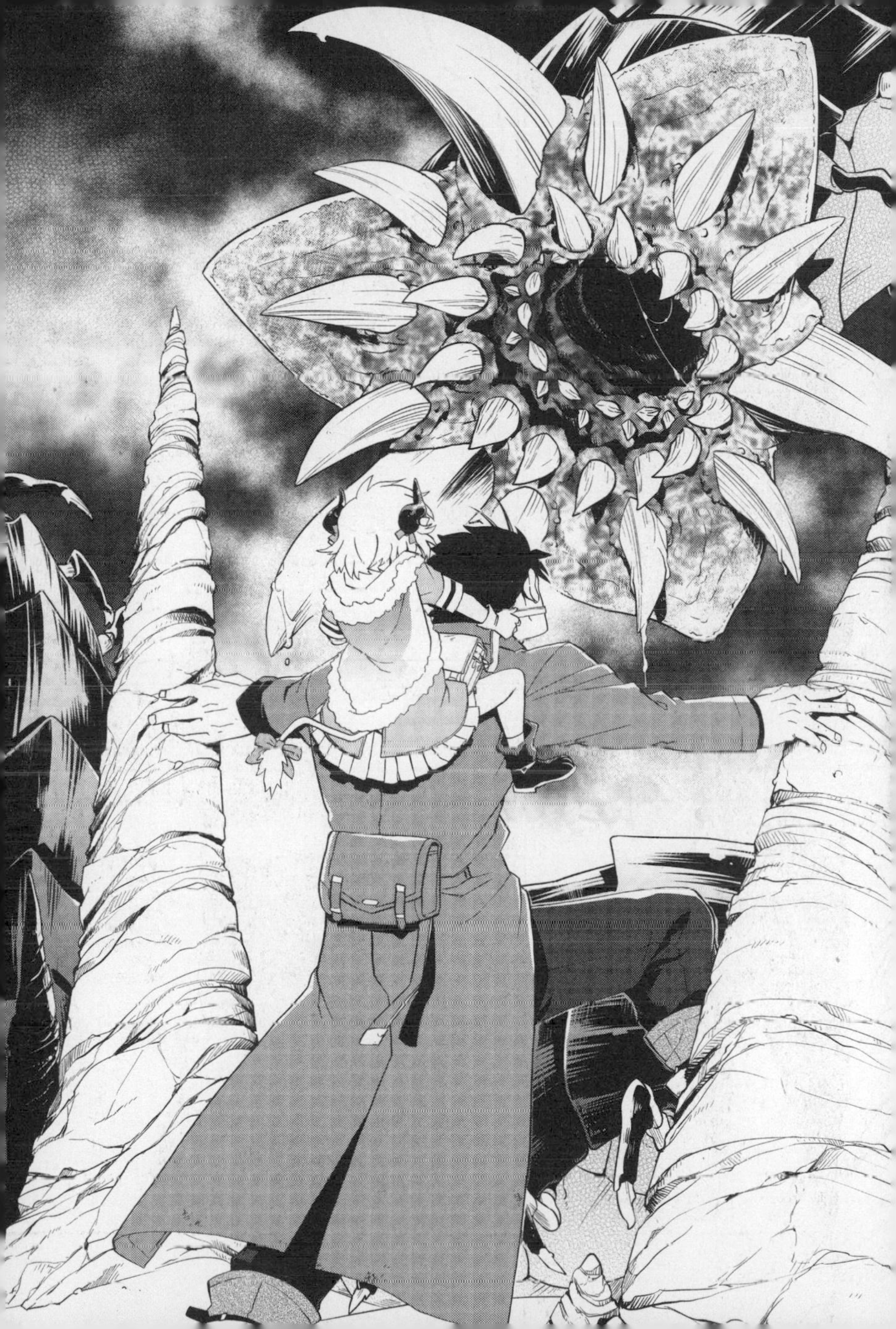

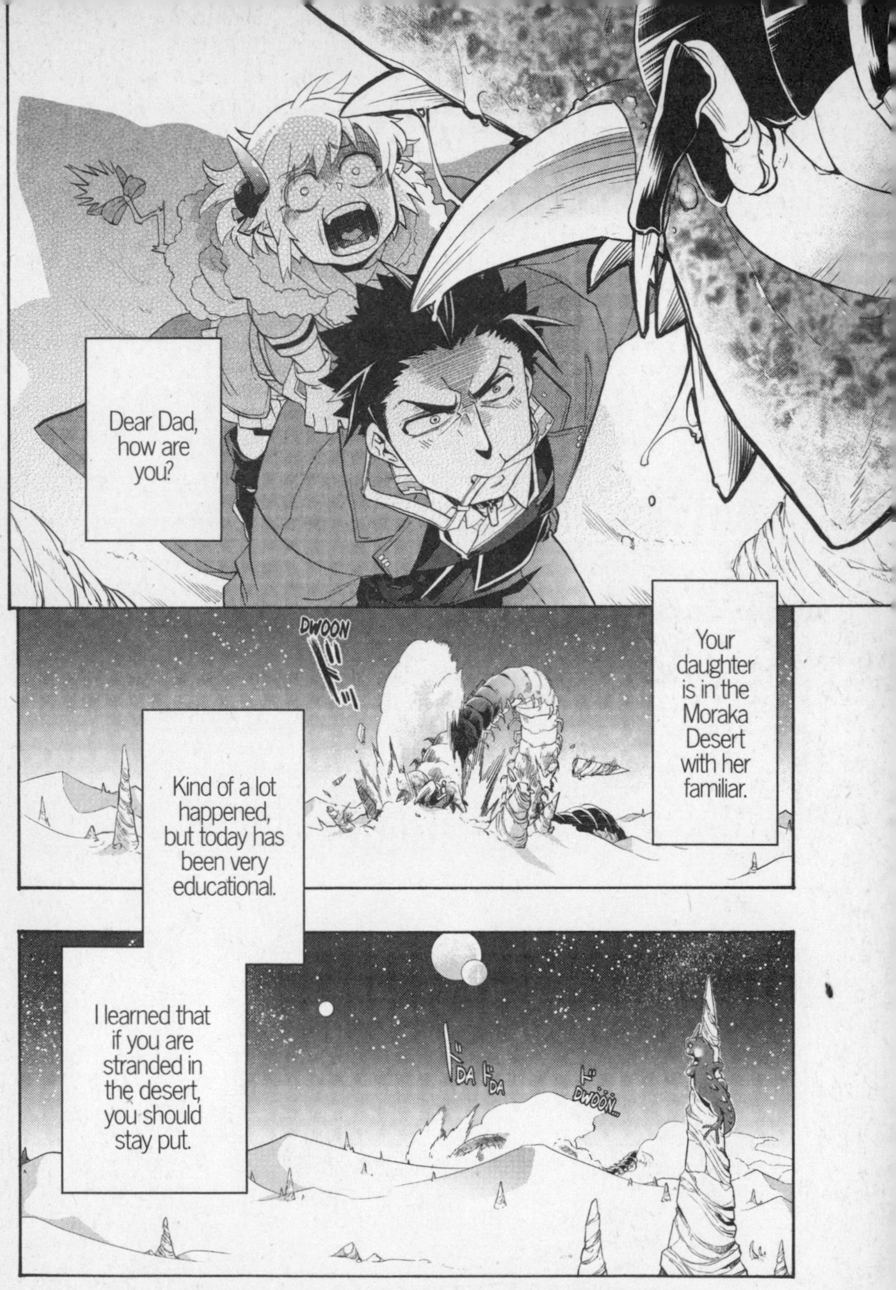
Dear Dad, how are you?
Your daughter is in the Moraka Desert with her familiar.
DWOON
Kind of a lot happened, but today has been very educational.
I learned that if you are stranded in the desert, you should stay put.
DWOON...
DA DA

Self-
Control

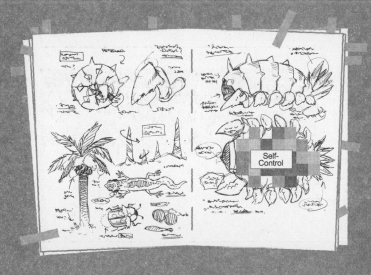

Sorry For My Familiar

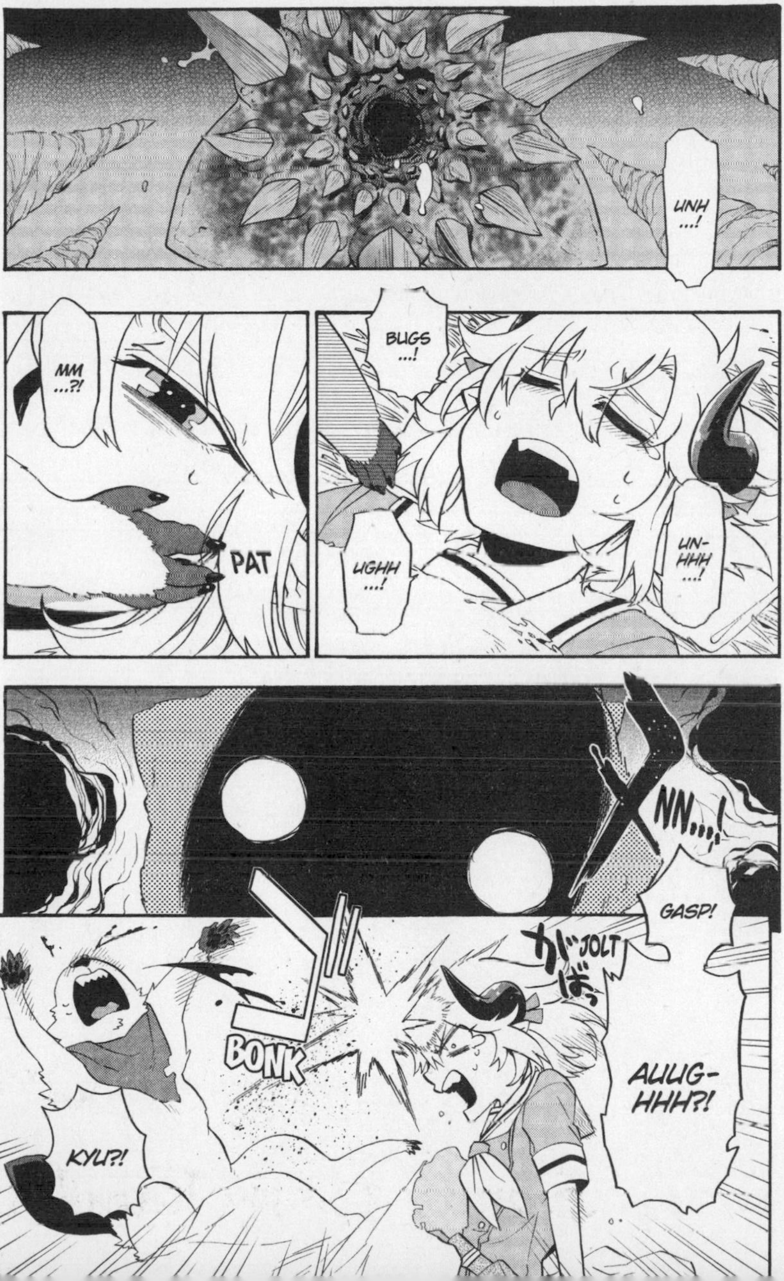
UNH ...!
BUGS ...!
UN-HHH ...!
UGHH ...!
MM ...?!
PAT
XNN...!
GASP!
がばっ
JOLT
BONK
AUUG-HHH?!
KYU?!

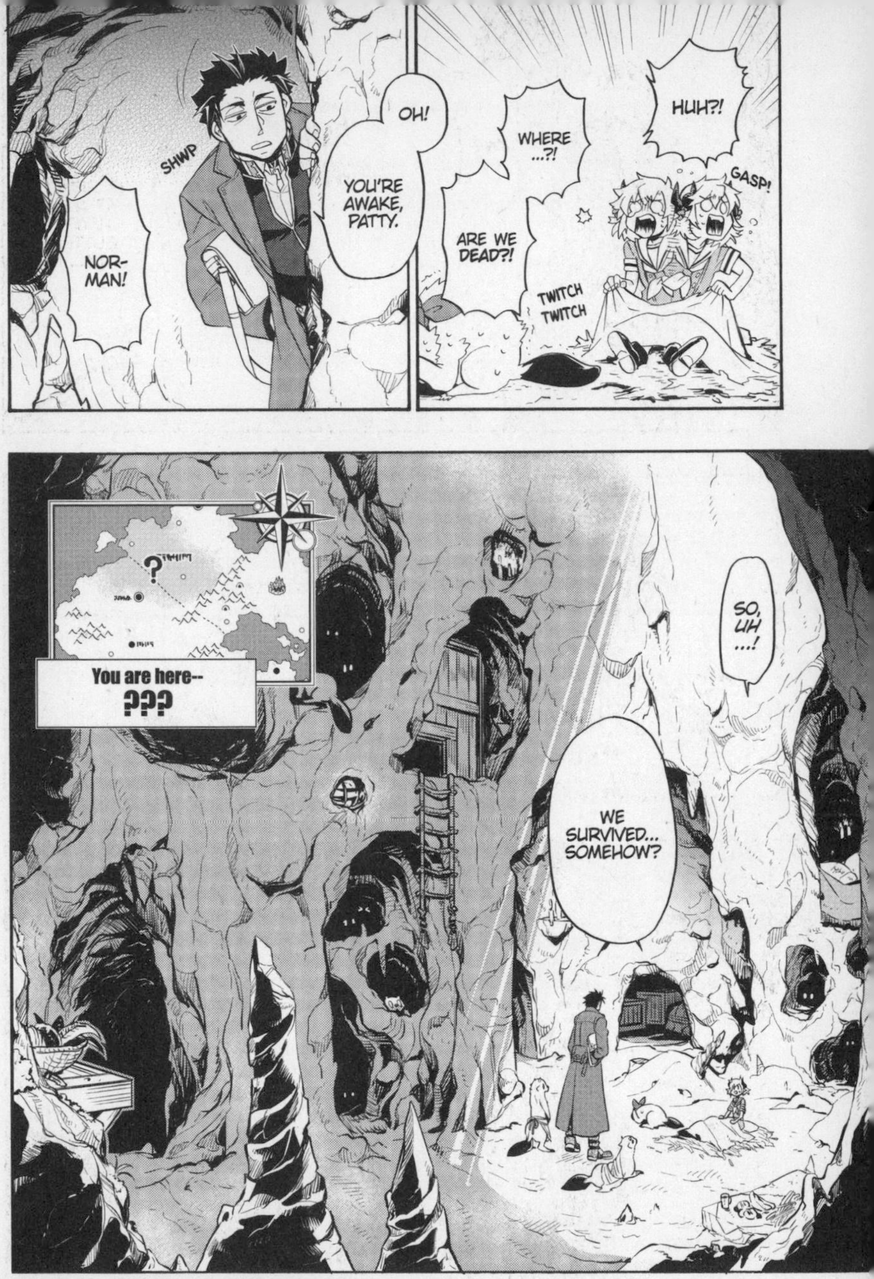
HUH?!
GASP!
WHERE ...?!
ARE WE DEAD?!
TWITCH TWITCH
OH!
SHWP
YOU'RE AWAKE, PATTY.
NOR-MAN!
SO, UH ...!
You are here-- ???
WE SURVIVED... SOMEHOW?

FILE 7: Moraka Desert

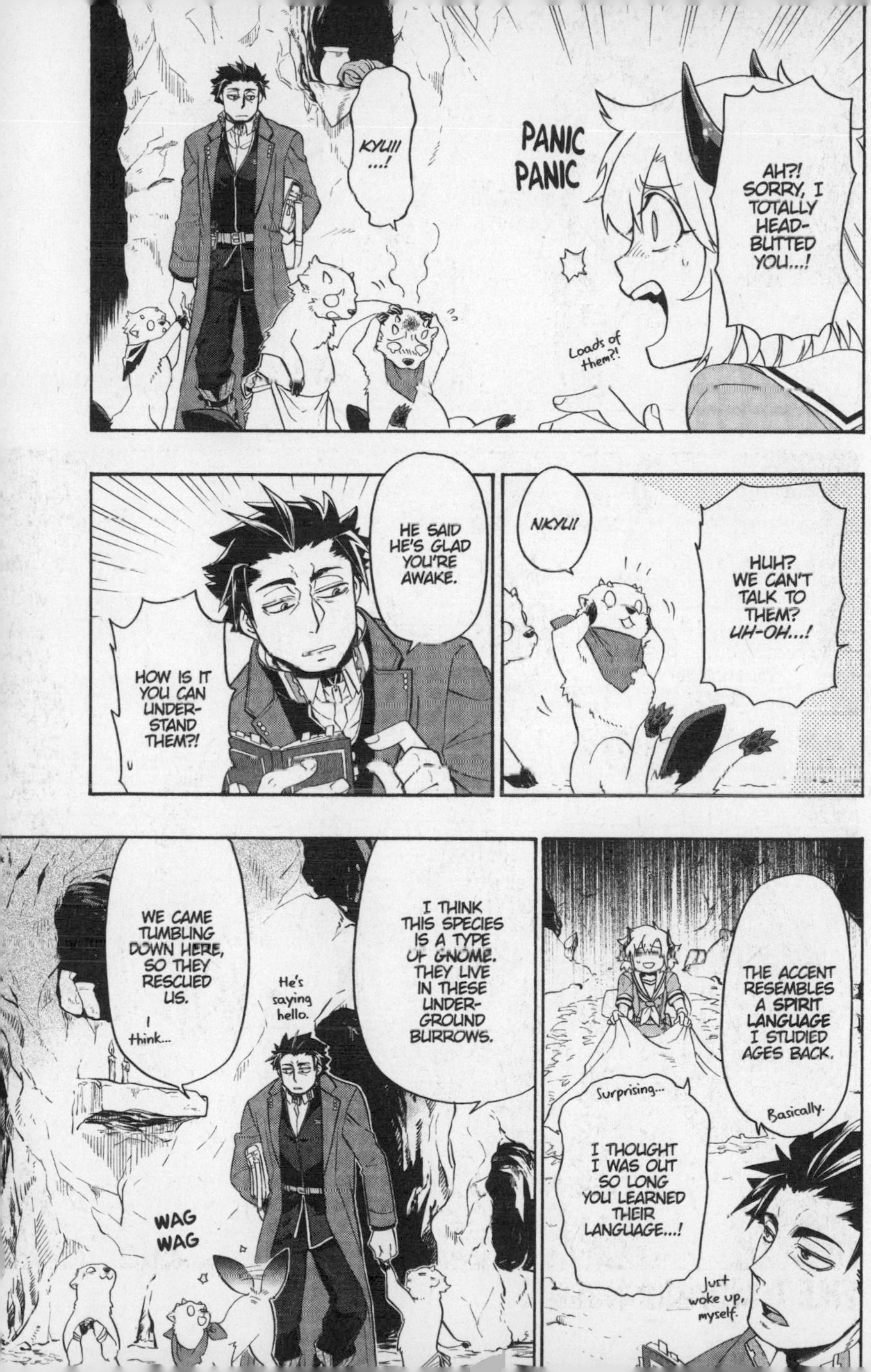
AH?! SORRY, I TOTALLY HEAD-BUTTED YOU...!
Loads of them?!
PANIC PANIC
KYUII ...!
HUH? WE CAN'T TALK TO THEM? UH-OH...!
NKYUI!
HE SAID HE'S GLAD YOU'RE AWAKE.
HOW IS IT YOU CAN UNDERSTAND THEM?!
THE ACCENT RESEMBLES A SPIRIT LANGUAGE I STUDIED AGES BACK.
Basically.
Surprising...
I THOUGHT I WAS OUT SO LONG YOU LEARNED THEIR LANGUAGE...!
Just woke up, myself.
I THINK THIS SPECIES IS A TYPE OF GNOME. THEY LIVE IN THESE UNDERGROUND BURROWS.
He's saying hello.
WE CAME TUMBLING DOWN HERE, SO THEY RESCUED US.
I think...
WAG WAG

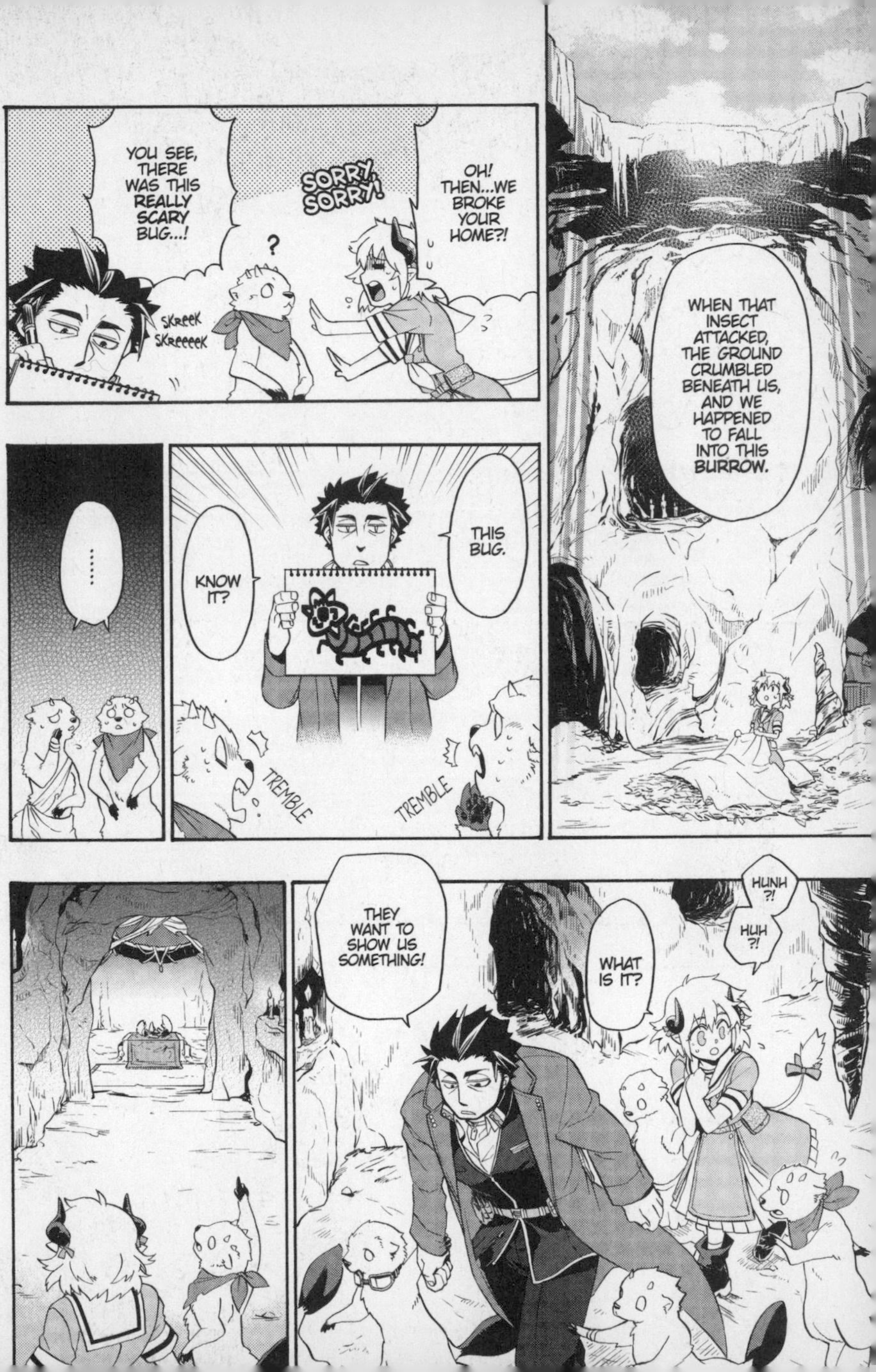
WHEN THAT INSECT ATTACKED, THE GROUND CRUMBLED BENEATH US, AND WE HAPPENED TO FALL INTO THIS BURROW.
OH! THEN...WE BROKE YOUR HOME?!
SORRY, SORRY!
?
YOU SEE, THERE WAS THIS REALLY SCARY BUG...!
SKREEK SKREEEEEK
THIS BUG.
KNOW IT?
TREMBLE
TREMBLE
......
HUNH ?!
HUH ?!
WHAT IS IT?
THEY WANT TO SHOW US SOMETHING!

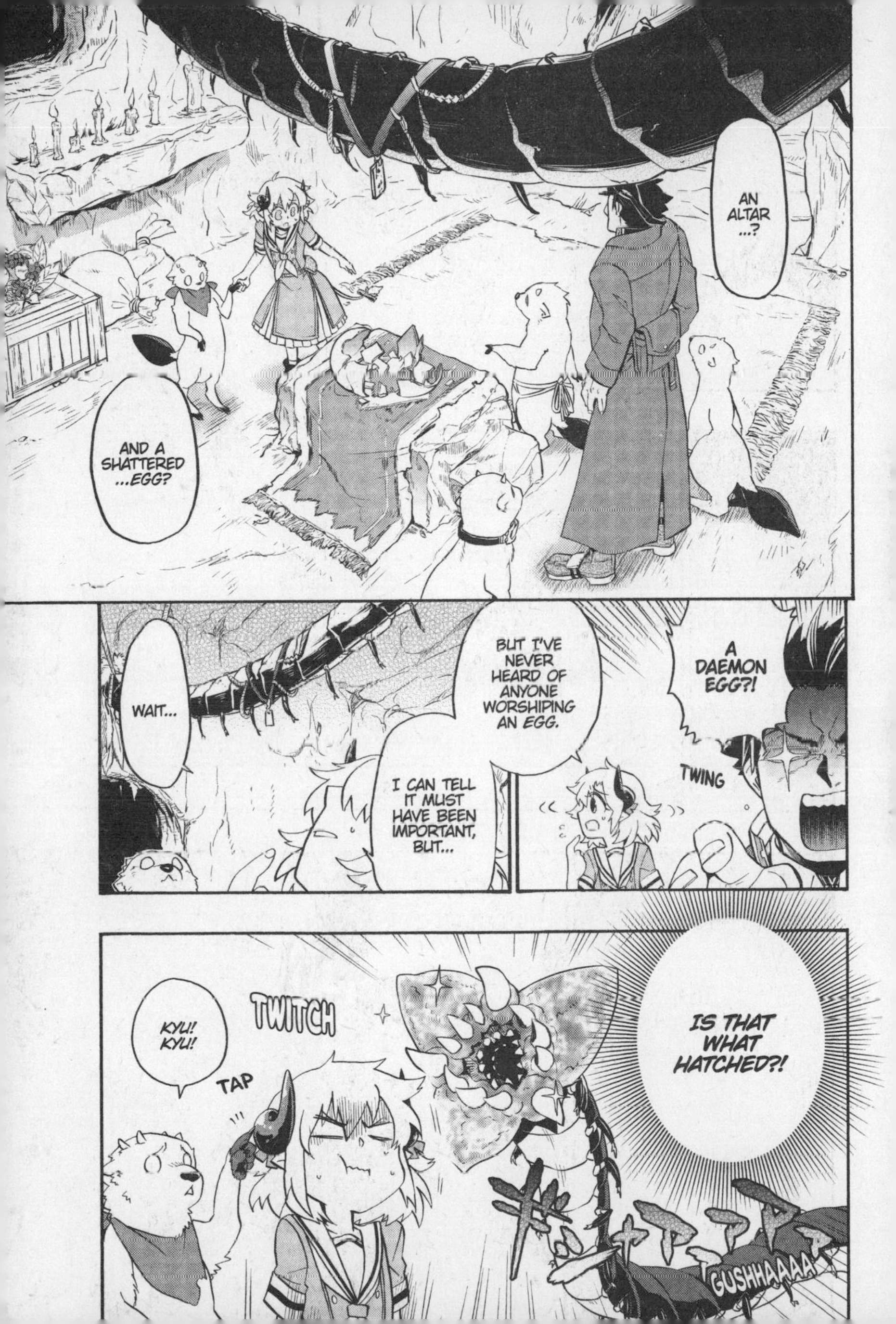
AN ALTAR ...?
AND A SHATTERED ...EGG?
A DAEMON EGG?!
TWING
I CAN TELL IT MUST HAVE BEEN IMPORTANT, BUT...
BUT I'VE NEVER HEARD OF ANYONE WORSHIPING AN EGG.
WAIT...
IS THAT WHAT HATCHED?!
GUSHHAAAA
TWITCH
KYU! KYU!
TAP

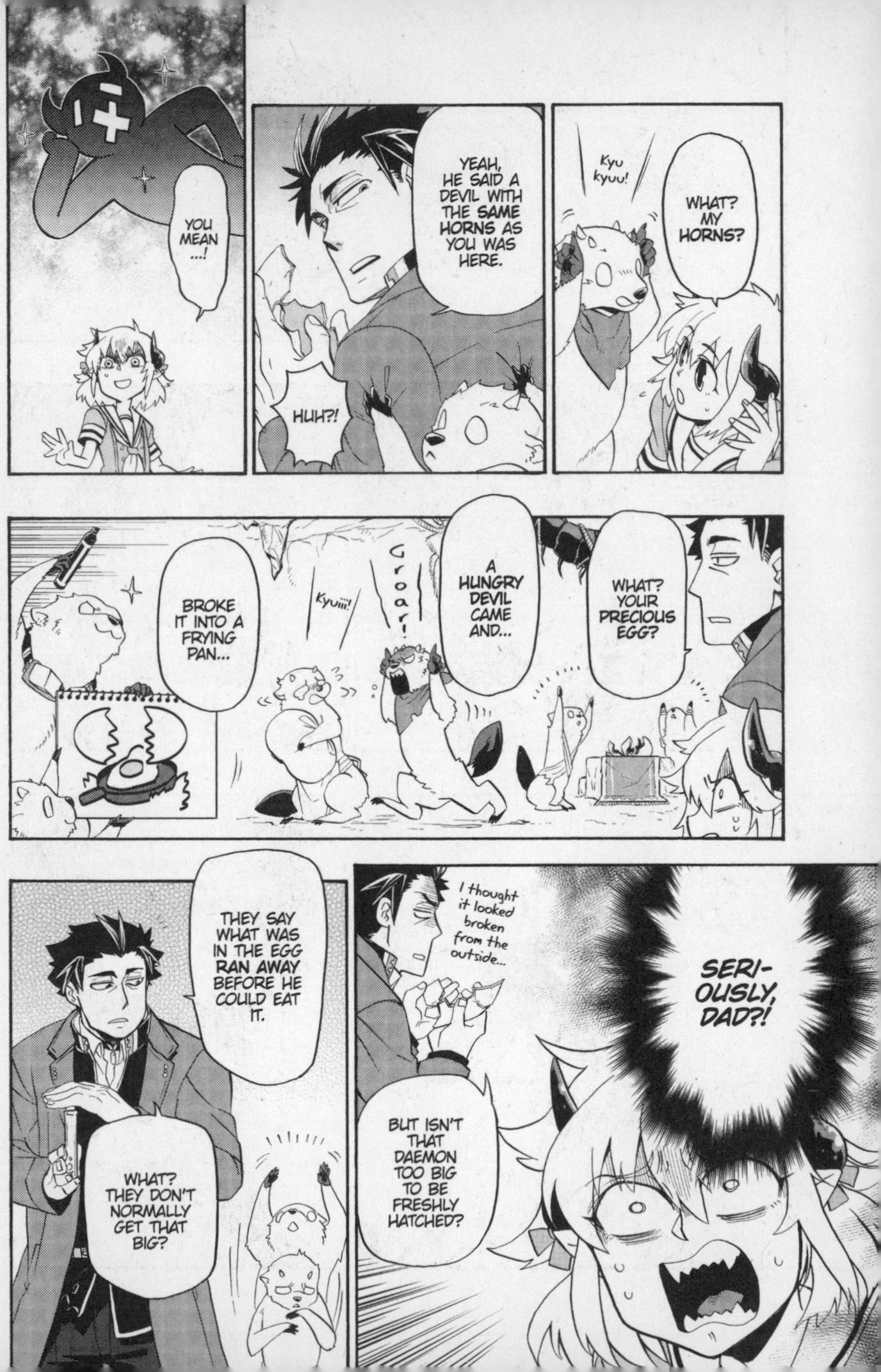
WHAT? MY HORNS?
Kyu kyuu!
YEAH, HE SAID A DEVIL WITH THE SAME HORNS AS YOU WAS HERE.
HUH?!
YOU MEAN ...!
WHAT? YOUR PRECIOUS EGG?
A HUNGRY DEVIL CAME AND...
Groar!
Kyuiii!
BROKE IT INTO A FRYING PAN...
SERI-OUSLY, DAD?!
I thought it looked broken from the outside...
BUT ISN'T THAT DAEMON TOO BIG TO BE FRESHLY HATCHED?
THEY SAY WHAT WAS IN THE EGG RAN AWAY BEFORE HE COULD EAT IT.
WHAT? THEY DON'T NORMALLY GET THAT BIG?

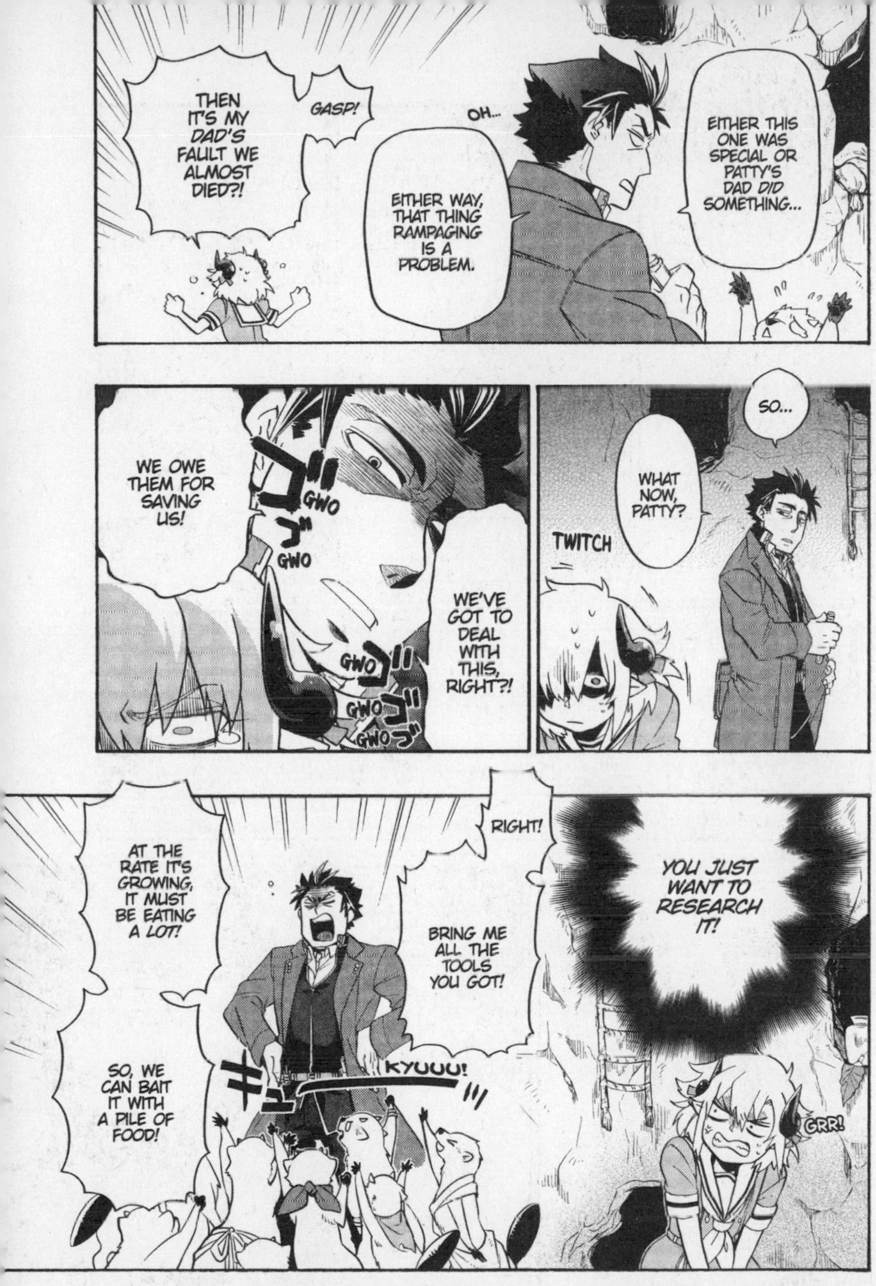
EITHER THIS ONE WAS SPECIAL OR PATTY'S DAD DID SOMETHING...
OH...
EITHER WAY, THAT THING RAMPAGING IS A PROBLEM.
GASP!
THEN IT'S MY DAD'S FAULT WE ALMOST DIED?!
SO...
WHAT NOW, PATTY?
TWITCH
WE'VE GOT TO DEAL WITH THIS, RIGHT?!
WE OWE THEM FOR SAVING US!
GWO GWO
GWO GWO GWO
YOU JUST WANT TO RESEARCH IT!
GRR!
RIGHT!
BRING ME ALL THE TOOLS YOU GOT!
AT THE RATE IT'S GROWING, IT MUST BE EATING A LOT!
SO, WE CAN BAIT IT WITH A PILE OF FOOD!
KYUUU!

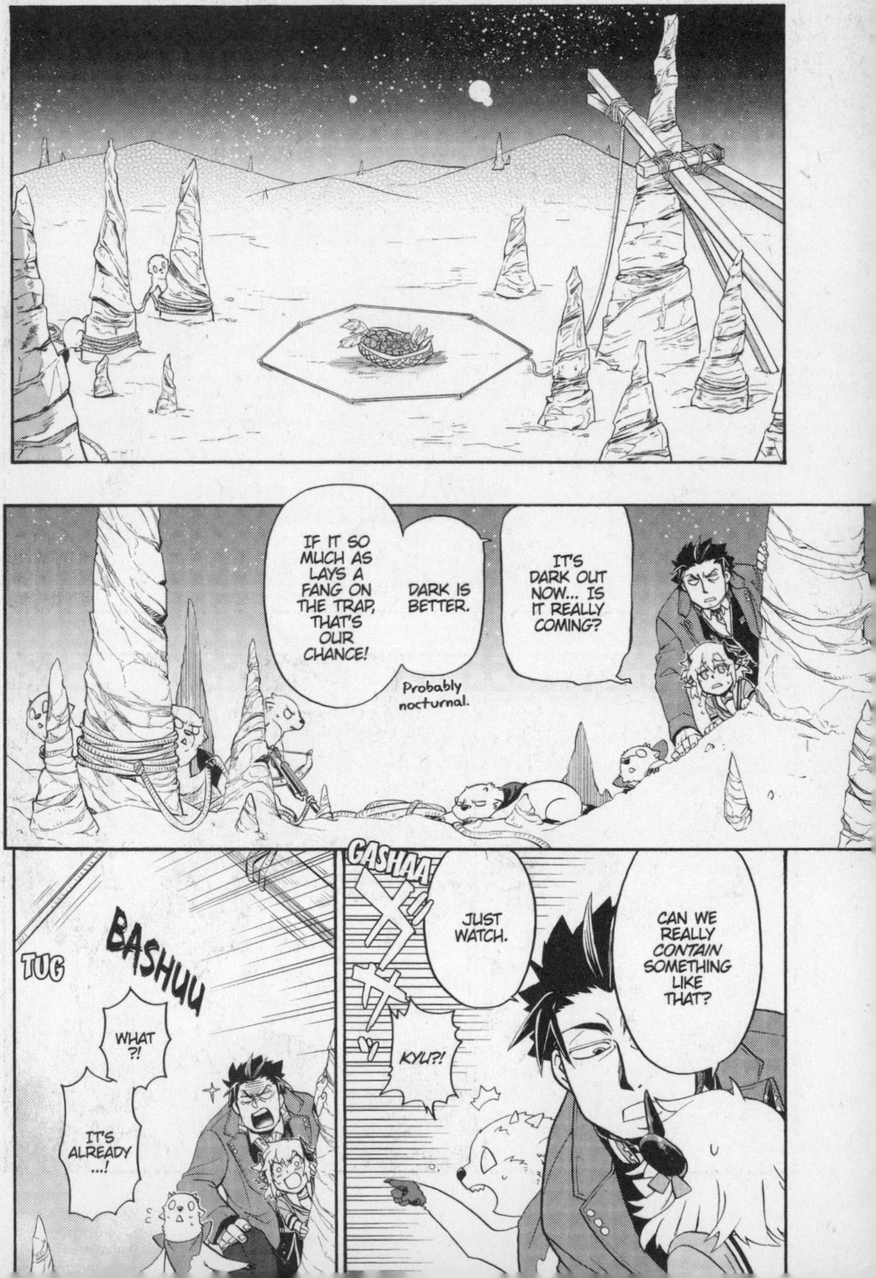
IT'S DARK OUT NOW... IS IT REALLY COMING?
DARK IS BETTER.
IF IT SO MUCH AS LAYS A FANG ON THE TRAP, THAT'S OUR CHANCE!
Probably nocturnal.
CAN WE REALLY CONTAIN SOMETHING LIKE THAT?
JUST WATCH.
GASHAA
KYU?!
BASHUU
TUG
WHAT?!
IT'S ALREADY...!

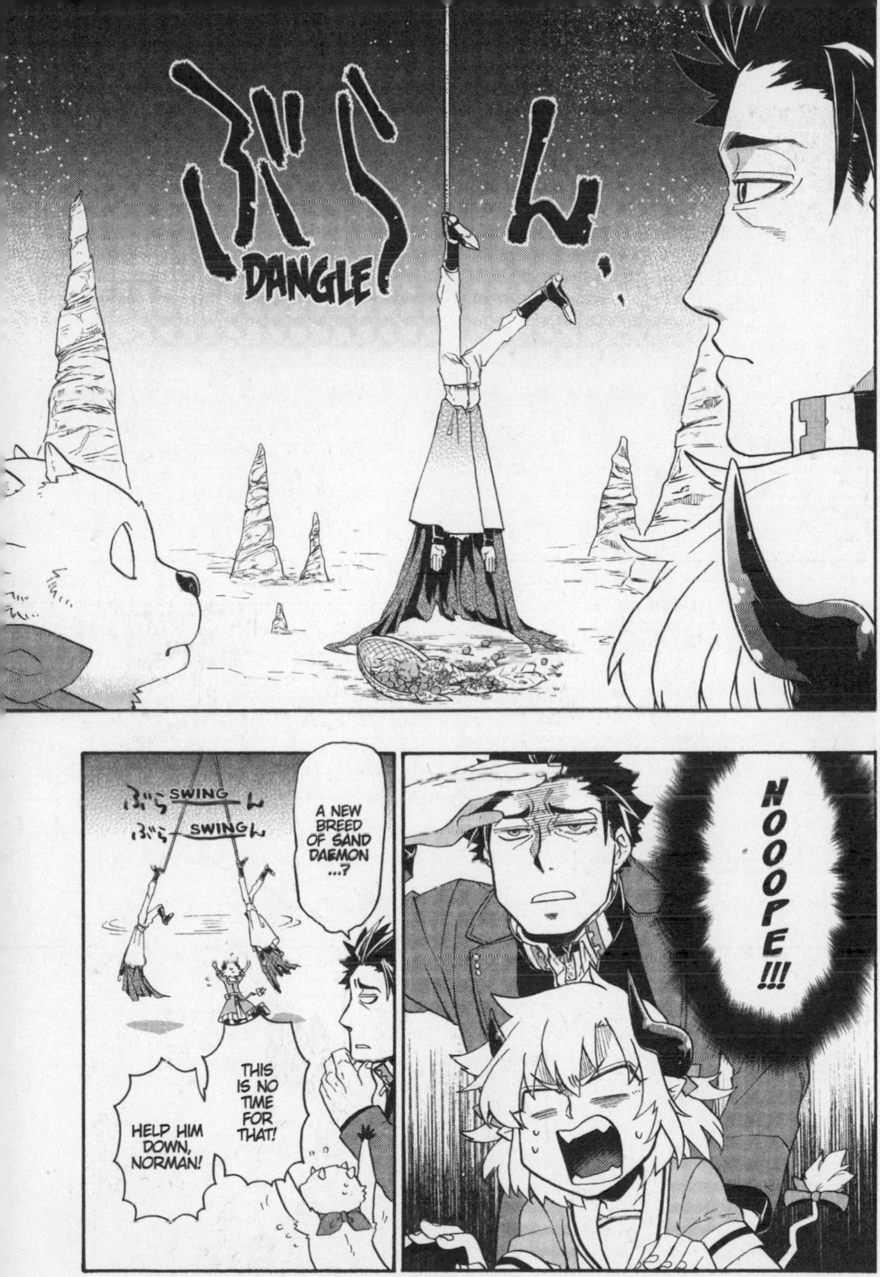
ぶらん
DANGLE
NOOOPE!!!
ぶら SWING ん
ぶら SWING ん
A NEW BREED OF SAND DAEMON ...?
THIS IS NO TIME FOR THAT!
HELP HIM DOWN, NORMAN!

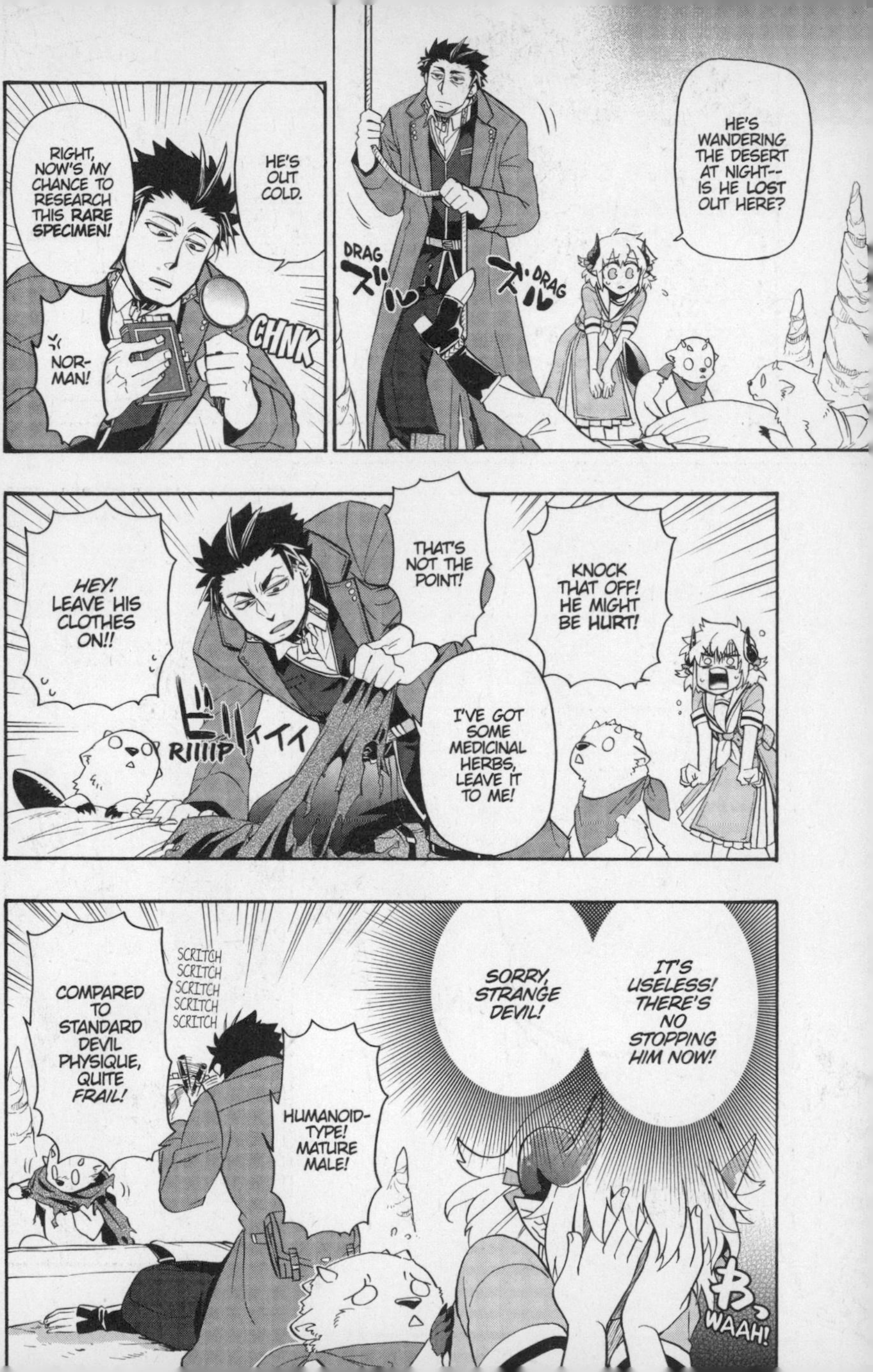
HE'S WANDERING THE DESERT AT NIGHT-- IS HE LOST OUT HERE?
DRAG
DRAG
HE'S OUT COLD.
RIGHT, NOW'S MY CHANCE TO RESEARCH THIS RARE SPECIMEN!
CHNK
NOR-MAN!
KNOCK THAT OFF! HE MIGHT BE HURT!
THAT'S NOT THE POINT!
I'VE GOT SOME MEDICINAL HERBS, LEAVE IT TO ME!
HEY! LEAVE HIS CLOTHES ON!!
RIIIIP
IT'S USELESS! THERE'S NO STOPPING HIM NOW!
SORRY, STRANGE DEVIL!
SCRITCH SCRITCH SCRITCH SCRITCH SCRITCH
HUMANOID-TYPE! MATURE MALE!
COMPARED TO STANDARD DEVIL PHYSIQUE, QUITE FRAIL!
WAAH!

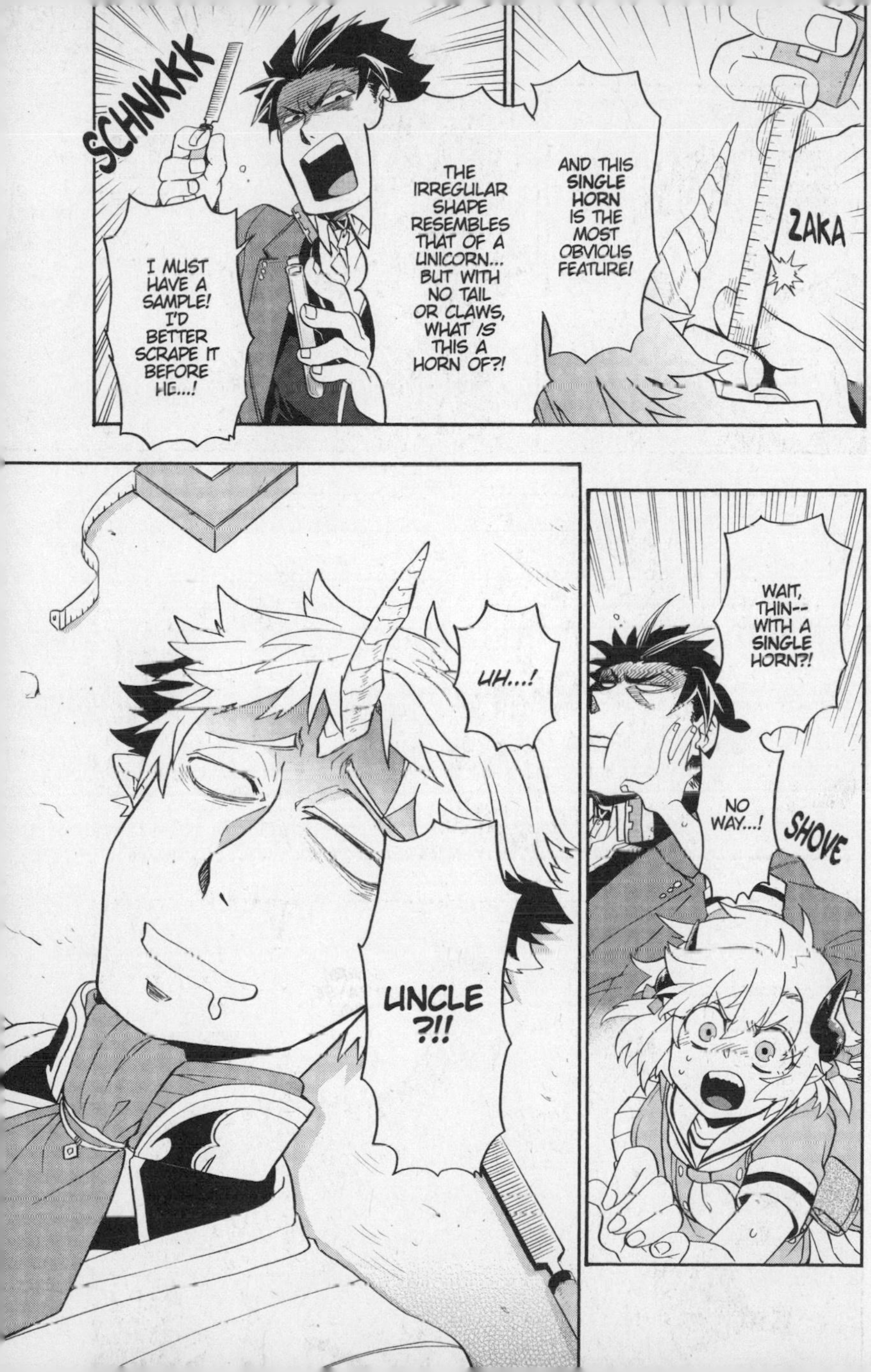
AND THIS SINGLE HORN IS THE MOST OBVIOUS FEATURE!
ZAKA
THE IRREGULAR SHAPE RESEMBLES THAT OF A UNICORN... BUT WITH NO TAIL OR CLAWS, WHAT *IS* THIS A HORN OF?!
SCHNKKK
I MUST HAVE A SAMPLE! I'D BETTER SCRAPE IT BEFORE HE...!
WAIT, THIN-- WITH A SINGLE HORN?!
NO WAY...!
SHOVE
UH...!
UNCLE ?!!

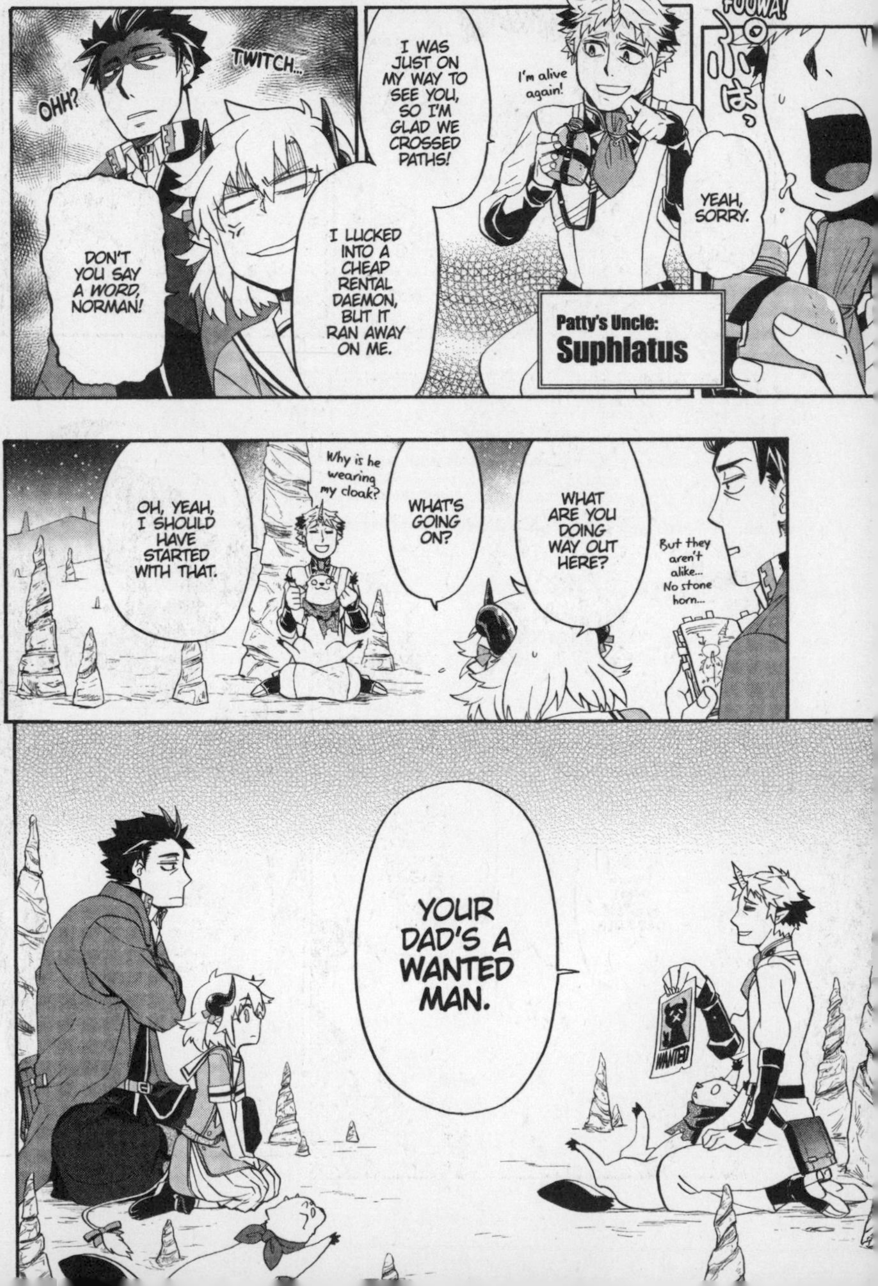
FUUWA!
ぷはっ
YEAH, SORRY.
I'm alive again!
I WAS JUST ON MY WAY TO SEE YOU, SO I'M GLAD WE CROSSED PATHS!
I LUCKED INTO A CHEAP RENTAL DAEMON, BUT IT RAN AWAY ON ME.
Patty's Uncle: Suphlatus
TWITCH...
OHH?
DON'T YOU SAY A WORD, NORMAN!
But they aren't alike... No stone horn...
WHAT ARE YOU DOING WAY OUT HERE?
WHAT'S GOING ON?
Why is he wearing my cloak?
OH, YEAH, I SHOULD HAVE STARTED WITH THAT.
YOUR DAD'S A WANTED MAN.
WANTED

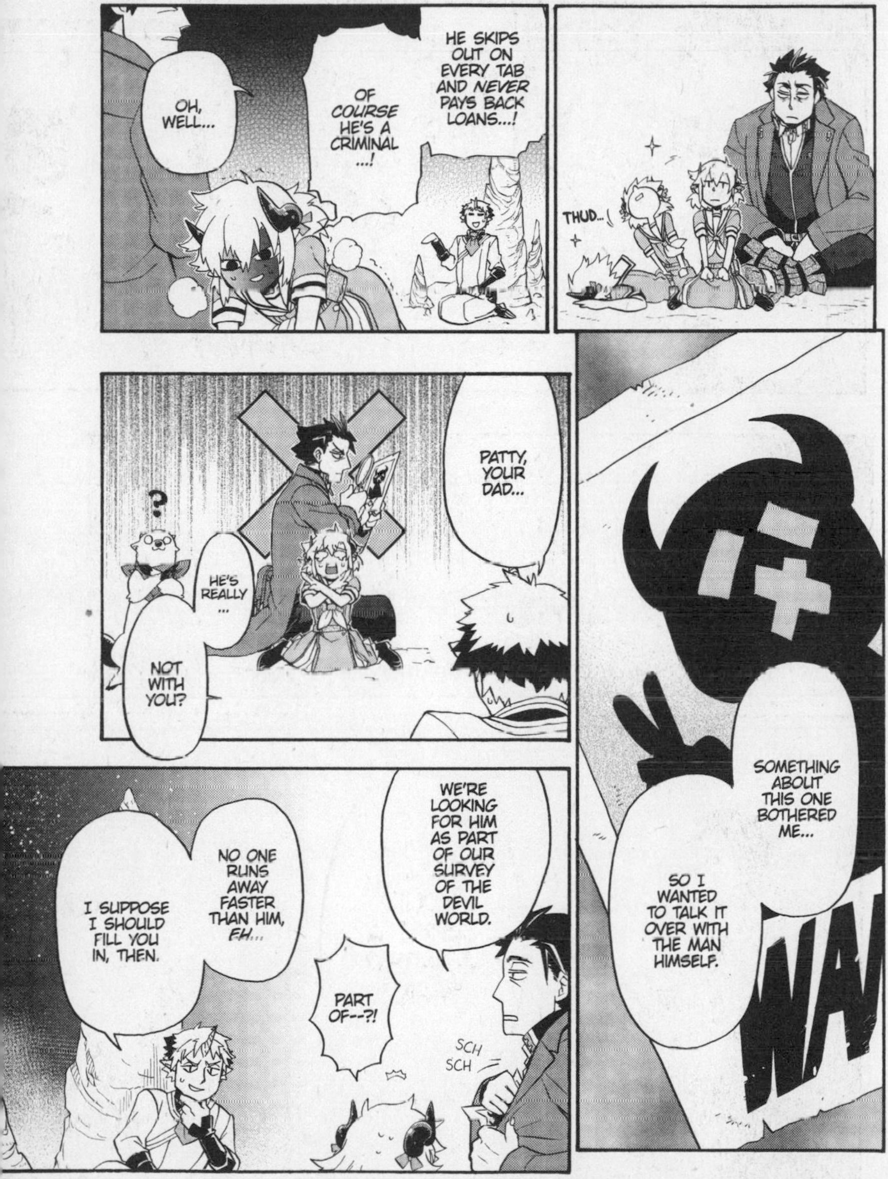
THUD...
HE SKIPS OUT ON EVERY TAB AND *NEVER* PAYS BACK LOANS...!
OF COURSE HE'S A CRIMINAL ...!
OH, WELL...
SOMETHING ABOUT THIS ONE BOTHERED ME...
SO I WANTED TO TALK IT OVER WITH THE MAN HIMSELF.
WA
PATTY, YOUR DAD...
HE'S REALLY ...
NOT WITH YOU?
?
WE'RE LOOKING FOR HIM AS PART OF OUR SURVEY OF THE DEVIL WORLD.
PART OF--?!
SCH SCH
NO ONE RUNS AWAY FASTER THAN HIM, *EH*...
I SUPPOSE I SHOULD FILL YOU IN, THEN.

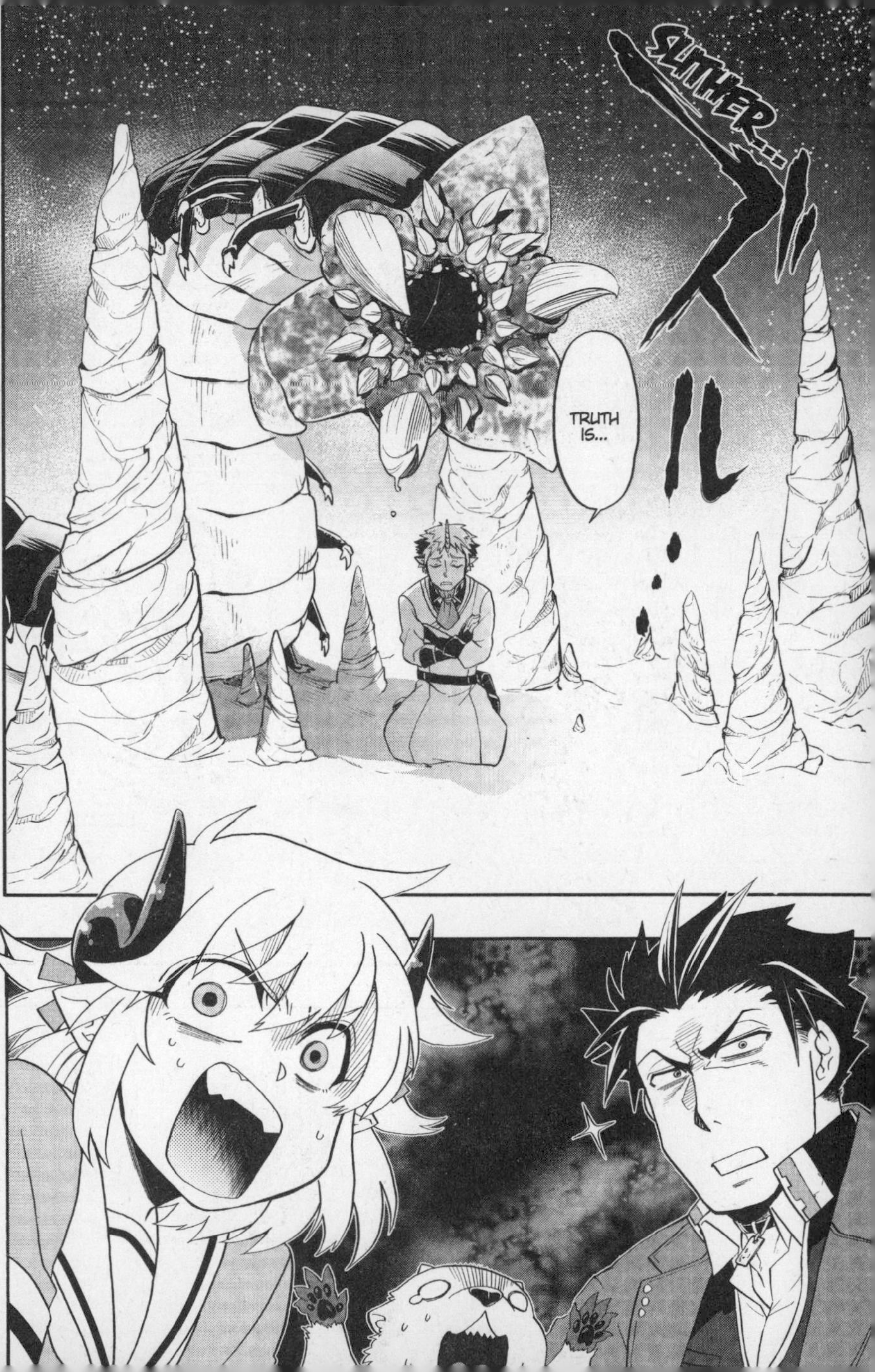
SLITHER...
TRUTH IS...

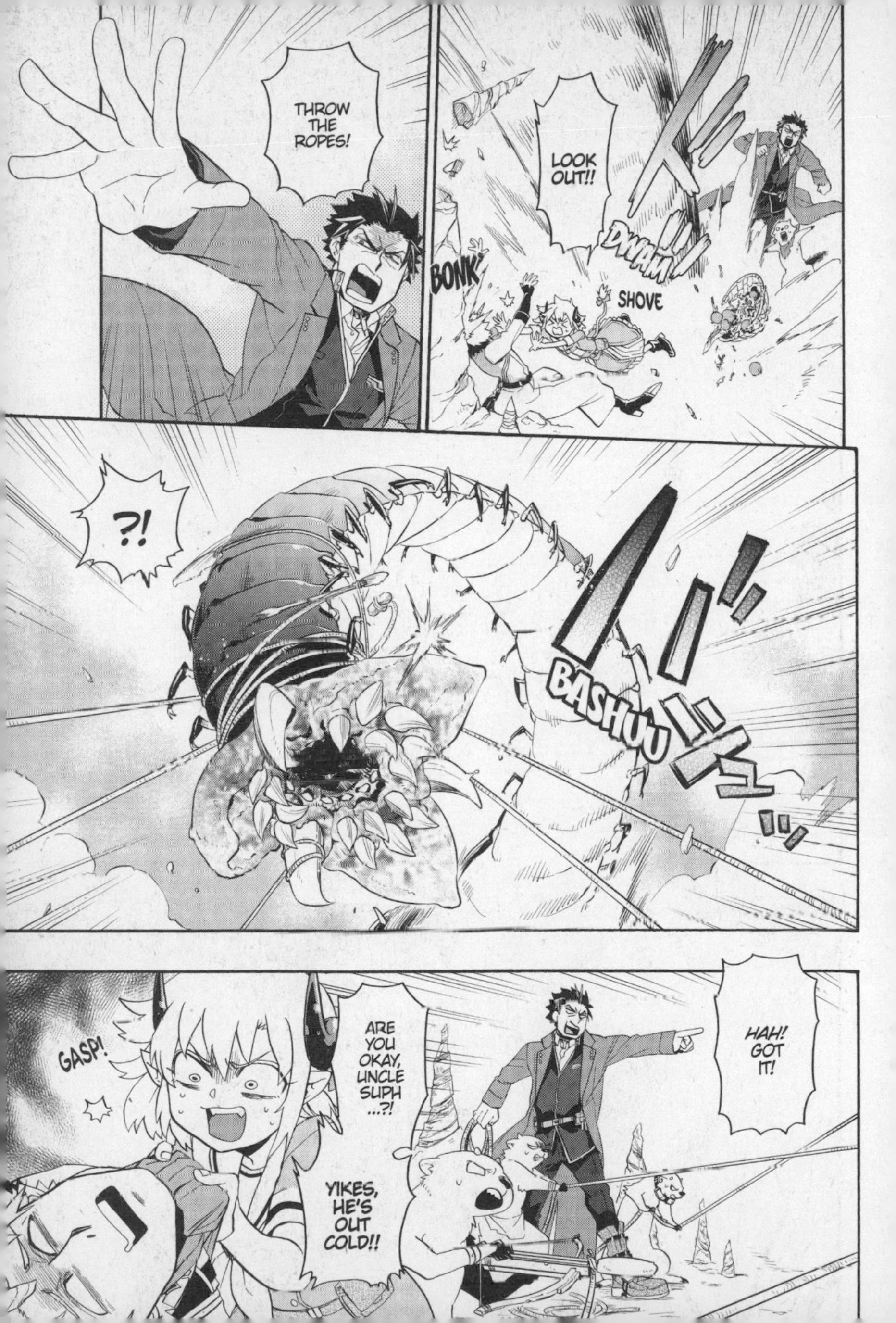
LOOK OUT!!
DWAM
SHOVE
BONK
THROW THE ROPES!
?!
BASHUU
HAH! GOT IT!
ARE YOU OKAY, UNCLE SUPH ...?!
YIKES, HE'S OUT COLD!!
GASP!

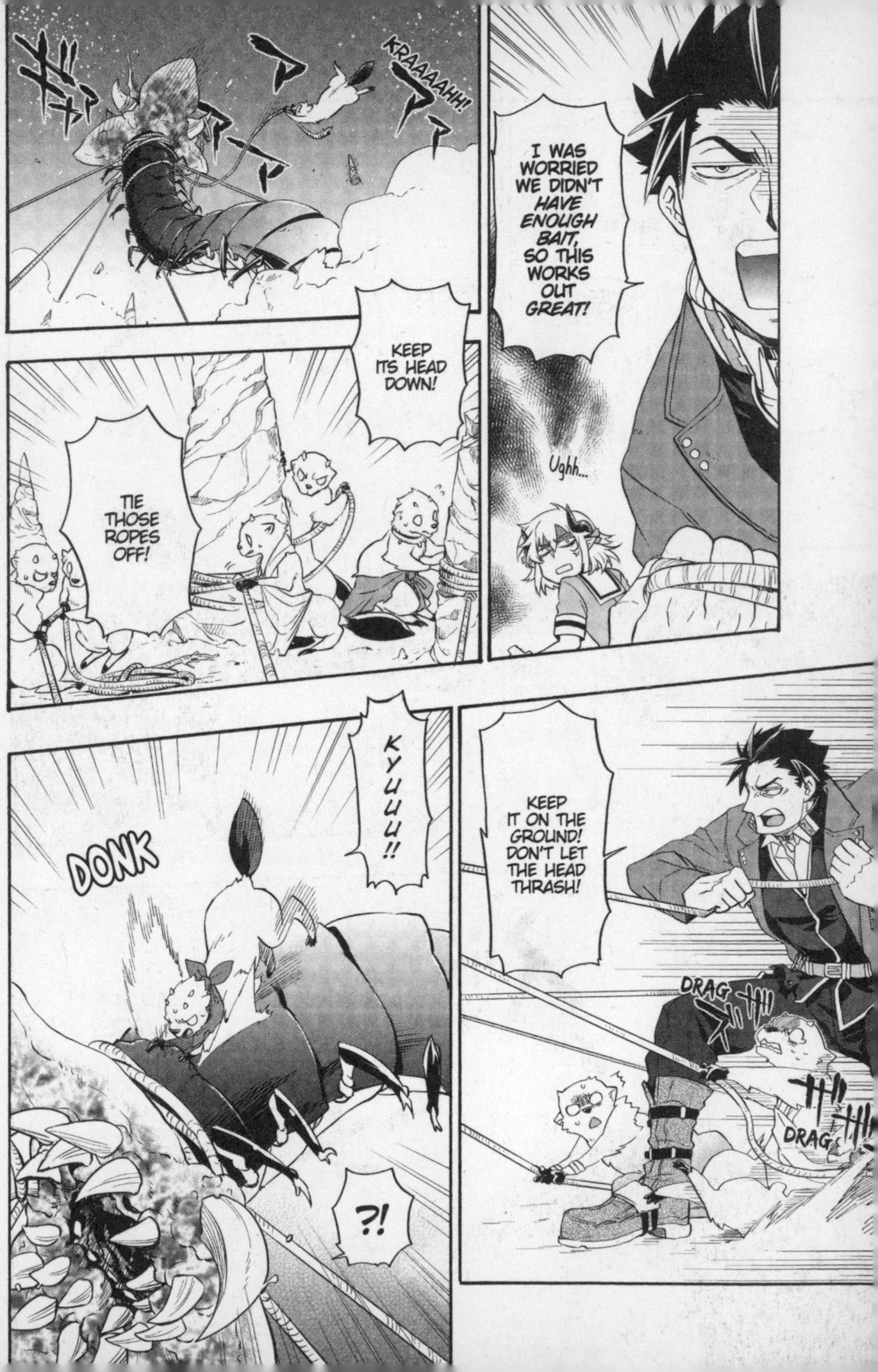
I WAS WORRIED WE DIDN'T HAVE ENOUGH BAIT, SO THIS WORKS OUT GREAT!
Ughh...
KRAAAAAHH!
KEEP ITS HEAD DOWN!
TIE THOSE ROPES OFF!
KEEP IT ON THE GROUND! DON'T LET THE HEAD THRASH!
DRAG
DRAG
KYUUUU!!
DONK
?!

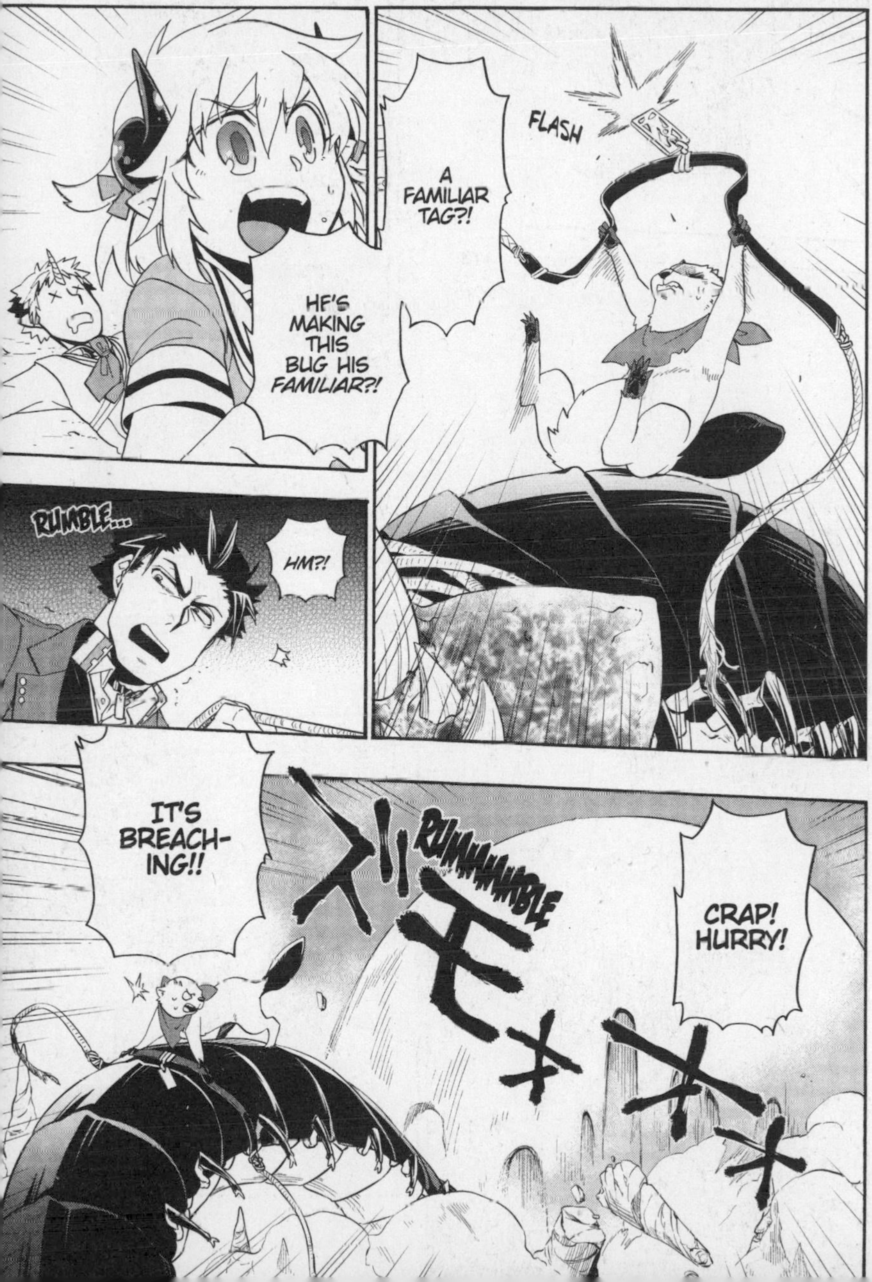
FLASH
A FAMILIAR TAG?!
HE'S MAKING THIS BUG HIS FAMILIAR?!
RUMBLE...
HM?!
CRAP! HURRY!
RUMMMMMBLE
IT'S BREACHING!!

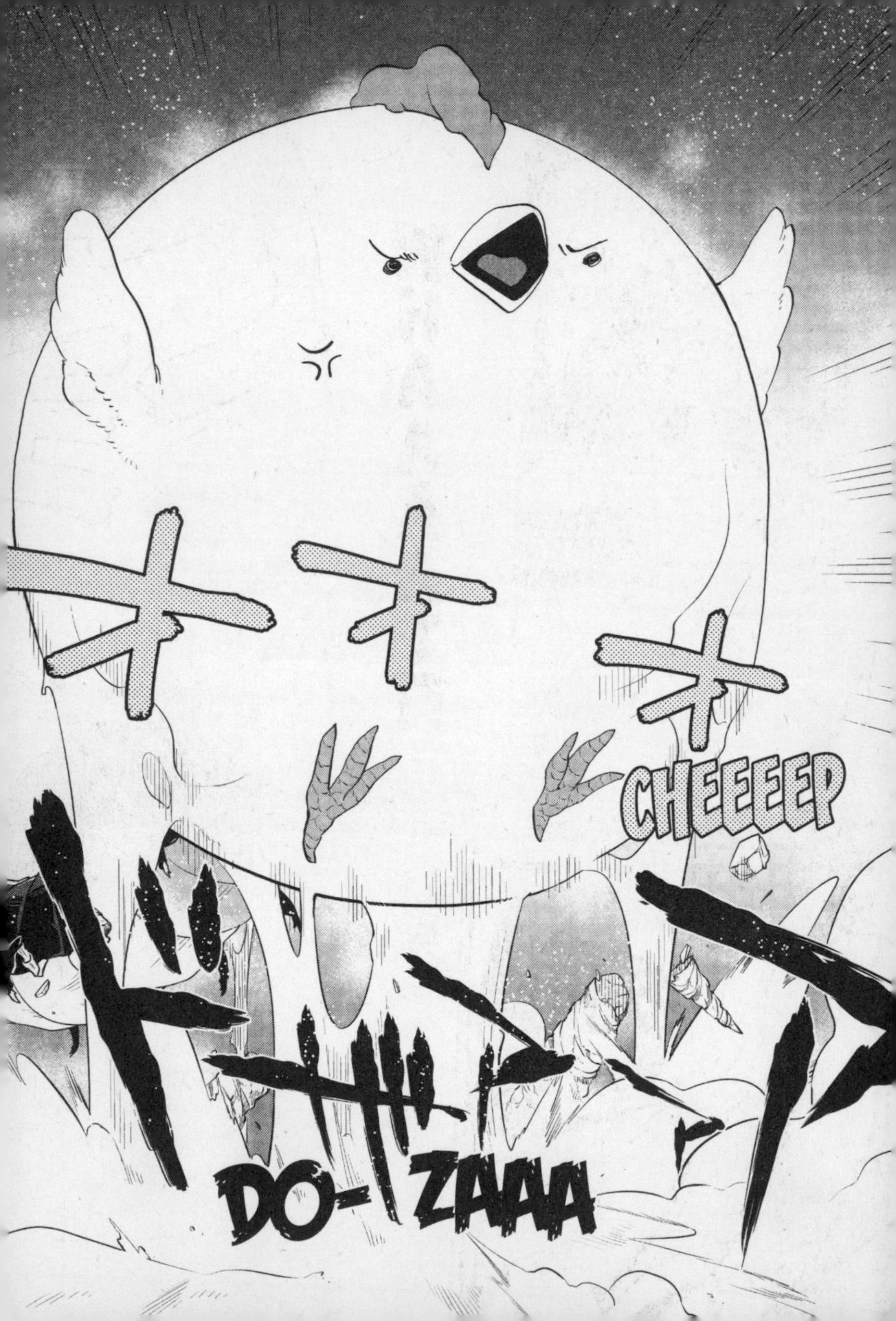
CHEEEEP
DO-ZAAA

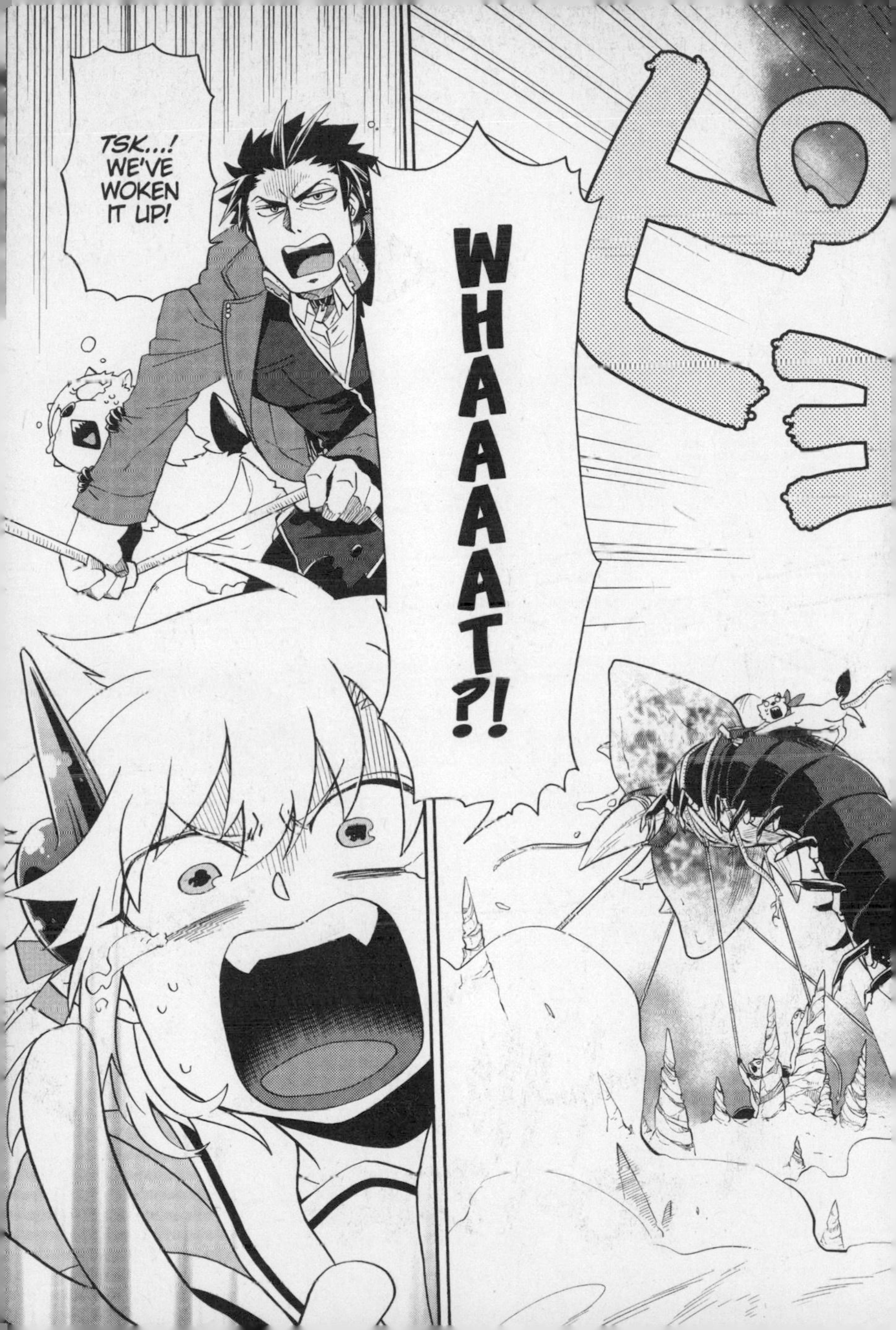
TSK...! WE'VE WOKEN IT UP!
WHAAAAT?!

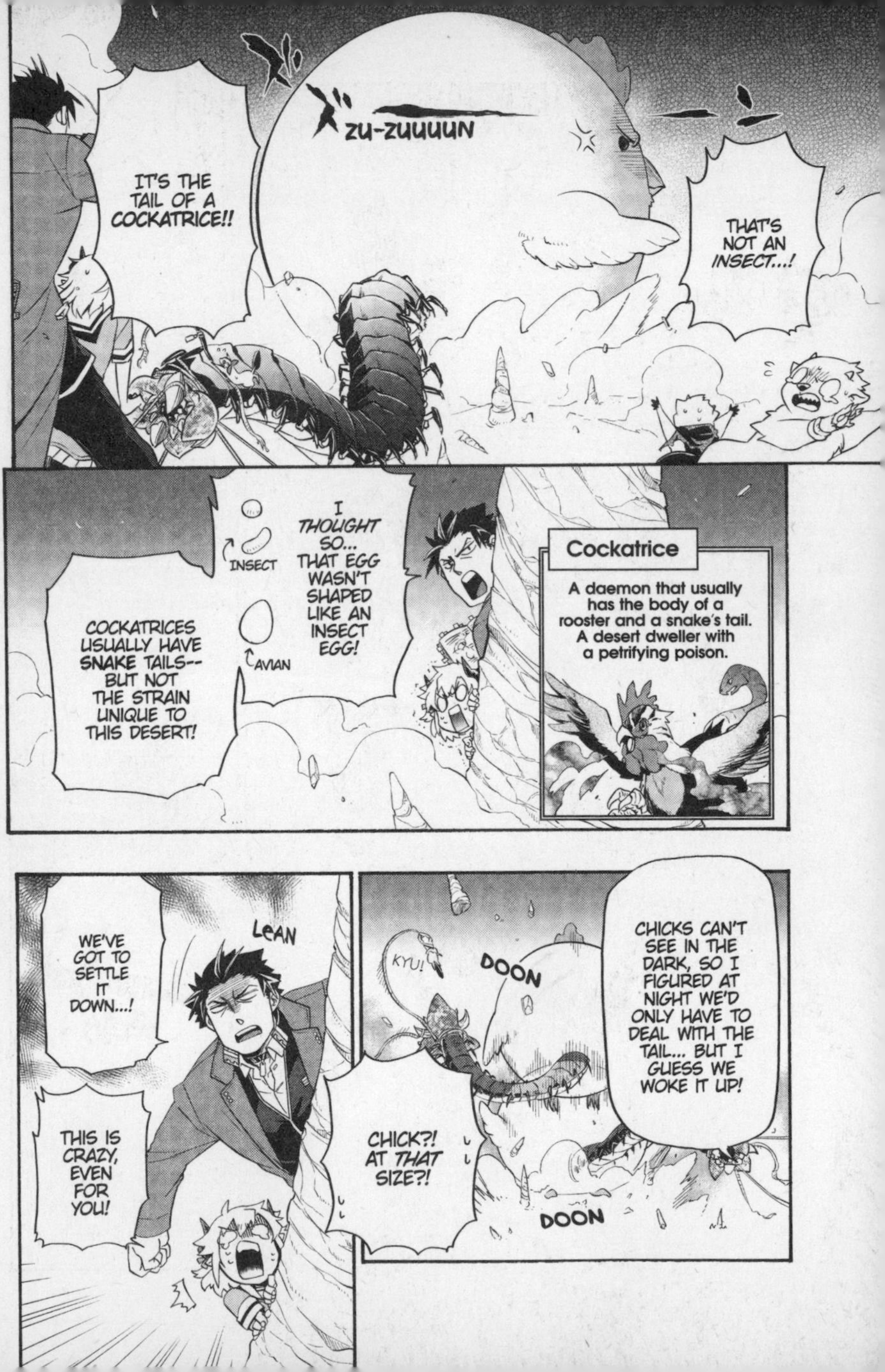
THAT'S NOT AN INSECT...!
zu-zuuuun
IT'S THE TAIL OF A COCKATRICE!!
Cockatrice
A daemon that usually has the body of a rooster and a snake's tail. A desert dweller with a petrifying poison.
I THOUGHT SO... THAT EGG WASN'T SHAPED LIKE AN INSECT EGG!
INSECT
AVIAN
COCKATRICES USUALLY HAVE SNAKE TAILS-- BUT NOT THE STRAIN UNIQUE TO THIS DESERT!
CHICKS CAN'T SEE IN THE DARK, SO I FIGURED AT NIGHT WE'D ONLY HAVE TO DEAL WITH THE TAIL... BUT I GUESS WE WOKE IT UP!
DOON
KYU!
CHICK?! AT THAT SIZE?!
DOON
Lean
WE'VE GOT TO SETTLE IT DOWN...!
THIS IS CRAZY, EVEN FOR YOU!

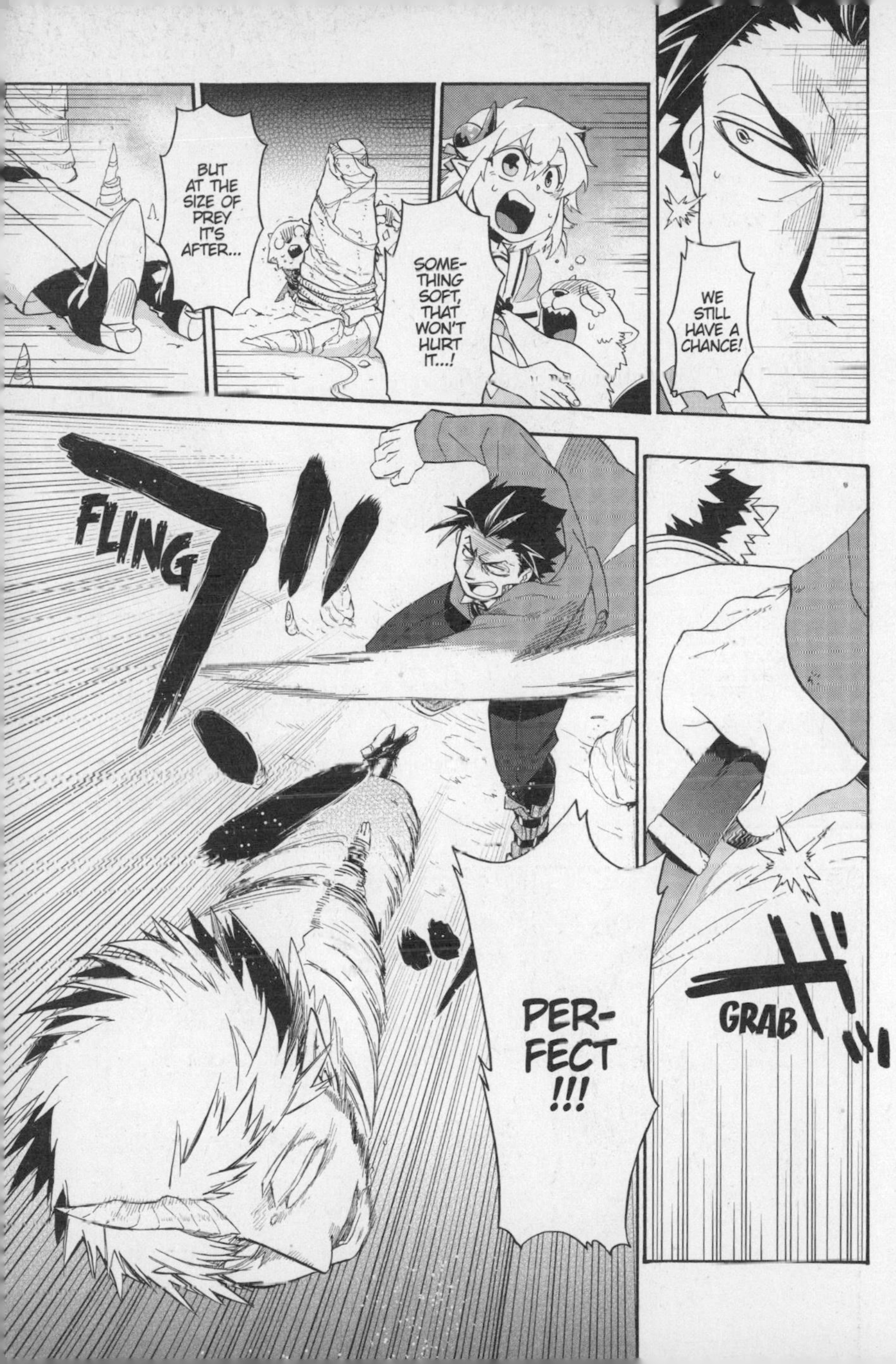
WE STILL HAVE A CHANCE!
SOME-THING SOFT, THAT WON'T HURT IT...!
BUT AT THE SIZE OF PREY IT'S AFTER...
GRAB
PER-FECT!!!
FLING

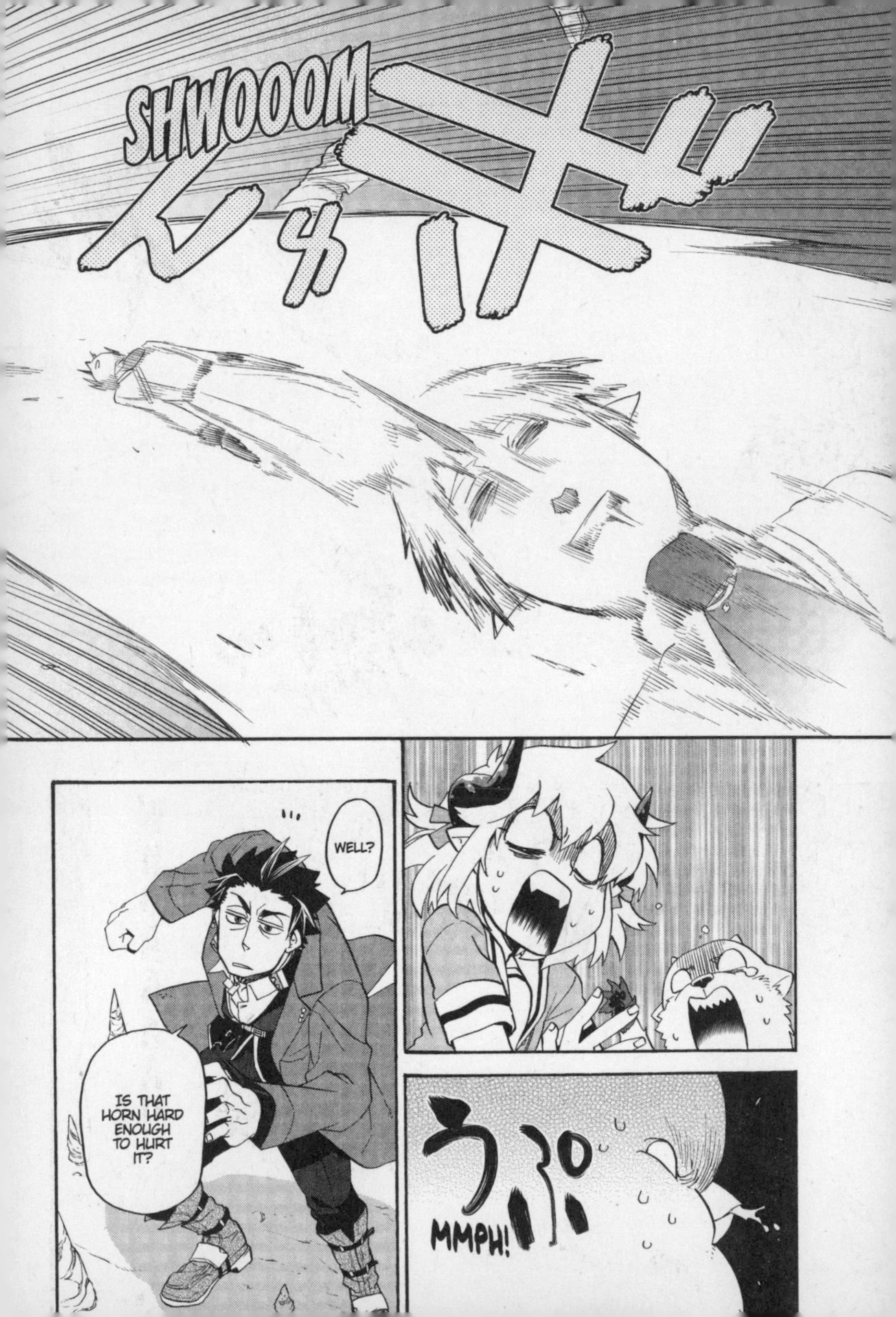
SHWOOOM
うぷ
MMPH!
WELL?
IS THAT HORN HARD ENOUGH TO HURT IT?

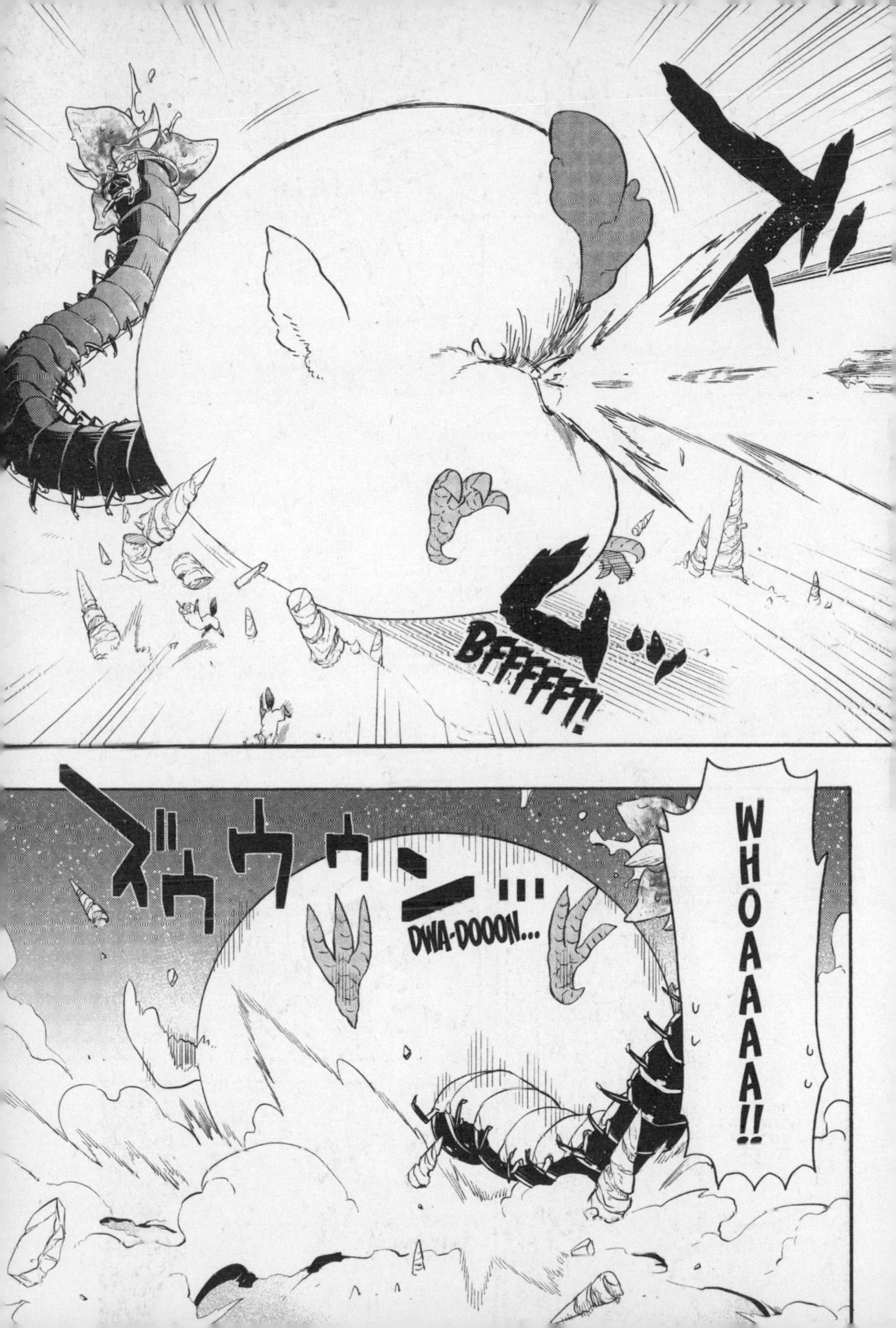
ズ
ム…
BFFFFFFT!
WHOAAAAA!!
ズウウウン…
DWA-DOOON...

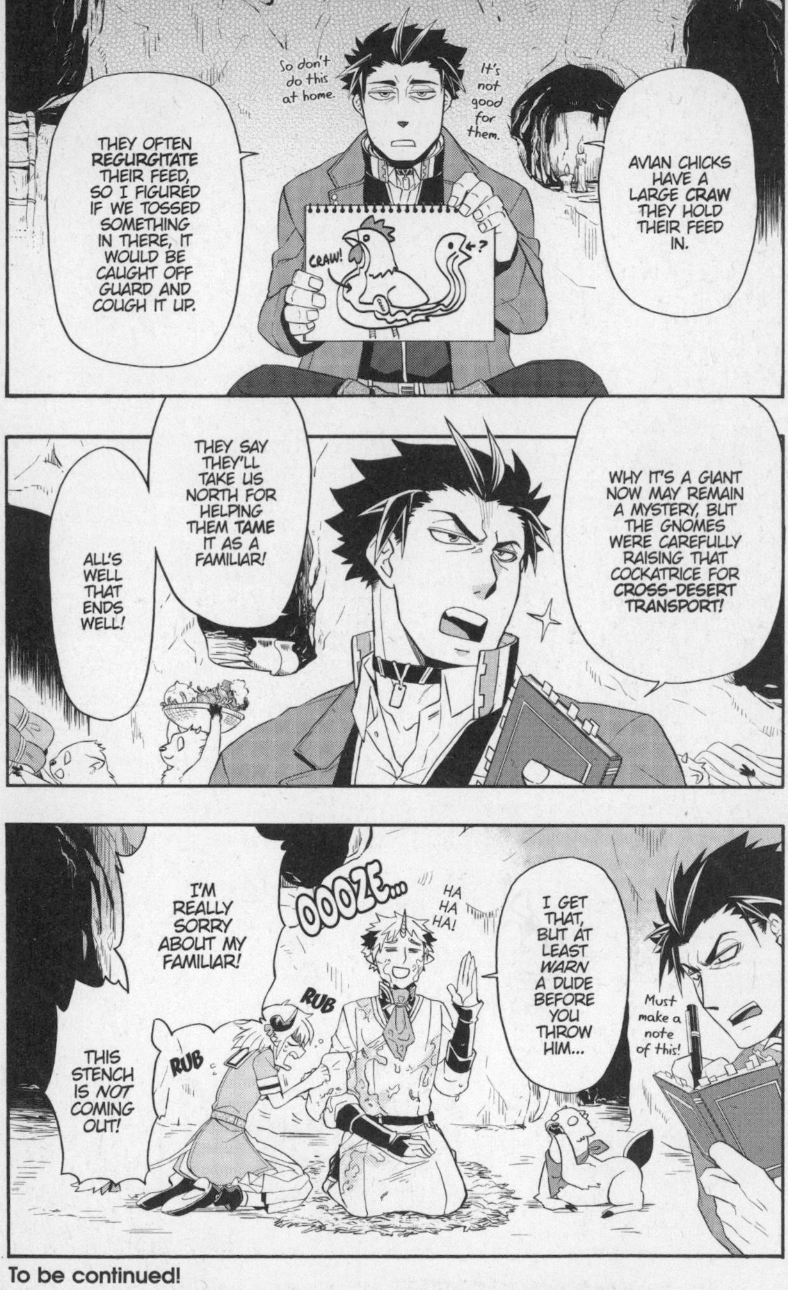
AVIAN CHICKS HAVE A LARGE CRAW THEY HOLD THEIR FEED IN.
It's not good for them.
So don't do this at home.
CRAW!
THEY OFTEN REGURGITATE THEIR FEED, SO I FIGURED IF WE TOSSED SOMETHING IN THERE, IT WOULD BE CAUGHT OFF GUARD AND COUGH IT UP.
WHY IT'S A GIANT NOW MAY REMAIN A MYSTERY, BUT THE GNOMES WERE CAREFULLY RAISING THAT COCKATRICE FOR CROSS-DESERT TRANSPORT!
THEY SAY THEY'LL TAKE US NORTH FOR HELPING THEM TAME IT AS A FAMILIAR!
ALL'S WELL THAT ENDS WELL!
Must make a note of this!
I GET THAT, BUT AT LEAST WARN A DUDE BEFORE YOU THROW HIM...
HA HA HA!
OOOZE...
I'M REALLY SORRY ABOUT MY FAMILIAR!
RUB
RUB
THIS STENCH IS NOT COMING OUT!

To be continued!

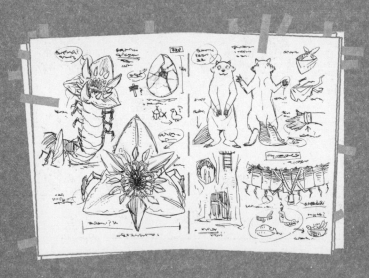

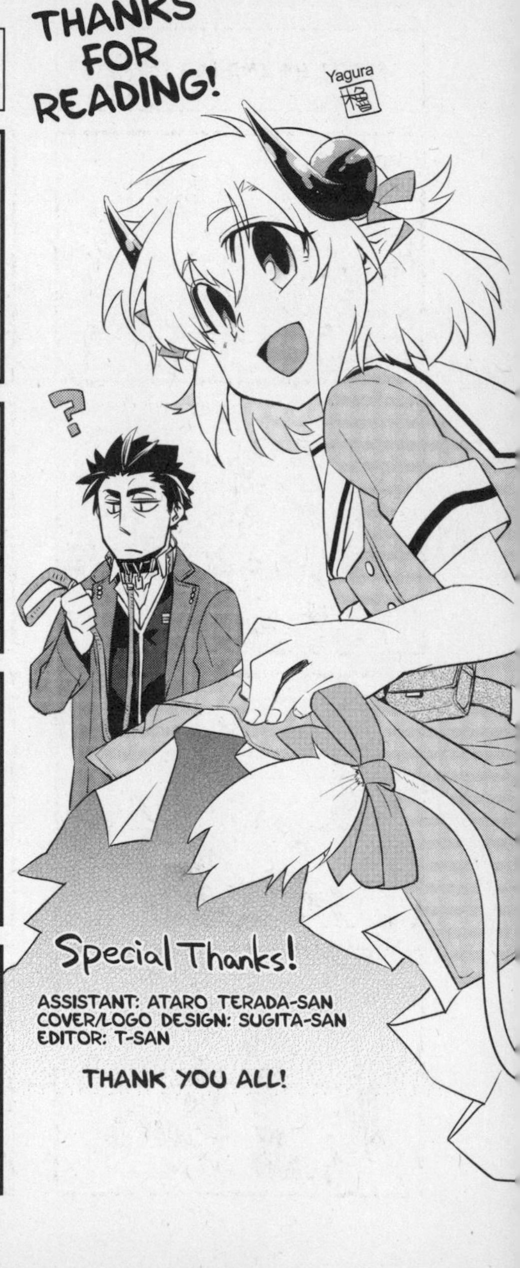
THANKS FOR READING!
Yagura
?
Special Thanks!
ASSISTANT: ATARO TERADA-SAN
COVER/LOGO DESIGN: SUGITA-SAN
EDITOR: T-SAN
THANK YOU ALL!

PATTY AND NORMAN'S NOTEBOOK

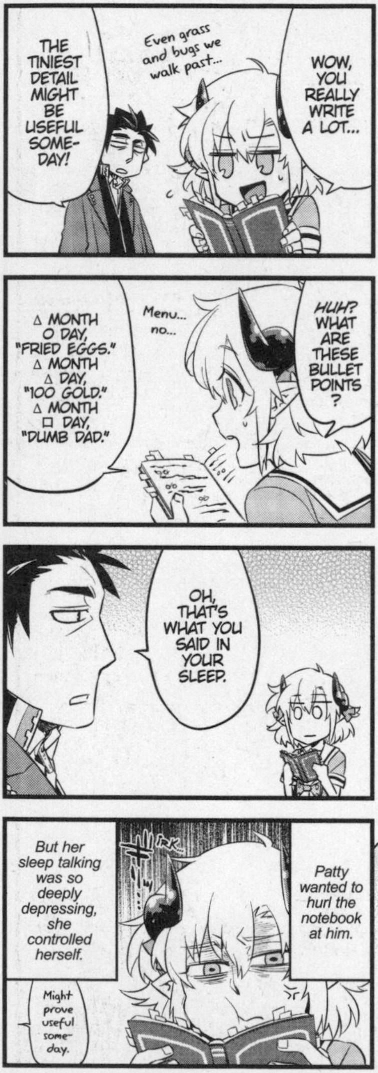
WOW, YOU REALLY WRITE A LOT...
Even grass and bugs we walk past...
THE TINIEST DETAIL MIGHT BE USEFUL SOME-DAY!
HUH? WHAT ARE THESE BULLET POINTS?
Menu... no...
△ MONTH ○ DAY, "FRIED EGGS." △ MONTH △ DAY, "100 GOLD." △ MONTH □ DAY, "DUMB DAD."
OH, THAT'S WHAT YOU SAID IN YOUR SLEEP.
Patty wanted to hurl the notebook at him.
IRK
But her sleep talking was so deeply depressing, she controlled herself.
Might prove useful some-day.

LITTLE KA AND MR. BO ①

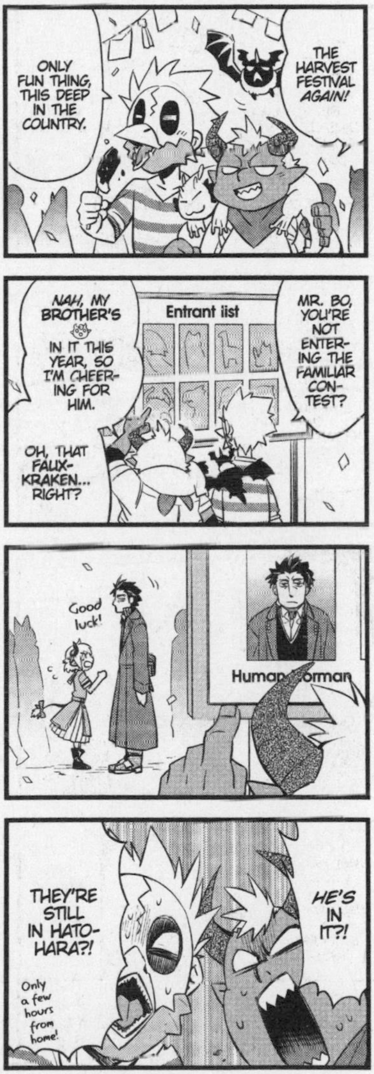

THE HARVEST FESTIVAL AGAIN!
ONLY FUN THING, THIS DEEP IN THE COUNTRY.
MR. BO, YOU'RE NOT ENTERING THE FAMILIAR CONTEST?
Entrant iist
NAH, MY BROTHER'S IN IT THIS YEAR, SO I'M CHEERING FOR HIM.
OH, THAT FAUX-KRAKEN... RIGHT?
Human
Good luck!
HE'S IN IT?!
THEY'RE STILL IN HATO-HARA?!
Only a few hours from home!

LITTLE KA AND MR. BO ②

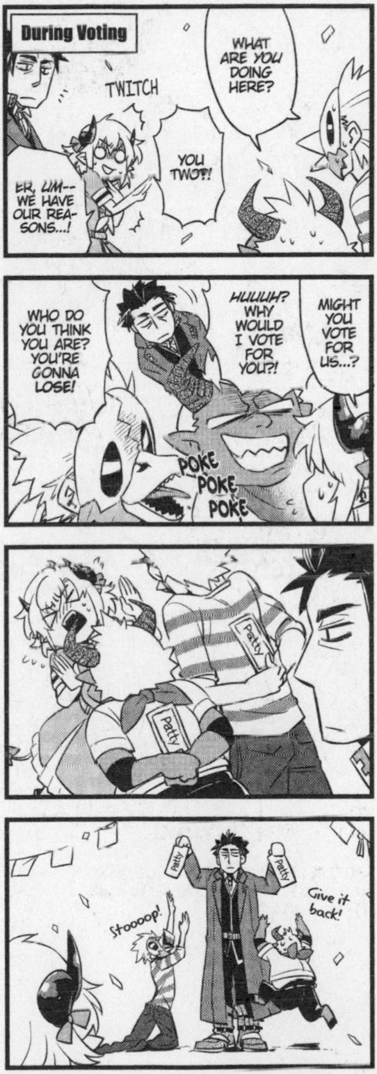

During Voting
WHAT ARE YOU DOING HERE?
YOU TWO?!
TWITCH
ER, UM-- WE HAVE OUR REASONS...!
MIGHT YOU VOTE FOR US...?
HUUUH? WHY WOULD I VOTE FOR YOU?!
WHO DO YOU THINK YOU ARE? YOU'RE GONNA LOSE!
POKE POKE POKE
Patty
Patty
Give it back!
Patty
Patty
Stoooop!

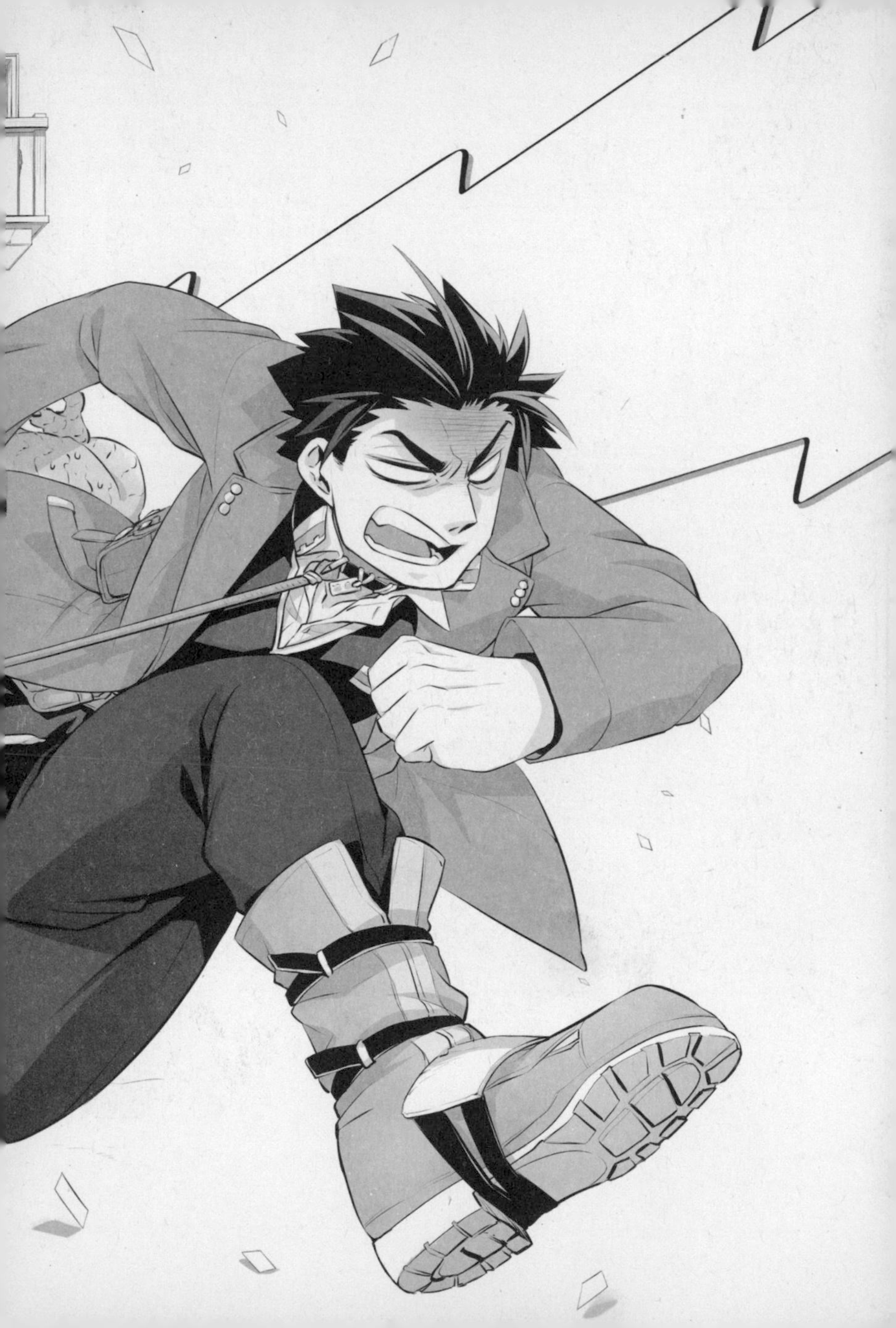

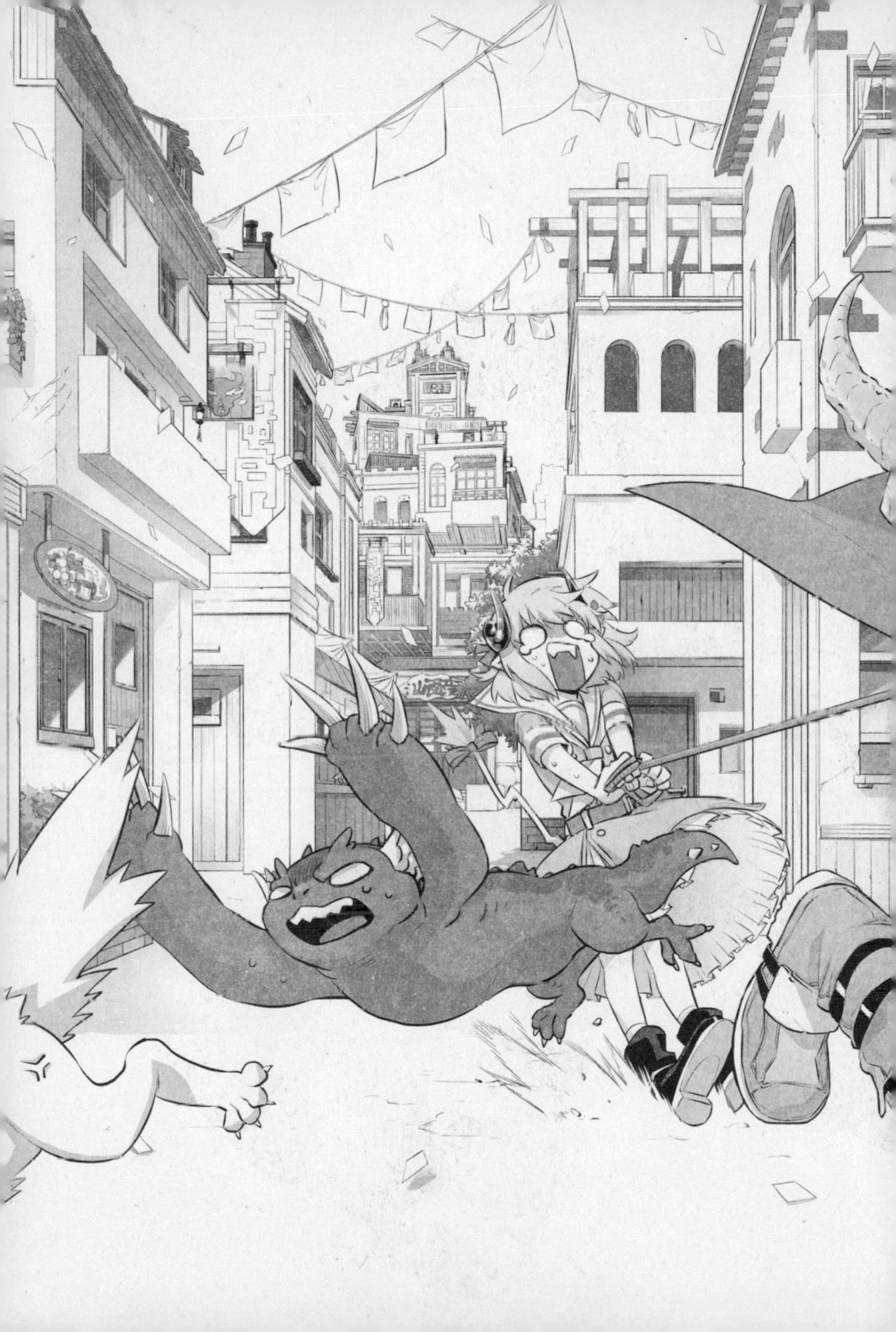

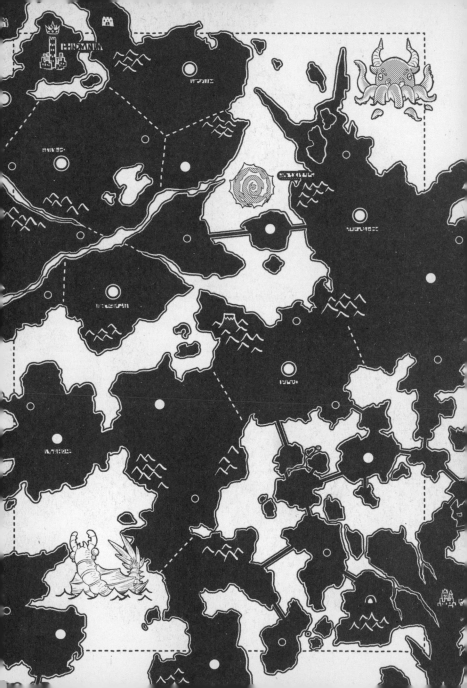

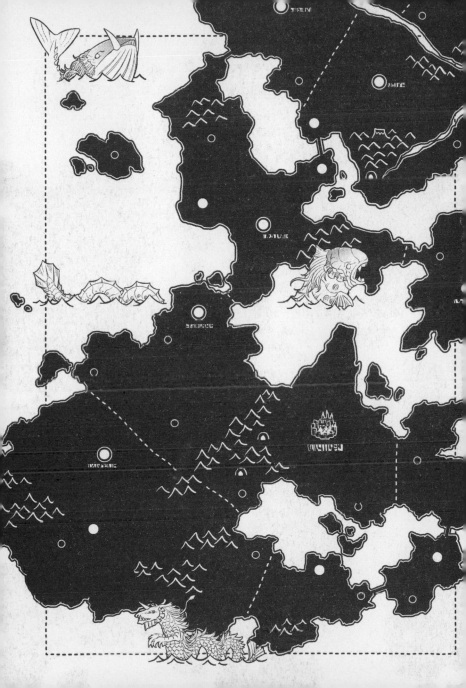

Sorry For My Familiar

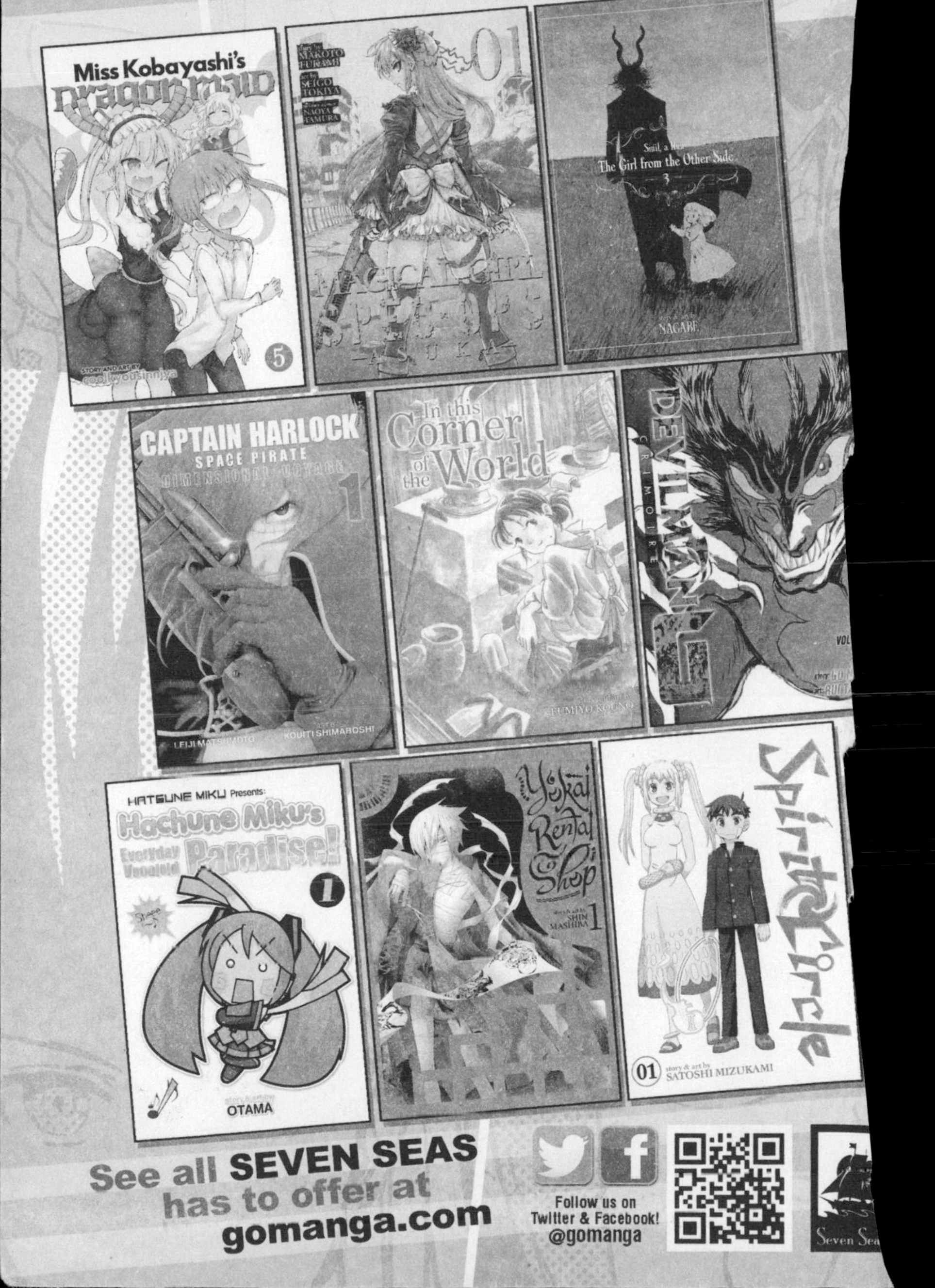
Miss Kobayashi's Dragon Maid
5
Story and art by coolkyousinnjya
01
story by MAKOTO FUKAMI
art by SEIGO TOKIYA
NAOYA TAMURA
Magical Girl Spec-Ops Asuka
Siúil, a Rún
The Girl from the Other Side
3
NAGABE
CAPTAIN HARLOCK
SPACE PIRATE
DIMENSIONAL VOYAGE
1
LEIJI MATSUMOTO
KOUITI SHIMABOSHI
In this Corner of the World
FUMIYO KOUNO
DEVILMAN GRIMOIRE
HATSUNE MIKU Presents:
Hachune Miku's Everyday Vocaloid Paradise!
1
OTAMA
Yokai Rental Shop
SHIN MASHIBA
1
Spirit Circle
01
story & art by
SATOSHI MIZUKAMI

SEVEN SEAS ENTERTAINMENT PRESENTS

Sorry For My Familiar

story and art by **TEKKA YAGURABA** **VOLUME 1**

TRANSLATION
Andrew Cunningham

ADAPTATION
Betsy Aoki

LETTERING AND RETOUCH
Kaitlyn Wiley

COVER DESIGN
Nicky Lim

PROOFREADER
Brett Hallahan
Kurestin Armada

ASSISTANT EDITOR
Jenn Grunigen

PRODUCTION ASSISTANT
CK Russell

PRODUCTION MANAGER
Lissa Pattillo

EDITOR-IN-CHIEF
Adam Arnold

PUBLISHER
Jason DeAngelis

SORRY FOR MY FAMILIAR VOLUME 1

First published in Japan in 2016 by Kodansha Ltd., Tokyo.
Publication rights for this English edition arranged through Kodansha Ltd., Tokyo.

ISBN: 978-1-626927-59-9

Printed in Canada

First Printing: March 2018

10 9 8 7 6 5 4 3 2 1

OLLOW US ONLINE: ***www.sevenseasentertainment.com***

READING DIRECTIONS

This book reads from ***right to left***, Japanese style. If this is your first time reading manga, you start reading from the top right panel on each page and take it from there. If you get lost, just follow the numbered diagram here. It may seem backwards at first, but you'll get the hang of it! Have fun!!

1
2
3
4
5
6
7
8
9

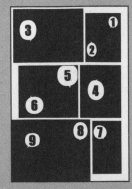